PENGUIN BOOKS

'This is not just a riveting read about how to understand others better. It's also a revealing look at how to be understood. Charles Duhigg delivers a winning combination of stories, studies, and guidance that might well transform the worst communicators you know into some of the best.' — Adam Grant, bestselling author of *Think Again* and *Hidden Potential*

'Charles Duhigg goes through a mountain of research – and some riveting stories – and unearths practical tactics to show that anyone can become a more effective listener, speaker, and even social media poster.' — David Epstein, bestselling author of *Range*

'Charles Duhigg does it again, with a book we all need to read . . . If you want to improve your communication skills at work and in life, this book is the place the start.' — Arthur C. Brooks, Professor, Harvard Kennedy School and Harvard Business School, and bestselling author of *From Strength to Strength*

'This is one of those books that stays with you for days after reading it . . . What makes us happiest in life is the quality of our connections and the relationships we forge . . . and that might just start with being able to understand what someone else is really trying to say. For, as Duhigg himself points out, the right conversation at the right moment can change everything.' — *Daily Mail*

'Duhigg's conversations with neurologists, psychologists and negotiation experts led him to learn that superior conversationalists have a lot in common . . . Following his tips to pay closer attention to non-verbal cues got me out of my thoughts, out of my apartment, and off the cursed Slack.' — *Guardian*

'A thoughtful and entertaining book. I even think it could make me a slightly better human.' — *Sunday Times*

'Duhigg's excellent book aims to explain how conversations work so we can connect more meaningfully in our relationships . . . As you would want in a book on communication, Duhigg is clear and engaging, linking research with his own interviews as he explores what really happens in successful – or difficult – conversation.' — *New Scientist*

Also by Charles Duhigg

The Power of Habit

Smarter Faster Better

ABOUT THE AUTHOR

CHARLES DUHIGG is a Pulitzer Prize-winning investigative reporter and the author of the international bestsellers *The Power of Habit* and *Smarter Faster Better.* His works have been translated into over forty-five languages. He is a winner of the National Academies of Sciences, National Journalism, and George Polk awards. A graduate of Harvard Business School and Yale College, he lives in California with his wife and two children.

charlesduhigg.com
X: @cduhigg

Supercommunicators

How to Unlock the Secret Language of Connection

Charles Duhigg

PENGUIN BOOKS

PENGUIN BOOKS

UK | USA | Canada | Ireland | Australia
India | New Zealand | South Africa

Penguin Books is part of the Penguin Random House group of companies whose addresses can be found at global.penguinrandomhouse.com

Penguin Random House UK,
One Embassy Gardens, 8 Viaduct Gardens, London SW11 7BW

penguin.co.uk
global.penguinrandomhouse.com

First published in the US by Random House, an imprint and division of Penguin Random House LLC, New York, 2024
First published in the UK by Cornerstone Press 2024
Published in Penguin Books 2025
003

Book design by Casey Hampton

Printed and bound in Great Britain by Clays Ltd, Elcograf S.p.A.

The authorised representative in the EEA is Penguin Random House Ireland, Morrison Chambers, 32 Nassau Street, Dublin D02 YH68

A CIP catalogue record for this book is available from the British Library

ISBN: 978–1–847–94364–4

Penguin Random House is committed to a sustainable future for our business, our readers and our planet. This book is made from Forest Stewardship Council® certified paper.

MIX
Paper | Supporting responsible forestry
FSC® C018179

To John Duhigg,
Susan Kamil,
and
Harry, Oli,
and Liz

CONTENTS

PROLOGUE

If there was one thing everyone knew about Felix Sigala, it was that he was easy to talk to. Exceptionally easy. People loved talking to him, because they always came away feeling a little smarter, funnier, more interesting. Even if you had nothing in common with Felix—which was unusual, because the conversation inevitably revealed all kinds of opinions or experiences or friends you shared—it felt as if he heard you, like you had some kind of bond.

That's why the scientists had sought him out.

Felix had been with the Federal Bureau of Investigation for two decades. He had joined after college and a stint in the military, and then had spent a few years as an agent in the field. That's where his superiors had first taken note of his easy way with others. A series of promotions soon followed, and eventually he landed as a senior regional administrator with a mandate to serve as an all-around negotiator. He was the guy who could coax statements from reluctant witnesses, or convince fugitives to turn themselves in, or console families as they grieved. He once persuaded a man who had barricaded himself in a room with six cobras, nineteen rattlesnakes, and an iguana to come out peacefully and then name his accomplices in an animal-smuggling ring. "The key was getting him to see things from the snakes' perspective," Felix told me. "He was a little weird, but he genuinely loved animals."

The FBI had a Crisis Negotiation Unit for hostage situations. When things got unusually complicated, they called someone like Felix.

There were lessons that Felix would share with younger agents when they asked for advice: Never pretend you're anything other than a cop. Never manipulate or threaten. Ask lots of questions, and, when someone becomes emotional, cry or laugh or complain or celebrate with them. But what ultimately made him so good at his job was a bit of a mystery, even to his colleagues.

So, in 2014, when a group of psychologists, sociologists, and other researchers were tasked by the Department of Defense to explore new methods for teaching persuasion and negotiation to military officers—essentially, how do we train people to get better at communication?—the scientists sought out Felix. They had learned about him from various officials who, when asked to name the best negotiators they had ever worked with, brought up his name, again and again.

Many of the scientists expected Felix to be tall and handsome, with warm eyes and a rich baritone. The guy who walked in for the interview, however, looked like a middle-aged dad, with a mustache, a little padding around the middle, and a soft, slightly nasal voice. He seemed . . . unremarkable.

Felix told me that, after introductions and pleasantries, one of the scientists explained the nature of their project, and then began with a broad question: "Can you tell us how you think about communication?"

"It might be better if I demonstrate it," Felix replied. "What's one of your favorite memories?"

The scientist Felix was speaking to had introduced himself as the head of a large lab. He oversaw millions of dollars in grants and dozens of people. He didn't seem like the kind of guy accustomed to idly reminiscing in the middle of the day.

The scientist paused. "Probably my daughter's wedding," he finally said. "My whole family was there, and my mother died just a few months later."

Felix asked a few follow-up questions, and occasionally shared memories of his own. "My sister got married in 2010," Felix told the man. "She's passed away now—it was cancer, which was hard—but she was so beautiful that day. That's how I try to remember her."

It went on this way for the next forty-five minutes. Felix would ask the scientists questions, and occasionally talk about himself. When someone revealed something personal, Felix would reciprocate with a story from his own life. One scientist mentioned problems he was having with a teenage daughter, and Felix responded by describing an aunt he couldn't seem to get along with, no matter how hard he tried. When another researcher asked about Felix's childhood, he explained that he had been painfully shy—but his father had been a salesman (and his grandfather a con man), and so, by imitating their examples, he had eventually learned how to connect with others.

As they got close to the end of their scheduled time together, a professor of psychology chimed in. "I'm sorry," she said, "this has been wonderful, but I don't feel any closer to understanding what you do. Why do you think so many people recommended we talk to you?"

"That's a fair question," Felix replied. "Before I answer, I want to ask: You mentioned you're a single mom, and I imagine there's a lot to juggling motherhood and a career. This might seem unusual, but I'm wondering: What would you tell someone who's getting a divorce?"

The woman went silent for a beat. "I guess I'll play along," she said. "I have lots of advice. When I separated from my husband—"

Felix gently interrupted.

"I don't really need an answer," he said. "But I want to point out that, in a room filled with professional colleagues, and after less than an hour of conversation, you're willing to talk about one of the most intimate parts of your life." He explained that one reason she felt so at ease was likely because of the environment they had created together, how Felix had listened closely, had asked questions that drew out people's vulnerabilities, how they had all revealed meaningful details about themselves. Felix had encouraged the scientists to explain how they saw the world, and then had proven to them that he had heard what they were saying. Whenever someone said something emotional—even when they didn't realize their emotions were on display—Felix had reciprocated by voicing feelings of his own. All those small choices they had made, he explained, had created an atmosphere of trust.

"It's a set of skills," he told the scientists. "There's nothing magical about it." Put differently, anyone can learn to be a supercommunicator.

• • •

Who would you call if you were having a bad day? If you had screwed up a deal at work, or had gotten into an argument with your spouse, or were feeling frustrated and sick of it all: Who would you want to talk to? There's likely someone that you know who will make you feel better, who can help you think through a thorny question or share a moment of heartbreak or joy.

Now, ask yourself: Are they the funniest person in your life? (Probably not, but if you paid close attention, you'd notice they laugh more than most people.) Are they the most interesting or smartest person you know? (What's more likely is that, even if they don't say anything particularly wise, you anticipate that *you* will feel smarter after talking to them.) Are they your most entertaining or confident friend? Do they give the best advice? (Most likely: Nope, nope, and nope—but when you hang up the phone, you'll feel calmer and more centered and closer to the right choice.)

So what are they doing that makes you feel so good?

This book attempts to answer that question. Over the past two decades, a body of research has emerged that sheds light on why some of our conversations go so well, while others are so miserable. These insights can help us hear more clearly and speak more engagingly. We know that our brains have evolved to crave connection: When we "click" with someone, our eyes often start to dilate in tandem; our pulses match; we feel the same emotions and start to complete each other's sentences within our heads. This is known as *neural entrainment,* and it feels wonderful. Sometimes it happens and we have no idea why; we just feel lucky that the conversation went so well. Other times, even when we're desperate to bond with someone, we fail again and again.

For many of us, conversations can sometimes seem bewildering, stressful, even terrifying. "The single biggest problem with communication," said the playwright George Bernard Shaw, "is the illusion it has taken place." But scientists have now unraveled many of the secrets of how successful conversations happen. They've learned that paying attention to someone's body, alongside their voice, helps us hear them better. They have determined that *how* we ask a question sometimes matters more than *what* we ask. We're better off, it seems, acknowledging social differences, rather than pretending they don't exist. Every discussion is influenced by emotions, no matter how rational the topic at hand. When starting a dialogue, it helps to think of the discussion as a negotiation where the prize is figuring out what everyone wants.

And, above all, the most important goal of any conversation is to *connect.*

• • •

This book was born, in part, from my own failures at communicating. A few years ago, I was asked to help manage a relatively complex work project. I had never been a manager before—but I had worked for plenty of bosses. Plus, I had a fancy MBA from Harvard Business School and, as a journalist, communicated as a profession! How hard could it be?

Very hard, it turned out. I was fine at drawing up schedules and planning logistics. But, time and again, I struggled with connecting. One day a colleague told me they felt their suggestions were being ignored, their contributions going unrecognized. "It's incredibly frustrating," they said.

I told them that I heard them and began suggesting possible solutions: Perhaps they should run the meetings? Or maybe we should draw up a formal organizational chart, clearly spelling out everyone's duties? Or what if we—

"You're not listening to me," they interrupted. "We don't need clearer roles. We need to do a better job of respecting each other." They wanted to talk about how people were treating one another, but I was obsessed with practical fixes. They had told me they needed empathy, but rather than listen, I replied with solutions.

The truth is, a similar dynamic sometimes played out at home. My family would go on vacation, and I would find something to obsess over—we didn't get the hotel room we were promised; the guy on the airplane had reclined his seat—and my wife would listen and respond with a perfectly reasonable suggestion: Why don't you focus on the positive aspects of the trip? Then I, in turn, would get upset because it felt like she didn't understand that I was asking for support—tell me I'm right to be outraged!—rather than sensible advice. Sometimes my kids would want to talk and I, consumed by work or some other distraction, would only half listen until they wandered away. I could see, in retrospect, that I was failing the people who were most important to me, but I didn't know how to fix it. I was particularly confused by these failures because, as a writer, I am supposed to communicate for a *living*. Why was I struggling to connect with—and hear—the people who mattered most?

I have a feeling I'm not alone in this confusion. We've all failed, at times, to listen to our friends and colleagues, to appreciate what they are trying to tell us—to *hear* what they're saying. And we've all failed to speak so we can be understood.

This book, then, is an attempt to explain why communication goes awry and what we can do to make it better. At its core are a handful of key ideas.

The first one is that many discussions are actually three different conversations. There are practical, decision-making conversations that focus on *What's This Really About?* There are emotional conversations, which ask *How Do We Feel?* And there are social conversations that explore *Who Are We?* We are often moving in and out of all three conversations as a dialogue unfolds. However, if we aren't having the same *kind* of conversation as our partners, at the same moment, we're unlikely to connect with each other.

What's more, each type of conversation operates by its own logic and requires its own set of skills, and so to communicate well, we have to know how to detect which kind of conversation is occurring, and understand how it functions.

The Three Conversations

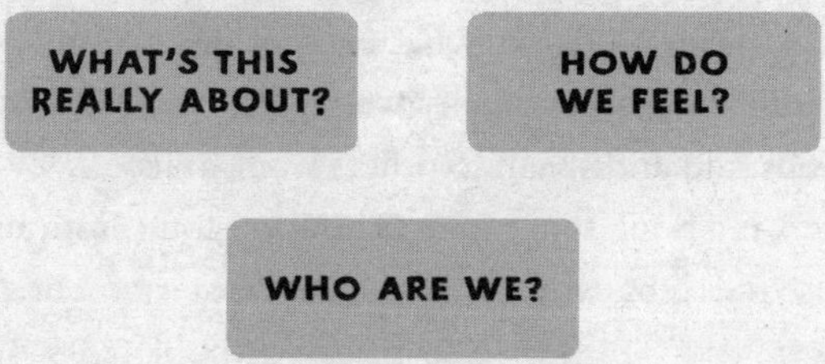

Which brings me to the second idea at the core of this book: Our goal, for the most meaningful discussions, should be to have a "learning conversation." Specifically, we want to learn how the people around us see the world and help them understand our perspectives in turn.

The last big idea isn't really an idea, but rather something I've learned: Anyone can become a supercommunicator—and, in fact, many of us already are, if we learn to unlock our instincts. We can all learn to hear more clearly, to connect on a deeper level. In the pages ahead, you'll see how executives at Netflix, the creators of *The Big Bang Theory,* spies and surgeons, NASA psychologists and COVID researchers have transformed how they speak and listen—and, as a result, have managed to connect with people across seemingly vast divides. And you will see how these lessons apply to everyday conversations: our chats with workmates, friends, romantic partners and our kids, the barista at the coffee shop and that woman we always wave to on the bus.

And that's important, because learning to have meaningful conversations is, in some ways, more urgent than ever before. It's no secret the world has become increasingly polarized, that we struggle to hear and be heard. But if we know how to sit down together, listen to each other and, even if we can't resolve every disagreement, find ways to hear one another and say what is needed, we can coexist and thrive.

Every meaningful conversation is made up of countless small choices. There are fleeting moments when the right question, or a vulnerable admission, or an empathetic word can completely change a dialogue. A silent laugh, a barely audible sigh, a friendly smile during a tense moment: Some people have learned to spot these opportunities, to detect what kind of discussion is occurring, to understand what others really want. They have learned how to hear what's unsaid and speak so others want to listen.

This, then, is a book that explores how we communicate and connect. Because the right conversation, at the right moment, can change everything.

THE THREE KINDS OF CONVERSATION

AN OVERVIEW

Conversation is the communal air we breathe. All day long, we talk to our families, friends, strangers, coworkers, and sometimes pets. We communicate via text, email, online posts, and social media. We speak via keyboards and voice-to-text, sometimes with handwritten letters and, occasionally, with grunts, smiles, grimaces, and sighs.

But not all conversations are equal. When a discussion is meaningful, it can feel wonderful, as if something important has been revealed. "Ultimately, the bond of all companionship, whether in marriage or in friendship, is conversation," wrote Oscar Wilde.

But meaningful conversations, when they *don't* go well, can feel awful. They are frustrating, disappointing, a missed opportunity. We might walk away confused, upset, uncertain if anyone understood anything that was said.

What makes the difference?

As the next chapter explains, our brains have evolved to crave connection. But consistently achieving alignment with other people requires understanding how communication functions—and, most important, recognizing that we need to be engaged in the same *kind* of conversation, at the same time, if we want to connect.

Supercommunicators aren't born with special abilities—but they have thought harder about how conversations unfold, why they succeed or fail, the nearly infinite number of choices that each dialogue offers that can bring us closer together or push us apart. When we learn to recognize those opportunities, we begin to speak and hear in new ways.

1

THE MATCHING PRINCIPLE

How to Fail at Recruiting Spies

If Jim Lawler was being honest with himself, he had to admit that he was terrible at recruiting spies. So bad, in fact, that he spent most nights worrying about getting fired from the only job he had ever loved, a job he had landed two years earlier as a case officer for the Central Intelligence Agency.

It was 1982 and Lawler was thirty years old. He had joined the CIA after attending law school at the University of Texas, where he had gotten mediocre grades, and then cycling through a series of dull jobs. One day, unsure what to do with his life, he telephoned a CIA headhunter he had once met on campus. A job interview followed, then a polygraph test, then a dozen more interviews in various cities, and then a series of exams that seemed designed to ferret out everything Lawler *didn't* know. (*Who,* he wondered, *memorizes rugby world champions from the 1960s?*)

Eventually, he made it to the final interview. Things weren't looking good. His exam performances had been poor to middling. He had no overseas experience, no knowledge of foreign languages, no military service or special skills. Yet, the interviewer noted, Lawler had flown himself to Washington, D.C., for this interview on his own dime; had persisted through each test, even when it was clear he didn't have the first clue how to answer most questions; had responded to every setback with what seemed like admirable, if misplaced, optimism.

Why, the man asked, did he want to join the CIA so badly?

"I've wanted to do something important my entire life," Lawler replied. He wanted to serve his country and "bring democracy to nations yearning for freedom." Even as the words came out, he realized how ridiculous they sounded. Who says *yearning* in an interview? So he stopped, took a breath, and said the most honest thing he could think of: "My life feels empty," he told the interviewer. "I want to be part of something meaningful."

A week later the agency called to offer him a job. He accepted immediately and reported to Camp Peary—the Farm, as the agency's training facility in Virginia is known—to be tutored in lock picking, dead drops, and covert surveillance.

The most surprising aspect of the Farm's curriculum, however, was the agency's devotion to the art of conversation. In his time there, Lawler learned that working for the CIA was essentially a communications job. A field officer's mandate wasn't slinking in shadows or whispering in parking lots; it was talking to people at parties, making friends in embassies, bonding with foreign officials in the hope that, someday, you might have a quiet chat about some critical piece of intelligence. Communication is so important that a summary of CIA training methods puts it right up front: "Find ways to connect," it says. "A case officer's goal should be to have a prospective agent come to believe, hopefully with good reason, that the case officer is one of the few people, perhaps the ONLY person, who truly understands him."

Lawler finished spy school with high marks and was shipped off to Europe. His assignment was to establish rapport with foreign bureaucrats, cultivate friendships with embassy attachés, and develop other sources who might be willing to have candid conversations—and thereby, his bosses hoped, open channels for discussions that make the world's affairs a bit more manageable.

• • •

Lawler's first few months abroad were miserable. He tried his best to blend in. He attended black-tie soirees and had drinks at bars near embassies. Nothing worked. There was a clerk from the Chinese delegation he met après-ski and repeatedly invited to lunch and cocktails. Eventually Lawler worked up the courage to inquire if his new friend, perhaps, wanted to earn some extra cash passing along gossip he heard inside his embassy. The man replied that his family was quite wealthy, thank you, and his bosses tended to execute people for things like that. He would pass.

Then there was a receptionist from the Soviet consulate who seemed promising until one of Lawler's superiors took him aside and explained that she, in fact, worked for the KGB and was trying to recruit *him*.

Eventually, a career-saving opportunity appeared: A CIA colleague mentioned that a young woman from the Middle East, who worked in her country's foreign ministry, was visiting. Yasmin was on vacation, the colleague explained, staying with a brother who had moved to Europe. A few days later, Lawler managed to "bump into" her at a restaurant. He introduced himself as an oil speculator. As they began talking, Yasmin mentioned that her brother was always busy, never available for sightseeing. She seemed lonely.

Lawler invited her to lunch the next day and asked about her life. Did she like her job? Was it hard living in a country that had recently undergone a conservative revolution? Yasmin confided that she hated the religious radicals who had come to power. She longed to move away, to live in Paris or New York, but for that she needed money, and it had taken months of saving just to afford this brief trip.

Lawler, sensing an opening, mentioned that his oil company was looking for a consultant. It was part-time work, he said, assignments she could do alongside her job at the foreign ministry. But he could offer her a signing bonus. "We ordered champagne and I thought she was going to start crying, she was so happy," he told me.

After lunch, Lawler rushed back to the office to find his boss. Finally, he had recruited his first spy! "And he tells me, 'Congratulations. Headquarters is gonna be overjoyed. Now you need to tell her you're CIA and you'll want information about her government.'" Lawler thought that was a terrible idea. If he was honest with Yasmin, she'd never speak to him again.

But his boss explained that it was unfair to ask someone to work for the CIA without being forthright. If Yasmin's government ever found out, she would be jailed, possibly killed. She had to understand the risks.

So, Lawler continued meeting with Yasmin, and tried to find the right moment to reveal his true employer. She became increasingly candid as they spent more time together. She was ashamed that her government was shutting down newspapers and prohibiting free speech, she told him, and despised the bureaucrats who had made it illegal for women to study certain topics in college and had forced them to wear hijabs in public. When she first sought out a job with the government, she said, she had never imagined things would get this bad.

Lawler took this as a sign. One night, over dinner, he explained that he was not an oil speculator, but, rather, an American intelligence officer. He told her that the United States wanted the same things she did: To undermine her country's theocracy, to weaken its leaders, to stop the repression of women. He apologized for lying about who he was, but the job offer was real. Would she consider working for the Central Intelligence Agency?

"As I talked, I watched her eyes get bigger and bigger, and she started gripping the tablecloth, and then shaking her head, no-no-no, and, when I finally stopped, she started crying, and I knew I was screwed," Lawler told me. "She said they murdered people for that, and there was no way she could help." There was nothing he could say to convince her to consider the idea. "All she wanted was to get away from me."

Lawler went back to his boss with the bad news. "And he says, 'I've already told everyone you recruited her! I told the division chief, and the chief of station, and they told D.C. Now you want me to tell them you can't close the deal?'"

Lawler had no idea what to do next. "No amount of money or promises would have convinced her to take a suicidal risk," he told me. The only possible way forward was convincing Yasmin that she could trust him, that he understood her and would protect her. But how do you do that? "They taught me, at the Farm, that to recruit someone, you have to convince them that you care about them, which means you have to *actually* care about them, which means you have to connect in some way. And I had no idea how to make that happen."

• • •

How do we create a genuine connection with another person? How do we nudge someone, through a conversation, to take a risk, embrace an adventure, accept a job, or go on a date?

Let's lower the stakes. What if you're trying to bond with your boss, or get to know a new friend: How do you convince them to let down their guard? How do you show you're listening?

Over the past few decades, as new methods for studying our behaviors and brains have emerged, these kinds of questions have driven researchers to examine nearly every aspect of communication. Scientists have scrutinized how our minds absorb information, and have found that connecting with others through speech is both more powerful, and more complicated, than we ever realized. *How* we communicate—the unconscious decisions we make as we speak and listen, the questions we ask and the vulnerabilities we expose, even our tone of voice—can influence who we trust, are persuaded by, and seek out as friends.

Alongside this new understanding, there's also been a flurry of research showing that at the heart of every conversation is the potential for neurological synchronization, an alignment of our brains and bodies—everything from how fast each of us breathes to the goose bumps on our skin—that we often fail to notice, but which influences how we talk, hear, and think. Some people consistently fail to synchronize with others, even when they're speaking to close friends. Others—let's call them *supercommunicators*—seem to synchronize effortlessly with just about anyone. Most of us lie somewhere in between. But we can learn to connect in more meaningful ways if we understand how conversations work.

For Jim Lawler, however, the path toward making a connection with Yasmin seemed murky. "I knew, at most, I had one more chance to talk to her," he told me. "I had to figure out how to break through."

WHEN BRAINS CONNECT

When Beau Sievers joined the Dartmouth Social Systems Lab in 2012, he still looked like the musician he had been a few years earlier. Some days he would rush to the laboratory after waking up, his blond hair in a frizzy nimbus and dressed in a ratty T-shirt from some jazz fest, sprinting past campus cops who were uncertain if he was a PhD candidate or a weed dealer servicing undergraduates.

Sievers had taken a circuitous route to the Ivy League. For college, he had attended a music conservatory where he studied drumming and music production at the exclusion of pretty much everything else. Soon, however, he began to suspect that no amount of practice would deliver the rarefied status of drummers-who-can-support-themselves-by-drumming. So he began exploring other careers. He had always been fascinated by how people communicate. In particular, he loved the voiceless musical dialogues that sometimes emerged onstage. There were moments when he was improvising with other musicians and suddenly everyone would click, as if they were sharing one brain. It felt as if the performers—as well as the audience, the guy at the mixing board, even the bartender—were suddenly all in sync. He sometimes felt the same thing during great late-night discussions, or successful dates. So he signed up for a few psychology classes, and, eventually, applied to a PhD program with Dr. Thalia Wheatley, one of the foremost neuroscientists researching how humans connect with one another.

"Why people 'click' with some people, but not others, is one of the great unsolved mysteries of science," Wheatley wrote in the journal *Social and Personality Psychology Compass.* When we align with someone through conversation, Wheatly explained, it feels wonderful, in part because our brains have evolved to crave these kinds of connections. The desire to connect has pushed people to form communities, protect their offspring, seek out new friends and alliances. It's one reason why our species has survived. "Human beings have the rare capacity," she wrote, "to connect with each other, against all odds."

Numerous other researchers have also been fascinated by how we form connections. As Sievers began reading science journals, he learned that in 2012, scholars at the Max Planck Institute for Human Development in Germany had studied the brains of guitarists playing Scheidler's Sonata in D Major. When the musicians played their guitars separately, with each person focused on their own musical score, their neural activity looked dissimilar. But when they segued into a duet, the electrical pulses within their craniums began to synchronize. To the researchers, it appeared as if the guitarists' minds had merged. What's more, that linkage often flowed through their bodies: They frequently began breathing at similar rates, their eyes dilated in tandem, their hearts began to beat in similar patterns. Frequently even the electrical impulses along their skin would synchronize. Then, when they stopped playing together—as their scores diverged or they veered into solos—the "between-brain synchronization disappeared completely," the scientists wrote.

Sievers found other studies showing this same phenomenon when people hummed together, or tapped their fingers side by side, or solved cooperative puzzles, or told each other stories. In one experiment, researchers at Princeton measured the neural activity of a dozen people listening to a young woman recount a long and convoluted tale about her prom night. As they monitored the speaker's brain alongside the brains of her listeners, they saw the listeners' minds synchronize with the narrator, until they were all experiencing the same feelings of stress and unease, joy and humor, at the same time, as if they were telling the story together. What's more, some listeners synchronized particularly closely with the speaker; their brains seemed to behave nearly precisely like her brain. When questioned afterward, those tightly aligned participants could distinguish between the story's characters more clearly and recall smaller details. The more people's brains had synchronized, the better they understood what was said. The "extent of speaker-listener neural coupling predicts the success of the communication," the researchers wrote in *The Proceedings of the National Academy of Sciences* in 2010.

SUPERCOMMUNICATORS

These and other studies make clear an essential truth: To communicate with someone, we must connect with them. When we absorb what someone is saying, and they comprehend what we say, it's because our brains have, to some degree, aligned. At that moment, our bodies—our pulses, facial expressions, the emotions we experience, the prickling sensation on our necks and arms—often start to synchronize as well. There is something about neural simultaneity that helps us listen more closely and speak more clearly.

Sometimes this connection occurs with just one other person. Other times, it happens within a group, or a large audience. But whenever it happens, our brains and bodies become alike because we are, in the language of neuroscientists, *neurally entrained.*

When we are not neurally aligned, we have trouble communicating.

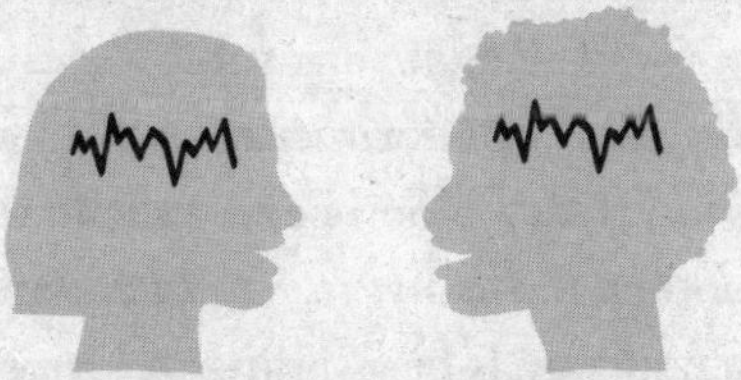

But when we start thinking alike, we understand each other better.

As researchers have scrutinized how entrainment occurs, they have discovered that some people are particularly skilled at this kind of synchronization. Some individuals are consistently better at connecting.

Scientists like Sievers don't call these people supercommunicators—they prefer terms like *high centrality participant* or *core information provider*—but Sievers knew what these kinds of people looked like: They were the friends everyone called for advice; the colleagues elected to leadership positions; the coworkers everyone welcomed into a conversation because they made it more fun. Sievers had performed onstage with supercommunicators, had sought them out at parties, had voted for them. He had even, at times, achieved moments of supercommunication himself, usually without understanding exactly how.

None of the studies Sievers read, however, seemed to explain why some people were better at synchronization than others. So Sievers decided to stage an experiment to see if he could figure it out.

• • •

To begin, Sievers and his colleagues gathered dozens of volunteers and asked them to watch a series of movie clips that were designed to be difficult to understand. Some, for example, were in a foreign language. Others were brief scenes from the middle of a film, completely decontextualized. To make the clips even harder to follow, the researchers had removed all audio and subtitles, so what participants saw were confusing, silent performances: A bald and irate man in strained conversation with a blond heavyset fellow. Are they friends or enemies? In another, a cowboy takes a bath while a second man observes from the doorway. Is he a sibling? A lover?

The volunteers' brains were monitored as they watched these clips, and researchers saw that each person reacted slightly differently. Some were confused. Others were entertained. But no two brain scans were alike.

Then, each participant was assigned to a small group and told to answer a few questions together: "Is the bald man angry at the blond man?" "Is the man in the doorframe sexually attracted to the man in the bath?"

After the groups spent an hour discussing their answers, they were put back into the brain scanners and shown the same clips.

This time, the researchers saw that participants' neural impulses had synchronized with those of their groupmates. Taking part in a conversation—debating what they had seen, discussing plot points—had caused their brains to align.

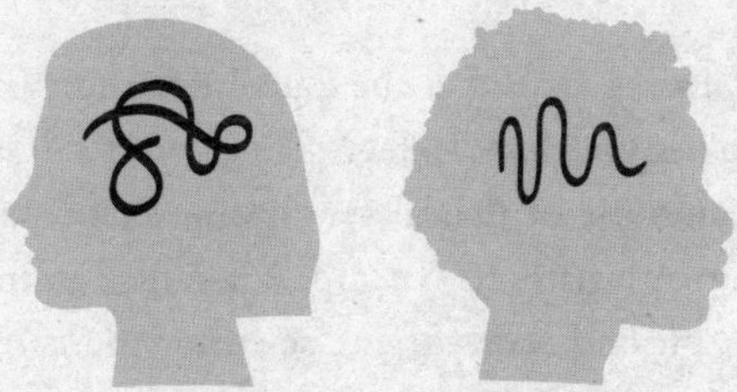

When people do things like watch movies separately, they think differently.

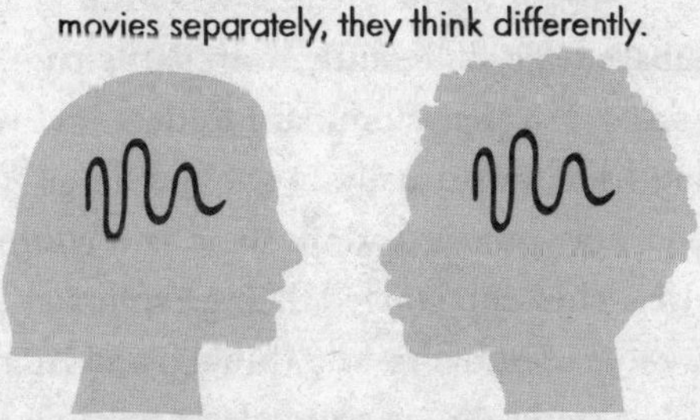

But when they begin to talk, their thoughts align.

However, there was a second, even more interesting discovery: Some of the groups had become *much* more synchronized than others. The brains of these participants looked strikingly alike during the second scan, as if they had all agreed to think precisely the same way.

Sievers suspected these groups included someone special, the type of person who made it easier for everyone to align. But who were they? His first hypothesis was that having a strong leader made synchronization easier. Indeed, in some groups, there was one person who had taken charge from the start. "I think it's gonna have a happy ending," one such leader, known as Participant 4 in Group D, told his teammates regarding a clip of a child who appeared to be looking for his parents. Participant 4 was talkative and direct. He assigned roles to his groupmates and kept everyone on task. Perhaps Participant 4, in addition to being a leader, was also a supercommunicator?

But when Sievers looked at the data, he found that strong leaders didn't help people align. In fact, groups with a dominant leader had the *least* amount of neural synchrony. Participant 4 made it harder for his groupmates to sync up. When he dominated the conversation, he pushed everyone else into their own, separate thoughts.

Rather, the groups with the greatest synchrony had one or two people who behaved very differently from Participant 4. These people tended to speak less than dominant leaders, and when they did open their mouths, it was usually to ask questions. They repeated others' ideas and were quick to admit their own confusion or make fun of themselves. They encouraged their groupmates ("That's really smart! Tell me more about what you think!") and laughed at others' jokes. They didn't stand out as particularly talkative or clever, but when they spoke, everyone listened closely. And, somehow, they made it easier for other people to speak up. They made conversations flow. Sievers began referring to these people as *high centrality participants.*

Here, for instance, are two high centrality participants discussing that bathtub scene, which featured the actors Brad Pitt and Casey Affleck:

High Centrality Participant 1: What's with that scene?*

High Centrality Participant 2: I have no idea. I was lost. *[Laughter.]*

Participant 3: Casey is watching Brad in the bath. Based on the length of the stare, we think Casey is attracted to Brad. *[Group laughter.]* Unrequited love.

High Centrality Participant 2: Oh, I like that! I don't know what "unrequited" means, but yeah!

Participant 3: Like, not returned.

High Centrality Participant 2: Oh, okay, yeah.

High Centrality Participant 1: What do you think will happen in the next scene?

Participant 3: I feel like they are gonna rob a bank. *[Laughter.]*

High Centrality Participant 1: I like that! I like that!

High Centrality Participant 2: Yeah. I was waiting for some other epiphany. *[Laughter.]*

High centrality participants tended to ask *ten to twenty times* as many questions as other participants. When a group got stuck, they made it easy for everyone to take a quick break by bringing up a new topic or interrupting an awkward silence with a joke.

But the most important difference between high centrality participants and everyone else was that the high centrality participants were constantly adjusting *how* they communicated, in order to match their companions. They subtly reflected shifts in other people's moods and attitudes. When someone got serious, they matched

* Because the transcript of this conversation is filled with asides and verbal overlaps, I have streamlined this exchange for brevity and clarity. I have removed trip-ups, noises like "umm," tangents, and dialogue unrelated to the issues at hand. I have not altered the meaning of anything said, nor put words in anyone's mouth. Throughout this book, anytime a verbatim transcript has been edited in this manner, it is mentioned in the endnotes.

that seriousness. When a discussion went light, they were the first to play along. They changed their minds frequently and let themselves be swayed by their groupmates.

In one conversation, when a participant brought up an unexpectedly serious idea—that a character in a clip had been abandoned, the participant's tone hinting that he might understand abandonment firsthand—the high centrality participant immediately matched his tone:

Participant 2: How do you think this movie will end?

Participant 6: I don't think it's a happy ending.

High Centrality Participant: You don't think it's a happy ending?

Participant 6: No.

High Centrality Participant: Why not?

Participant 6: I don't know. This movie seemed to be more darker than . . .

[Silence.]

. . .

High Centrality Participant: How will it end?

. . .

Participant 6: It might be the nephew and the parents died or something like this, and they . . .

Participant 3: He's just been abandoned.

High Centrality Participant: Yeah, abandoned for the night. Yeah.

Within moments of that exchange, the entire group became serious-minded and started discussing what abandonment felt like. They made room for Participant 6 to discuss his emotions and experiences. The High Centrality Participant matched Participant 6's gravity, which nudged others to do so as well.

High centrality participants, Sievers and his coauthors wrote in their results, were much more "likely to adapt their own brain activity to the group," and "played an outsized role in creating group alignment by facilitating conversation." But they didn't merely mirror others—rather, they gently led people, nudging them to hear one another, or to explain themselves more clearly. They matched their groupmates' conversational styles, making room for seriousness or laughter, and invited others to match them in return. And they had enormous influence on how people ended up answering the questions they had been assigned. In fact, whichever opinion the high centrality participants endorsed usually became the group's consensus answer. But that influence was almost invisible. When polled afterward, few people realized how much the high centrality participants had swayed their own choices. Not every group had such a person—but those that did all seemed closer to one another afterward, and their brain scans showed they were more aligned.

When Sievers looked at the lives of high centrality participants, he found they were unusual in other respects. They had much larger social networks than the average person and were more likely to be elected to positions of authority or entrusted with power. Other people turned to them when they needed to discuss something serious or ask for advice. "And that makes sense," Sievers told me. "Because if you're the kind of person who's easy to talk to, then lots of people are going to want to talk to you."

In other words, the high centrality participants were supercommunicators.

THE THREE MINDSETS

So, to become a supercommunicator, all we need to do is listen closely to what's said and unsaid, ask the right questions, recognize and match others' moods, and make our own feelings easy for others to perceive.

Simple, right?

Well, no, of course not. Each of those tasks is difficult on its own. Together, they can seem impossible.

To understand how supercommunicators do what they do, it's useful to explore what happens inside our brains when we're in a conversation. Researchers have studied how our minds function during different sorts of discussions and have found that various neural networks and brain structures become active during different types of dialogue. Simplifying greatly, there are three *kinds* of conversation that dominate most discussions.

The Three Conversations

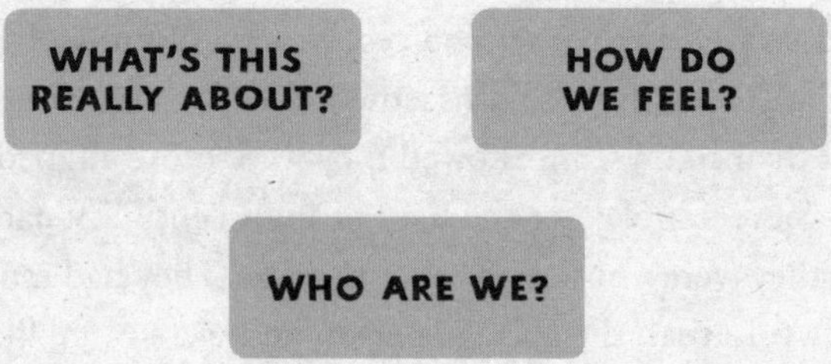

These three conversations—which correspond to practical decision-making conversations, emotional conversations, and conversations about identity—are best captured by three questions: *What's This Really About?*, *How Do We Feel?*, and *Who Are We?* Each of these conversations, as we will see, draws on a different type of mindset and mental processing. When we have a conversation about, say, a choice—a *What's This Really About?* conversation—we're activating different parts of our brains from when we discuss our feelings—the *How Do We Feel?* discussion—and if our mind doesn't align with the brains of our conversational partners, we'll all feel like we didn't fully understand one another.

The first mindset—the *decision-making mindset*—is associated with the *What's This Really About?* conversation, and it's active whenever we're thinking about practical matters, such as making choices or analyzing plans. When someone says, "What are we going to do about Sam's grades?," our brains' frontal control network, the command center for our thoughts and actions, becomes active. We have to make a series of decisions, often subconsciously, to evaluate the words we heard, but also to consider what motives or desires might be lurking underneath. "Is this discussion serious or playful?" "Should I offer a solution or just listen?" The *What's This Really About?* conversation is integral to thinking about the future, negotiating options, discussing intellectual concepts, and determining what we *want* to discuss, our goals for this conversation, and *how* we should discuss it.

The Three Conversations

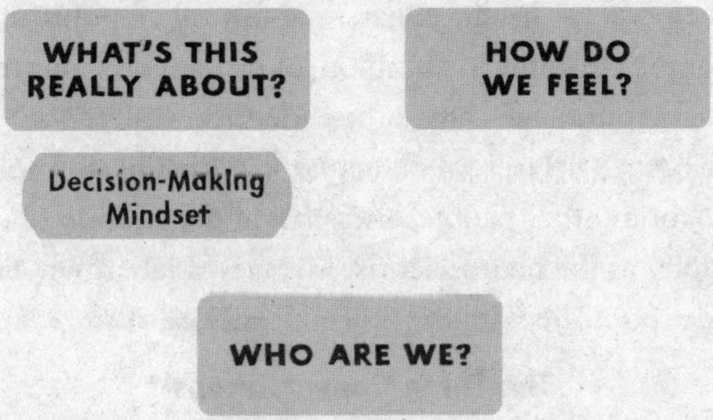

The second mindset—the *emotional mindset*—emerges when we discuss *How Do We Feel?* and draws on neural structures—the nucleus accumbens, the amygdala, and the hippocampus, among others—that help shape our beliefs, emotions, and memories. When we tell a funny story, or have an argument with our spouse, or experience a rush of pride or sorrow during a conversation, that's the emotional mindset at work. When a friend complains to us about their boss, and we sense they're asking for empathy, rather than advice, it's because we're attuned to *How Do We Feel?*

The Three Conversations

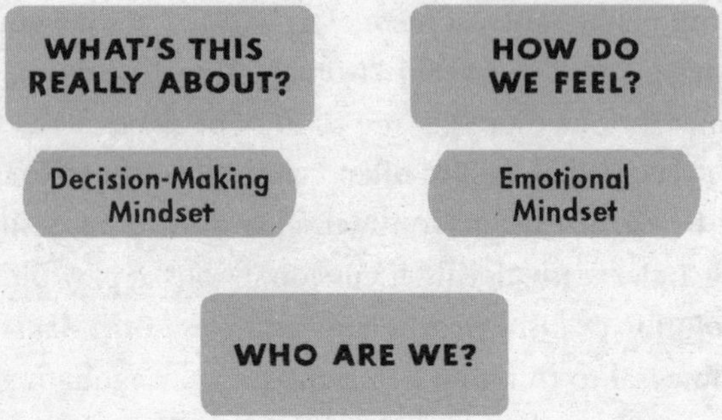

The third conversational mindset—the *social mindset*—emerges when we discuss our relationships, how we are seen by others and see ourselves, and our social identities. These are *Who Are We?* discussions. When we, for instance, gossip about office politics, or figure out the people we know in common, or explain how our religion or family background—or any other identity—influences us, we're using our brain's default mode network, which plays a role in how we think "about other people, oneself, and the relation of oneself to other people," as the neuroscientist Matthew Lieberman wrote. One 1997 study published in the journal *Human Nature* found that

The Three Conversations

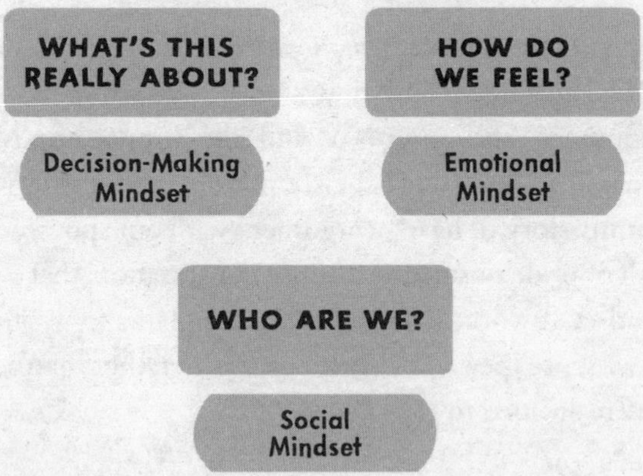

70 percent of our conversations are social in nature. During those dialogues the social mindset is constantly shaping how we listen and what we say.

Each of these conversations—and each mindset—is, of course, deeply intertwined. We often use all three during a single dialogue. The important thing to understand is that these mindsets can shift as a conversation unfolds. For example, a discussion might begin when a friend asks for help thinking through a work problem (*What's This Really About?*) and then proceeds to admit he's feeling stressed (*How Do We Feel?*) before finally focusing on how other people will react when they learn about this issue (*Who Are We?*).

If we could see inside our friend's skull during this conversation, we would see—and I'm simplifying greatly here—the decision-making mindset becoming dominant at first, and then the emotional mindset assuming primacy, and then the social mindset asserting influence.

Miscommunication occurs when people are having different *kinds* of conversations. If you are speaking emotionally, while I'm talking practically, we are, in essence, using different cognitive languages. (This explains why, when you complain about your boss—"Jim is driving me crazy!"—and your spouse responds with a practical suggestion—"What if you just invited him to lunch?"—it's more apt to create conflict than connection: "I'm not asking you to solve this! I just want some empathy.")

Supercommunicators know how to evoke synchronization by encouraging people to match how they're communicating. Psychologists who study married couples, for instance, have found that the happiest spouses frequently mirror each other's speaking styles. "The underlying mechanism that maintains closeness in marriage is symmetry," one prominent researcher, John Gottman, wrote in the *Journal of Communication.* Happy couples "communicate agreement not with the speaker's point of view or content, but with the speaker's affect." Happy couples ask each other more questions, repeat what the other person said, make tension-easing jokes, get serious together. The next time you feel yourself edging toward an argument, try asking your partner: "Do you want to talk about our emotions? Or do we need to make a decision together? Or is this about something else?"

The importance of this insight—that communication comes from connection and alignment—is so fundamental that it has become known as the *matching principle*: Effective communication requires recognizing what *kind* of conversation is occurring, and then *matching* each other. On a very basic level, if someone seems emotional, allow yourself to become emotional as well. If someone is intent on decision making, match that focus. If they are preoccupied by social implications, reflect their fixation back to them.

The Matching Principle

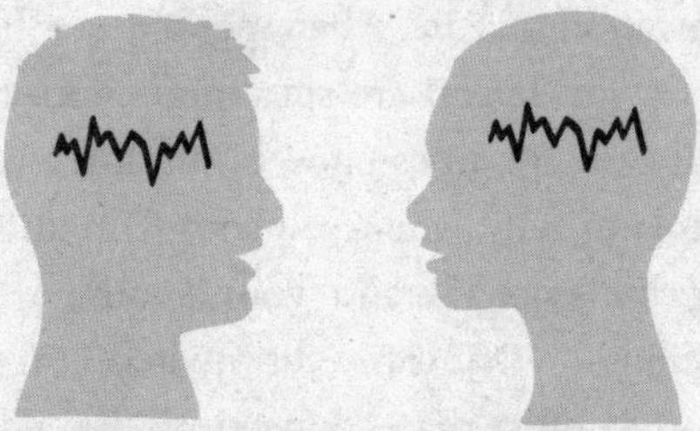

Successful communication requires recognizing what *kind* of conversation is occurring, and then *matching* each other.

It is important to note that matching isn't mimicry. As you'll see in the forthcoming chapters, we need to genuinely understand what someone is feeling, what they want, and who they are. And then, to match them, we need to know how to share ourselves in return. When we align, we start to connect, and that's when a meaningful conversation begins.

TO RECRUIT A SPY, CONNECT

After the disastrous dinner where he had revealed that he worked for the CIA and Yasmin had fled, it didn't seem to Lawler like there was much hope left. This was his only potential recruitment after nearly a year of work. He had completely messed things up and was fairly certain this failure was going to cost him his job. Only one option remained: To call Yasmin and beg her to join him for one last meal. "I filled up a notebook with ideas for what to say to her, but I knew it was pointless," Lawler told me. "Nothing was going to break through."

Yasmin agreed to a final dinner. They went to a fancy restaurant where she sat, quiet and on edge, through the entire meal. Her anxiety wasn't just due to Lawler's proposal, she told him. She was flying home soon and was nervous and discouraged. She had hoped this trip would reveal something to her, show her how to live a more meaningful life. But here she was, about to go home, and everything was the same. She felt like she had disappointed herself.

"She was so sad," Lawler told me. "So I tried to cheer her up—you know, little jokes, funny stories."

Lawler talked about a landlord who had kept forgetting his name, and reminisced about sightseeing trips they had taken together. Yasmin remained glum. Eventually, it was time for dessert. A silence crept in. Lawler wondered if he should try one more pitch. Should he offer to get her a visa to America for her cooperation? Too risky, he decided. She might just stand up and leave.

The silence extended. Lawler had no idea what to say. The last time he had felt this lost was before he had joined the CIA, when he had worked for his father selling steel components in Dallas. "I had never sold a thing in my life before that," he told me. "I was terrible at it." There was this one day, after months of discouraging sales calls, when he had visited a potential client—a woman running a small construction firm in West Texas—who was on the phone when he arrived, her five-year-old son playing with blocks alongside her desk.

When the woman hung up, she listened to Lawler's pitch for steel joists and thanked him for stopping by. Then, she began talking about the challenges of juggling work and motherhood. It was a constant struggle, she said. She always felt as if she was letting someone down, having to choose between being a good businesswoman or a good mom.

Lawler was in his early twenties at the time, and didn't have children. He had nothing in common with this woman, and had no idea how to reply. But he had to say *something.* So he started rambling about his own family. It was hard working for his dad, he told her. His brother was a better salesman, and that had caused tension between them. "She'd been honest with me, and so I was honest back," Lawler told me. "It felt good to tell the truth." He ended up sharing more than he intended, more than seemed appropriate, to be honest. But she didn't seem to mind.

Then Lawler returned to his sales spiel, and "she told me she didn't need any components, but she appreciated the conversation," he said. "And I left, thinking, well, there's another screwup."

Two months later the woman called and placed a huge order. "I told her, 'I'm not sure we can give you the pricing you're looking for'—that's how bad a salesman I was," Lawler told me. "And she said, 'That's okay, I feel like we have a connection.'"

That experience had reshaped Lawler's approach to sales. From then on, whenever he spoke to clients, he listened closely to their moods and concerns and enthusiasms, and tried to relate to them—to show that he understood, at least a little bit, what they were feeling. He slowly became a better salesman. Not great, but better. "I learned that if you listen for someone's truth, and you put your truth next to it, you might reach them." His goal, during sales calls, became simply to connect. He didn't try to pressure or impress clients. He just tried to find something they shared. "It didn't work all the time," he said. "But it worked enough."

Eating dessert with Yasmin, it occurred to Lawler that he had forgotten this lesson. He had been thinking of recruiting spies as very different from selling steel. But, at some level, they were the same basic activity. In both situations, he needed to connect with someone, which meant he had to show them he was hearing what they were trying to say.

But he hadn't done that with Yasmin, he realized, not in an honest way, not like he had with the mother in West Texas. He hadn't proved that he heard Yasmin's anxieties and hopes, hadn't been authentic about himself. He hadn't shared with her the way she had with him.

So, once the dishes were cleared, Lawler started talking about how he felt. He told Yasmin he was worried he wasn't cut out for this life. He had worked so hard to get into the CIA, but he found himself lacking something, some kind of confidence that he saw in his peers. He told her about all the times he'd clumsily approached foreign officials, how terrified he was they would report him and he'd get deported. He described his embarrassment when a colleague had explained that he was trying to recruit a KGB officer who was simultaneously seeking to recruit him. He told her he was worried he was a failure just for admitting all this to her—but he understood, a little, what she was feeling when she thought about returning home. He had felt the same way back in Texas, when he was desperate for a life that mattered.

Instead of trying to cheer up Yasmin, he talked about his own frustrations and disappointments, the same way she had. It felt like the most honest thing he could do. "I wasn't trying to be manipulative," Lawler told me. "She'd already refused me, and I knew I wasn't going to change her mind. So I stopped trying. It felt good to stop pretending I had all the answers."

Yasmin listened. She told Lawler she understood. The worst part, she said, was that she felt as if she were betraying herself. She wanted to do something, but she felt powerless. She began to cry.

"I'm sorry," Lawler told her. "I didn't mean to make you sad."

This was all a mistake, he thought. *I should have left her alone.* He would have to report this discussion, in detail, to the agency. It would be one final embarrassment to cap off a humiliating year.

Then Yasmin gathered herself. "I can do this," she whispered.

"What do you mean?" Lawler said.

"I can help you," she replied.

"You don't have to!" he said. He was caught so off guard that he blurted the first thought in his mind. "We don't have to see each other ever again! I promise I'll leave you alone."

"I want to do something important," she said. "This matters. I can do it. I know I can."

Two days later, Yasmin underwent polygraph testing and training in secure communication methods at a CIA safe house. "You've never seen someone so nervous," Lawler told me. "But she stuck with it. She never said she was having second thoughts." Once she was back home, Yasmin began sending Lawler messages detailing the memos she had seen, the officials the foreign minister had hosted, the gossip she'd overheard. "She became one of the best sources in the region," said Lawler. "She was a gold mine." For the next two decades, as Yasmin's career inside the foreign ministry thrived, she communicated regularly with the CIA, helping them understand what was happening behind the scenes, putting context around governmental declarations, making quiet introductions. Her assistance was never discovered by the authorities.

Lawler still has no real idea why Yasmin changed her mind that night. In the years that followed, he asked her to explain it numerous times, but even she struggled to say what had caused the shift. She told him that somehow, during dinner, when it became clear they were both so uncertain of themselves, she suddenly felt safe with him. They understood each other. She could hear, for the first time, what he had been trying to tell her: This could be important. You could make a difference. And she felt genuinely heard. They agreed to trust each other.

When we match someone's mindset, a permission is granted: To enter another person's head, to see the world through their eyes, to understand what they care about and need. And we give them permission to understand—and hear—us in return. "Conversations are the most powerful thing on earth," Lawler told me.

But matching is also hard. Simply mirroring another person's gestures, or moods, or tone of voice doesn't forge a real connection. Giving in to someone else's desires and preoccupations doesn't work, either. Those aren't real conversations. They're dueling monologues.

Instead, we have to learn to distinguish a decision-making conversation from an emotional conversation from a social conversation. We need to understand which kinds of questions and vulnerabilities are powerful, and how to make our own feelings more visible and easier to read. We need to prove to others that we are listening closely. When Lawler managed to connect with Yasmin at dinner, it was more luck than anything else. Afterward, he would spend years trying to repeat that success and failing, until he had polished his skills and understood how to make authentic connections.

Eventually Lawler became one of the CIA's most successful recruiters of overseas assets. By the time he retired in 2005, he had convinced dozens of foreign officials to participate in sensitive conversations. Then he began teaching his methods to other case officers. Today, Lawler's techniques are woven into the agency's training materials. As one document on recruiting foreign agents puts it: "A case officer creates an ever-deeper relationship through the process—from becoming an 'associate' then a 'friend' in the assessment phases and then moving to the role of 'sounding board' and 'confidant' as development moves to recruitment. . . . The agent then can look forward to each meeting as a chance to spend quality time with a comrade he can trust with his life."

In other words, CIA recruiters are taught how to synchronize. "Once you understand how it works, it's completely learnable," an officer trained by Lawler told me. "I've always been an introvert, and so I hadn't thought much about communication before I started my training. But once someone shows you how a conversation works, how to pay attention to what's going on, you start noticing all these things you missed before." These aren't just skills she uses at work, this officer told me. She uses them with her parents, her boyfriend, the people she sees at the grocery store. She notices when her colleagues use their training in everyday meetings: Nudging each other to align better, listen more closely, speak in ways that make it easier for others to understand. "From the outside, it seems like a Jedi mind trick, but it's just something you learn, and then practice, and then do," she told me.

In other words, it's a set of skills anyone can use. The chapters ahead explain how.

A GUIDE TO USING THESE IDEAS

PART I

The Four Rules for a Meaningful Conversation

Happily married couples, successful negotiators, persuasive politicians, influential executives, and other kinds of supercommunicators tend to have a few behaviors in common. They are as interested in figuring out what *kind* of conversation everyone wants as the *topics* they hope to discuss. They ask more *questions* about others' feelings and backgrounds. They talk about their own *goals* and *emotions*, and are quick to discuss their vulnerabilities, experiences, and the various identities they possess—and to ask others about their emotions and experiences. They inquire how others see the world, prove they are listening, and share their own perspectives in return.

In other words, during the most meaningful conversations, the best communicators focus on four basic rules that create a *learning conversation*:

THE LEARNING CONVERSATION

Rule One:

Pay attention to what *kind* of conversation is occurring.

Rule Two:

Share your goals, and ask what others are seeking.

Rule Three:

Ask about others' feelings, and share your own.

Rule Four:

Explore if identities are important to this discussion.

Each of these rules will be explored in a series of guides throughout this book. For now, let's focus on the first one, which draws on what we have learned about the *matching principle*.

First Rule:

Pay attention to what *kind* of conversation is occurring.

The most effective communicators pause before they speak and ask themselves: Why am I opening my mouth?

Unless we know what kind of discussion we're hoping for—and what type of discussion our companions want—we're at a disadvantage. As the last chapter explained, we might want to discuss practicalities while our partner wants to share their feelings. We might want to gossip while they want to make plans. If we're not having the same *kind* of conversation, we're unlikely to connect.

So the first goal in a learning conversation is identifying what kind of dialogue we're seeking—and then looking for clues about what the other parties want.

This can be as simple as taking a moment to clarify, for yourself, what you hope to say and how you want to say it: "My goal is to ask Maria if she wants to vacation together, but in a way that makes it easy for her to say no." Or it might consist of asking a spouse, as he describes a hard day, "Do you want me to suggest some solutions, or do you just need to vent?"

In one project examining how a group of investment bankers communicated among themselves inside a high-pressure firm, researchers tested a simple method to make daily discussions easier. Within this company, screaming matches occurred regularly, and colleagues were in competition for deals and bonuses. Disagreements sometimes led to prolonged fights, and meetings were often tense. But the researchers believed they could make these battles less fierce by asking everyone to write out just one sentence, before each meeting, explaining their goals for the upcoming discussion. So, for a week, before each gathering, every attendee scribbled out a goal: "This is to choose a budget that everyone agrees on," or "This is to air our complaints and hear each other out." The exercise never took more than a few minutes. Some people would share what they wrote at the meeting's start; others did not.

Then, during each meeting, the researchers studied what people had written, and took notes on what everyone said. They noticed two things: First, the sentences that people had written out usually indicated what *kind* of conversation they were seeking, as well as a mood they hoped to establish. They would typically specify an aim ("air our complaints") and a mindset ("hear each other out"). Second, if everyone scribbled their goals ahead of time, verbal arguments declined significantly. People still disagreed with one another. They were still competitive and got upset. But they were more likely to walk away from a meeting satisfied, like they had been heard and had understood what others were saying. Because they had determined what kind of conversation they wanted, they could convey their intents more clearly and listen as others declared their own goals.

Before we phone a friend or chat with a spouse, we don't need to write out a sentence about our goals, of course—but, if it's an important conversation, taking a moment to formulate what we hope to say, and how we hope to say it, is a good idea. And then, during the discussion, try to observe your companions: *Are they emotional? Do they seem practical minded? Do they keep bringing up other people or social topics?*

We all send clues, as we speak and listen, about what kind of conversation we want. Supercommunicators notice these clues, and think a bit harder about where they hope a conversation will go.

Notice:
Do your companions seem emotional, practical, or focused on social topics?
Have people said their goal for this conversation? Have you?
***Ask others:* What do you want to talk about?**

Some schools have trained teachers to ask students questions designed to elicit their goals, because it helps everyone communicate what they want and need. When a student comes to a teacher upset, for instance, the teacher might ask: "Do you want to be helped, hugged, or heard?" Different needs require different types of communication, and those different kinds of interaction—*helping, hugging, hearing*—each correspond to a different kind of conversation.

Do you want to be:

Helped?
A practical *What's This Really About?* conversation

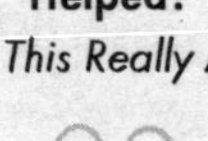

Hugged?
An emotional *How Do We Feel?* conversation

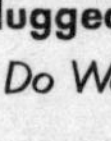

Or Heard?
A more social *Who Are We?* conversation

When a teacher—or anyone—asks a question like "Do you want to be helped, hugged, or heard?," what they are actually asking is: "What kind of conversation are you looking for?" Simply by asking someone what they need, we encourage a learning conversation, a dialogue that helps us discover what everyone most wants.

Most of the time, when we're talking to close friends or family, we engage in these kinds of learning conversations without thinking about it. We don't need to ask what someone wants, because we intuit what kind of discussion they are aiming for. It feels natural to ask people how they're feeling, and to provide them with a hug or advice or simply to listen.

But not every conversation is so easy. In fact, the most important ones rarely are.

In a learning conversation, our goal is to understand what's going on inside others' heads, and to share what's happening within our own. A learning conversation nudges us to pay better attention, listen more closely, speak more openly, and express what might otherwise go unsaid. It elicits alignment by convincing everyone that we all want to genuinely understand one another, and by revealing ways to connect.

THE *WHAT'S THIS REALLY ABOUT?* CONVERSATION

AN OVERVIEW

The beginnings of conversations are often awkward and fraught. We need to make decision after decision, at rapid speed ("What tone is appropriate?" "Is it okay to interrupt?" "Should I tell a joke?" "What does this person think of me?"), and there are lots of opportunities to miss something or fail to notice what goes unsaid.

This is when the *What's This Really About?* conversation can begin. *What's This Really About?* has two goals: The first is to determine what *topics* we want to discuss—what everyone needs from this dialogue. The second is to figure out *how* this discussion will unfold—what unspoken rules and norms we have agreed upon, and how we will make decisions together.

What's This Really About? often occurs at the start of a conversation. But it can also emerge mid-discussion, particularly when we are focused on making choices, considering plans, or thinking practically about costs and benefits. As the next chapter explores, within every conversation there is a quiet negotiation, where the prize is not winning, but rather determining what everyone *wants*, so that something meaningful can occur.

If the *What's This Really About?* conversation doesn't happen, what follows can feel frustrating and directionless. You've probably walked away from discussions feeling this way yourself: "We kept talking about completely different things" or "All we did was monologue at each other." The solution is learning to recognize when a *What's This Really About?* conversation has begun, and then knowing how to negotiate over how it will unfold.

2

EVERY CONVERSATION IS A NEGOTIATION

The Trial of Leroy Reed

"Okay, ladies and gentlemen," the court bailiff says to the twelve people around the table. He points to a stack of papers. "These are the instructions that the judge read to you"—he points to another stack—"these are the verdict forms."

The room contains seven men and five women with little in common except that they all live in Wisconsin and have appeared at this courthouse, as ordered, on a cold November morning in 1985. Now they are a jury, charged with deciding the fate of a man named Leroy Reed.

Over the previous two days, they had learned all about Reed, a forty-two-year-old ex-convict. He had been released from the state penitentiary nine years earlier and, since then, had lived a quiet life in a run-down part of Milwaukee. There had been no arrests or missed parole meetings. No fights or complaints from neighbors. By all accounts, he was a model citizen—until, that is, he was arrested for possession of a firearm. Because Reed was a felon, it was illegal for him to own a gun.

At the trial's start, Reed's lawyer had acknowledged that the evidence against his client was compelling. "First thing I'll tell you right now," he told the jurors, "Leroy Reed is a convicted felon. And on December seventh of last year, eleven months ago, he bought a gun. I'll tell you that right off the top. There's gonna be no dispute about that."

Under Wisconsin Statute 941.29, that meant Reed should go to prison for up to ten years. But "he ought to be acquitted anyway," the lawyer continued, because Reed had serious mental disabilities that, when combined with the strange circumstances of his arrest, suggested he hadn't intended to commit a crime. A psychologist testified that Reed could read only at a second-grade level and his intelligence was "substantially sub-average." When, over a decade earlier, he had been convicted for unknowingly serving as the getaway driver for a friend who robbed a convenience store, he was released early, in part, because authorities suspected that, even after his conviction, Reed hadn't understood that a crime had occurred.

Now, at this trial, the jurors were learning about the odd events leading up to Reed's latest arrest. Reed had been trying to get a steady job for years when, one day, he saw an advertisement in a magazine for a private-detective correspondence course. He mailed in the required $20 and, in return, received a fat envelope containing a tin badge and instructions telling him to, among other things, exercise regularly and buy a pistol. Reed followed the directions scrupulously. He jogged most mornings and, about a week after receiving the envelope, took the bus to a sporting goods store and filled out the appropriate paperwork, and then walked out with a .22 caliber gun.

Afterward, he went home and put the weapon, still in its box, in his closet. As far as anyone could tell, he never touched it again.

The purchase of the gun would likely have gone unnoticed except that, one day, he was hanging around the courthouse, hoping someone might hire him to solve a crime, when a police officer asked for identification. Reed handed over the only item in his pocket bearing his name: The bill of sale from the sporting goods store.

"Are you carrying this weapon?" the officer asked.

"It's at home," Reed replied.

The cop told Reed to bring the gun, in its box, to the sheriff's station. When Reed arrived, an officer ran his name against a database of felons and promptly arrested him.

Now he was on trial to determine if he would go back to prison. The prosecutor offered a simple argument for conviction: No matter Reed's mental limitations, "ignorance of the law is not a defense," he said. The jury might wish the law were different, but Reed had effectively admitted his guilt. He should go to jail.

The judge seemed to agree. He told the jury, before sending them off to deliberate, that Statute 941.29 dictated there were three questions they needed to answer:

Was Reed a felon?

Had he acquired a gun?

Did he know he had acquired a gun?

If the answer to all three was yes, then Reed was guilty.

The jury's duty, the judge told them, was to "not be swayed by sympathy, prejudice, or passion.... You are to decide only whether the defendant is guilty or not guilty of the offense." If mercy was required, the judge could apply it later, during sentencing.

Now, however, sitting inside the deliberation room, the jurors seem uncertain how to begin.

"Let's choose a foreperson," one says.

"You're it," another juror replies.

No one will be allowed to leave the room, except for short bathroom breaks, until they have a unanimous verdict. If the deliberations go late, they'll start again early the next morning. No one will be permitted to withdraw from the conversation, or remain silent, or defer debate simply because they are tired of talking. They will have to argue over facts and theories, try to persuade and cajole one another, until everyone agrees.

But first, they need to figure out how to start the conversation. They need to negotiate the unspoken rules for how they will speak and listen—and determine what everyone wants and needs. This is a negotiation we all participate in whenever a conversation begins, whether we realize it or not. And it's more complicated than we think.

HOW DO WE DECIDE WHAT TO TALK ABOUT?

Try to recall your last meaningful conversation. Perhaps you and a loved one were discussing how to divvy up household chores. Or maybe it was a work meeting about next year's budget. Possibly you were debating with friends about who should be the next president, or gossiping about whether your neighbors Pablo and Zach are going to break up.

As the conversation started, how did you know what everyone wanted to discuss? Did someone announce a topic ("We need to decide who's driving Aimee to school tomorrow") or did a focus emerge gradually? ("Hey, just wondering, did Pablo seem distracted at dinner last night?")

Once you figured out what to talk about, how did you intuit the conversation's tone? How did you know if you should speak casually? If making jokes was appropriate? If it was okay to interrupt?

You probably didn't think about those questions, and yet they all got answered somehow. When researchers have studied conversations, they've found a delicate, almost subconscious dance that usually occurs at a discussion's start. This back-and-forth emerges via our tone of voice, how we hold our bodies, our asides and sighs and laughs. But until we arrive at a consensus on how a dialogue ought to proceed, the real conversation can't begin.

Occasionally, a conversation's aims are stated explicitly ("We're here to discuss this quarter's projections") until we realize, midway through, that people's real preoccupations lie elsewhere ("What we're actually worried about is whether there're going to be layoffs"). Sometimes we cycle through various starts—someone tells a joke; someone else gets overly formal; there's an awkward silence until a third person takes the lead—and, eventually, the conversation's focus is tacitly agreed upon.

Some researchers call this process a *quiet negotiation*: A subtle give-and-take over which topics we'll dive into and which we'll skirt around; the rules for how we'll speak and listen.

The first goal of this negotiation is determining what everyone *wants* from a conversation. These desires are often revealed via a series of offers and counteroffers, invitations and refusals, that are nearly subconscious but expose if people are willing to play along. This back-and forth can take just a few moments, or last as long as the conversation itself. And it serves a crucial purpose: To help us find a set of subjects that we are all willing to embrace.

The second goal in this negotiation is to figure out the rules for how we will speak, listen, and make decisions together. We don't always explicitly state these rules aloud. Rather, we conduct experiments to see which norms will stick. We introduce new topics, send signals via our tone of voice and expressions, react to what people say, project various moods, and pay attention to how others respond.

However, regardless of how this quiet negotiation unfolds, the goals are the same: First, to decide *what* we all need from this conversation. Second, to determine *how* we will speak and make decisions. Or, put differently, to figure out: What does everyone *want*? And how will we make choices *together*?

The Three Conversations

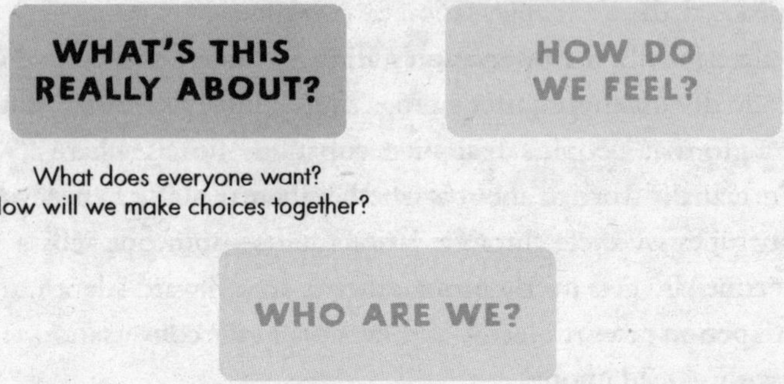

The *What's This Really About?* conversation often emerges when we confront a decision. Sometimes, these decisions are about the conversation itself—*Is it okay to openly disagree, or should we sugarcoat our differences? Is this a friendly chat or a serious talk?* Other decisions ask us to think practically ("Should we submit an offer for the house?") or make a judgment ("What do you think of Zoe's work?") or analyze a choice ("Do you want me to pick up the groceries or get the kids?").

Underneath all those straightforward decisions are other, potentially more serious choices: *If we openly disagree, can we remain friends? Can we afford to pay that much for a home? Is it fair for me to pick up the kids when I have so much work to do?* Unless we come to a basic agreement about what we're actually discussing, and how we should discuss it, it's hard to make progress.

But once we know what everyone wants from a conversation, and how we'll make decisions together, a more meaningful dialogue can emerge.

HOW A SURGEON LEARNED TO COMMUNICATE

In 2014, a prominent surgeon at Memorial Sloan Kettering Cancer Center in New York City—someone admired for his warmth, kindness, and medical acumen—realized that, for years, he had been talking to patients all wrong.

Dr. Behfar Ehdaie specialized in treating prostate cancer. Every year, hundreds of men sought his advice after receiving the terrifying news that a tumor had been discovered deep inside their groin. And every year, many of those patients, despite Ehdaie's best efforts, failed to hear what he was desperately trying to tell them regarding their disease.

Treating prostate cancer involves a complicated trade-off: The surest course of action is surgery or radiation to prevent the cancer from spreading. But because the prostate gland is located alongside nerves involved in urination and sexual function, some patients, after treatment, experience incontinence and impotence, sometimes for the rest of their lives.

So for most people with prostate tumors, doctors advise against surgery or any other form of treatment. Low-risk patients, instead, are counseled to choose "active surveillance": Blood tests every six months and a prostate biopsy every two years to see if the tumor is growing. But, otherwise, no surgery, radiation, or anything else. Active surveillance carries its own risks, of course: The tumor might metastasize. But prostate cancer usually grows very slowly—in fact, there's a saying among physicians that older patients will usually die of old age before their prostate cancer kills them.

Nearly every day, a new patient would enter Ehdaie's office, overwhelmed by a recent diagnosis, and confront a difficult choice: Have surgery and face a potential lifetime of incontinence and sexual dysfunction? Or leave it alone and hope, if the cancer grows, the tests will catch it in time?

Ehdaie believed these patients had come to him for practical medical advice, so he followed what, to him, seemed a logical script: For the vast majority of people, he felt active surveillance was the right decision, and he provided evidence supporting the wisdom of that approach. He typically began by showing patients data indicating that, for 97 percent of men who opt for active surveillance, the risk of the cancer spreading is roughly the same as for those undergoing invasive treatments, and so they are better off with a wait-and-see approach. He would hand over studies—with the important sentences highlighted in yellow—explaining that the risks of waiting were minuscule, while the downsides of surgery were potentially life changing. Ehdaie tends to speak in full paragraphs, like a medical textbook come to life, but he kept these conversations short and sweet: The right choice was active surveillance. "I thought these would be some of the easiest discussions of my life," he told me. "I figured they'd be overjoyed to hear they could avoid surgery."

However, again and again, his patients failed to hear what he was saying. Ehdaie was talking about treatment options, but running through patients' minds were questions of a very different sort: *How will my family react to this news? Am I willing to risk dying so I can continue enjoying my life? Am I ready to confront my mortality?*

As a result, the patients, instead of looking at the charts and studies and feeling relief, would inevitably begin asking questions: What about the 3 percent of patients who *hadn't* benefited from active surveillance? Had they died? Were their deaths painful? "We'd spend the entire meeting talking about the three percent," said Ehdaie. "And then, when we'd meet again, the three percent was all they'd remember, and they'd say they wanted the surgery."

It was bewildering. Ehdaie had spent his life perfecting his knowledge of prostate tumors—these patients had sought him out because he was an expert!—and yet, no matter how much he told them they didn't need surgery, many of them insisted on going under his knife. Sometimes patients would take the highlighted studies home and start searching online for counterevidence, diving into obscure journals and medical abstracts until they had convinced themselves the data was all contradictory, or the doctors didn't know what they were talking about.

"Then they'd come back suspicious," Ehdaie said. "They'd say, 'Are you the active surveillance guy? Is that why you're suggesting this?'" Other patients would simply ignore his advice. "They'd say, 'I have a friend who had prostate cancer and he told me the surgery was fine.' Or 'I have a neighbor who had brain cancer and she died in two months, so it's too risky to wait.'"

This problem wasn't limited to Ehdaie. Surveys indicate that, even today, an estimated 40 percent of prostate cancer patients opt for unnecessary surgeries. That's more than fifty thousand people, each year, who fail to hear—or decide to ignore—the advice their physicians are giving them.

"When it happens again and again, you start to realize: This isn't a problem with my patients," Ehdaie told me. "This is a problem with me. I'm doing something wrong. I'm failing at this conversation."

• • •

Ehdaie started asking friends for advice and, eventually, a colleague recommended he speak with a professor from Harvard Business School named Deepak Malhotra. Ehdaie sent a long email asking if they could talk.

Malhotra was part of a group of professors studying how negotiations occur in the real world. In 2016, one of his colleagues had helped the president of Colombia negotiate a peace deal to end a fifty-two-year civil war that had killed more than two hundred thousand people. After the 2004 National Hockey League lockout, which canceled half the season, Malhotra analyzed why discussions between players and team owners had broken down and what it took to get them back on track.

When he received Ehdaie's email, Malhotra was intrigued. His scholarship sometimes describes formal negotiations where, say, union leaders and managers battle around a conference table. But Ehdaie's situation was different: The doctor and his patients were engaged in high-stakes negotiations—only, most of the time, no one recognized they were negotiating with each other.

How to Figure Out What This Is Really About

First, recognize that this is a negotiation.

Malhotra flew to Sloan Kettering to gather more information and, as he shadowed Ehdaie, saw opportunities where these conversations could improve. "An important step in any negotiation is getting clarity on what all the participants want," Malhotra told me. Often, what people desire from a negotiation isn't obvious at first. Sometimes a union leader might say her goal is higher wages. But then, over time, other goals are revealed: She also wants to look good to her members, or one union faction hopes to take power from another faction, or the workers value autonomy on a par with higher paychecks, but they don't know how to express that at the bargaining table. It can take time, and the right inquiries, to help define people's desires. So an important task in any negotiation is asking lots of questions.

But as Ehdaie interacted with patients, he wasn't asking the most important questions. He wasn't asking patients what mattered to them. He wasn't asking: Did they want to extend their lives if the treatment robbed them of things like travel and sex? Would you want an extra five years of life if the trade-off was constant pain? How much of someone's decision depended on their own desires versus what their family wanted? Was the patient secretly hoping the doctor would just tell him what to do?

Ehdaie's biggest mistake was assuming, at the start of a conversation, that he knew what the patient wanted: Objective medical advice, an overview of options to make an informed choice.

"But you don't want to begin a negotiation assuming you know what the other side wants," Malhotra said. This is the first part of the *What's This Really About?* conversation: Figuring out what everyone wants to talk about. The simplest method for uncovering everyone's desires, of course, is simply asking *What do you want?* But that approach can fail if people don't know, or are embarrassed to say, or aren't certain how to express their desires, or worry that revealing too much will put them at a disadvantage.

How to Figure Out What This Is Really About

First, recognize that this is a negotiation.

Next determine: What does everyone *want*?

So Malhotra suggested that Ehdaie take a different approach. Instead of starting the conversation by presenting patients with an overview of options, he should ask open-ended questions designed to get them talking about their values and what they wanted out of life.

"What does this cancer diagnosis mean to you?" Ehdaie asked a sixty-two-year-old patient a few weeks later.

"Well," the man said, "it makes me think of my dad because he died when I was young, which was tough on my mom. I would hate to put my family through that." The man talked about his kids and how he didn't want to traumatize them. He spoke about his worries regarding the world his grandchildren were inheriting, what with climate change and all.

Ehdaie had expected the man to talk about his medical concerns or his mortality, or to ask questions about pain. Instead, his preoccupations were focused on his family. What he really wanted to know was which treatment would make his wife and kids worry least. He didn't care about data. He wanted to discuss how to avoid upsetting the people he loved.

A similar pattern emerged in other conversations. Ehdaie would start with a broad question—"What did your wife say when you told her about your diagnosis?"—and instead of talking about their disease, patients spoke about their marriages, or memories of a parent's illness, or about nonmedical traumas such as divorces or bankruptcies. Some spoke about the future, how they hoped to spend their retirements, what they wanted to leave behind as a legacy. They started working out how to fit the *idea* of cancer into their lives, debating over what this disease *means.* That's how a quiet negotiation works: It is a process of people deciding, together, what topics we'll discuss, and how we'll discuss them. It is an attempt to figure out what we all want from a conversation, even if we're not, ourselves, sure at first.

Some patients, Ehdaie's questions revealed, were scared and wanted emotional reassurance. Others wanted to feel in control. Some—seeking social proof they weren't taking unusual risks—needed to hear how other people had made this decision. Still others wanted the most cutting-edge treatments.

Often, Ehdaie only managed to figure out what a patient wanted to talk about by asking them the same basic questions, again and again, in different ways. "Eventually they would say something that revealed what was important to them," he told me. This explained why Ehdaie had failed to communicate with so many patients over the years: He hadn't been asking the right questions. He hadn't been asking about their needs and desires, what they *wanted* from this conversation. He had assumed he already knew. And because he hadn't bothered to figure out what mattered, he had deluged patients with information they didn't care about. He resolved to change how he communicated, to stop lecturing and start asking better questions, to begin having proper dialogues.

Within six months of Ehdaie's adopting this more inclusive approach, the number of his patients opting for surgery fell by 30 percent. Today, he's training other surgeons to negotiate about topics such as opioid use, treatments for breast cancer, and end-of-life decisions. It's an approach we can all use, even in less dire discussions, when we're talking to a friend about, say, their dating life, or a work colleague about an upcoming project, or our partner about how we should raise our kids. In many conversations, there's a surface topic—but also a deeper, more meaningful subject that, when we bring it into the light, reveals what everyone wants most from the conversation. "It's important to ask what they want," Ehdaie told me. "It's an invitation for people to tell you who they are."

THE SUPERCOMMUNICATOR IN THE JURY ROOM

"I know some juries like to take a vote right off the bat," the freshly appointed foreperson tells his fellow jurors. But maybe, he suggests, they could avoid committing to positions right away and, instead, go around the room and offer their general impressions of the trial.

His goal is obviously to sidestep kneejerk reactions, but some jurors can't help immediately taking a side. One, a firefighter named Karl, says there's no question in his mind that Leroy Reed is guilty. "To me, they proved it beyond a reasonable doubt," he says. "The extenuating circumstances, as far as what his intent was, his awareness of the law, his ability to read and understand, is not for us to determine, as far as guilt or innocence. That's for the judge to take into consideration in the sentencing." He reminds everyone of the three questions the judge instructed them to answer: Was Reed a felon? Had he acquired a gun? Did he know he had acquired a gun?

"As far as I'm concerned, they met the three points, the burden of proof," Karl says.

Two other jurors quickly agree with Karl: Leroy Reed is guilty.

Others, though, are less certain. "I feel that the defendant is guilty on all three accusations technically, but I guess I feel that we should also take into consideration the fact that he does have a reading disability," says a public schoolteacher named Lorraine. Another juror, Henry, is also unsure. "Technically, the man is guilty, guilty as sin," he says. "But I want to acquit Leroy because I don't think he was fully aware of the rules."

After everyone in the room speaks, it appears there are three people certain they want to convict Reed, two who are strongly leaning toward acquittal, and seven on the fence. "We have a very philosophical argument on our hands," says one of the undecided, a psychologist named Barbara. "Are we obligated, as a jury, to follow the letter of the law and find him guilty? Or are we obligated, as a jury, to use our special level of conscience?"

If, at this point, an educated observer were asked to guess how this would turn out, the answer would be easy: Leroy Reed is going to prison. Numerous studies have found that juries, regardless of initial uncertainties, usually eventually vote to convict, particularly if the defendant has a criminal record.

However, there is something different about this jury. It's imperceptible at first, but it slowly becomes apparent when a juror in his midthirties, a man named John Boly, starts talking. Boly seems to understand that all the jurors are involved in a negotiation with one another. He also recognizes that the first step in this negotiation is figuring out what everyone *wants* from this conversation.

"I'm really not at all sure what I think or what I feel on this case," Boly tells the others when it's his turn to speak. "There's no question but that this man is a felon and there's no question but that he purchased a firearm." His tone is a bit formal. "This guy's reading magazines and living in a fantasy world," Boly says. "I'm not sure . . ." he starts. "I want to listen to other people and I want to talk about and figure this out together as we go along."

The other jurors seem a bit mystified by Boly. Some of them are dressed in jeans while he is in a suit. Some have indicated they are retired, or work in factories or are stay-at-home parents. Boly is a professor of contemporary literature at Marquette University, where his specialty is Jacques Derrida. As one juror later told me, "When he started going on about Kafka and trials at one point, I was like, what are you talking about, man? What planet are you from?"

However, Boly is also different in another, less obvious way: He's a supercommunicator. He knows he must figure out what each juror wants from this discussion, what they need, and he knows that requires, as a first step, asking lots of questions. So he starts posing them as the conversation moves around the room: *What do you think of handguns? What did you think when Leroy got flummoxed? Do you own a gun? Can we talk about what "possession" means? What is justice?*

To the other jurors, these questions seem innocent, almost like casual asides. But Boly is listening closely to how people answer, cataloging each juror in his mind, trying to figure out what each person wants to discuss. Some want to talk about morality and fairness ("I don't care what the law says. Has justice been done?") or autonomy ("I am not a computer. . . . I want to sit here and talk about it and think about it and not just say, right off the bat, he's convicted on these three counts, he's therefore guilty") or are simply bored ("We can argue about semantics and we could do that forever").

As Boly listens, he keeps a list in his head of what each person is seeking: Henry wants guidance. Barbara wants compassion. Karl wants to go by the book. He is engaging in the first part of the *What's This Really About?* conversation: Figuring out what everyone wants.

But there's also a second part to *What's This Really About?*: Determining how we will talk to one another and cooperate in making decisions. There are lots of decisions that occur during every conversation, ranging from the unimportant (*Will we interrupt each other?*) to the crucial ("Should we send this man to jail?"). So, amid our negotiation, we must also figure out how we will make choices *together.*

How to Figure Out What This Is Really About

First, recognize that this is a negotiation.

Next determine: What does everyone *want*?

Then, how will we make choices *together*?

A NEGOTIATOR'S GOAL IS EXPANDING THE PIE

Our understanding of this second part of the *What's This Really About?* discussion—*how will we make choices together?*—has been transformed in the past forty years.

In 1979, a now-famous group of professors—Roger Fisher, William Ury, and Bruce Patton—founded the Harvard Negotiation Project. Their goal was to "improve the theory and practice of negotiation and conflict management," which, up to that point, had received relatively scant scholarly attention. Two years later, they published a book based on their research, *Getting to Yes,* that turned popular understanding of negotiations upside down.

Until then, many people had assumed that negotiations were zero-sum games: Any time I gained something at the bargaining table, you lost. "A generation ago," reads *Getting to Yes,* "in contemplating a negotiation, the common question in people's minds was,

'Who is going to win and who is going to lose?'" But Fisher, a Harvard law professor, thought that approach was all wrong. As a young man, he had helped implement the Marshall Plan in Europe and, later, aided in finding ways to end the Vietnam War. He had worked on the Camp David Accords in 1978 and in securing the release of fifty-two American hostages from Iran in 1981.

In those and other negotiations, Fisher saw something different at work: The best negotiators didn't battle over who should get the biggest slice of pie. Rather, they focused on making the pie itself larger, finding win-win solutions where everyone walked away happier than before. The concept that both sides could "win" in a negotiation, Fisher and his colleagues wrote, might seem impossible, but "it is increasingly recognized that there are cooperative ways of negotiating our differences and that even if a 'win-win' solution cannot be found, a wise agreement can still often be reached that is better for both sides."

Since *Getting to Yes* was first published, hundreds of studies have found ample evidence to support this idea. Elite diplomats have explained that their goal at a bargaining table isn't seizing victory, but rather convincing the other side to become collaborators in uncovering new solutions that no one thought of before. Negotiation, among its top practitioners, isn't a battle. It's an act of creativity.

This approach has become known as *interest-based bargaining*, and its first step looks a lot like what Boly did in the jury room or what Dr. Ehdaie did with his patients at Sloan Kettering: Ask open-ended questions and listen closely. Get people talking about how they see the world and what they value most. Even if you don't learn, right away, what others are seeking—they might not know themselves—you'll at least inspire them to listen back. "If you want the other side to appreciate your interests," Fisher wrote, "begin by demonstrating that you appreciate theirs."

Listening, though, is just the first step. The next task is addressing the second question inherent in a *What's This Really About?* conversation: How will we make decisions together? What are the rules for this dialogue?

Frequently, the best way to figure out those rules is by testing out various conversational approaches, and seeing how others react. For instance, negotiators often conduct experiments—*first I'll interrupt you, and then I'll be polite, and then I'll bring up a new topic or make an unexpected concession, and watch what you do*—until everyone decides, together, which norms are accepted, and how this conversation should unfold. These experiments can take the form of proposals or solutions, or unanticipated suggestions or new topics that are suddenly introduced. In each case, the goal is the same: To see if this probe reveals a path forward. "Great negotiators are artists," said Michele Gelfand, a professor at Stanford's business school. "They take conversations in unexpected directions."

Among the surest methods for sparking this kind of experimentation is introducing new themes and questions to a discussion, adding items to the table until the conversation has changed enough that new possibilities are revealed. "If you're negotiating over salaries, for instance, and you're stuck," Gelfand said, "then drag something new in: 'We've been focused on wages, but what if, instead of increasing paychecks, we give everyone more sick days? What if we let them work from home?'"

"The challenge is not to eliminate conflict," Fisher wrote in *Getting to Yes*, "but to transform it." All of us conduct these kinds of experiments in our everyday conversations, frequently without realizing it. When we make a joke, or ask a probing question, or suddenly get serious or silly, we are, in a sense, conducting a test to see if our companions will accept our invitation, if they'll play along.

Like interest-based bargaining, the *What's This Really About?* conversation succeeds by transforming a conversation from a tussle over where the dialogue is going into a collaboration, a group experiment, where the aim is figuring out what everyone is seeking and the goals and values we all share. To an outside observer, it might seem as if we're simply discussing who will pick up the kids and the groceries. But we—the people participating in this quiet negotiation—are aware of subtexts and undercurrents, the experiments under way. We're asking open-ended questions ("Am I doing enough to help?") and adding items to the table ("What if I do grocery pickup and wash the dishes, and you get the kids and fold the laundry?") until the conversation has changed enough to make clear what everyone actually wants and the rules we've all agreed on: "I want to respect your time, and work is important, so what if I get takeout and ask Uncle Arvind to get the kids, so we can both come home late?"

The *What's This Really About?* conversation is a negotiation—only the goal is not to win, but to help everyone agree on the topics we'll discuss, and how we'll make decisions together.

• • •

Back in the jury room, Boly has done the first part of *What's This Really About?*: He has asked questions and sought to understand what each of his fellow jurors want.

Some of what Boly hears indicates a guilty verdict is becoming increasingly likely. The foreperson says that he intends to convict, and then another juror, who was previously on the fence, agrees with him. Karl, the fireman, jumps in with support. Leroy Reed didn't hurt anyone this time, he says, but what about next time? "That's why the law is there, why felons cannot own guns," Karl says. Others chime their assent: "What if Mr. Reed would've bought a gun and killed some innocent bystander somewhere along the line?"

This, studies of courtroom dynamics indicate, is when a jury's verdict often starts to gel. This is the moment—when one or two jurors take a strong stance, and others, because of indecisiveness or pliability, climb aboard the bandwagon—that a guilty verdict becomes inevitable.

But Barbara, the school psychologist, isn't quite ready. "I wonder if we could find some room," she says, "that perhaps he didn't, in the full sense of the word, *know* he was a felon, and didn't, in the full sense of the word, *know* that he possessed a firearm."

"The only thing that bothers me," the foreperson shoots back, is that the judge said "something to the effect that ignorance is no excuse." The conversation is getting heated. Voices are rising.

It's at this point that Boly speaks again, but in a different way from before. He's done asking questions. It's time for the second part of a *What's This Really About?* conversation: Figuring out how everyone will make choices together.

He begins by introducing something new to the conversation and imagining what it's like to be Leroy Reed.

"One of the things I noticed," Boly says, interrupting the growing tension with a light tone, is something about Reed's gun. If you look closely at it, he says, it "looks like a toy." This comment comes out of left field. The others look at Boly with confusion. "Now, I'd be willing to bet, if I bought a gun," Boly continues, "and I got a holster with it, the first thing I'd wanna do is stick it here," he gestures at his belt, "and go around Milwaukee and, you know, every time I walk past that bridge or under that underpass, or something like that, I don't have to worry about what's gonna step out from behind a lamppost. I'm ten feet tall! I'm packing a rod!"

His fellow jurors are befuddled. What's going on? What is "packing a rod"? The only thing everyone knows for certain is that Boly should never be given a weapon.

But Boly isn't really talking about guns. He's talking about something bigger. He's conducting an experiment.

"Now," Boly continues, "the fact that, you know, he handles it almost like it was this sacramental thing, and he locks it up and he puts it in his closet and he shuts the door," that's an important detail, he tells them. "He doesn't put it in the holster or in his pocket or wear it on his hip or anything like that."

One of the other jurors—someone who, until now, seemed willing to ride the momentum to a guilty verdict—picks up the thread. "Right," he says, "he didn't take it out of the box."

Another juror jumps in: "We can't even say that he knew how to use a gun."

This is pure conjecture. No evidence was offered during the trial suggesting that Leroy Reed is ignorant of how to use a firearm. But the jurors are now building a story in their minds: *Maybe he doesn't know how to load a gun. Maybe he doesn't even realize that a gun needs bullets.* Within a few minutes, a whole new version of Leroy Reed has materialized: Someone who, even if he *possessed* a gun, might not have *understood* he possessed it. In which case the judge's third question—"Did he know he had acquired a gun?"—has taken on a new dimension.

Boly has shifted the conversation. He has reframed this discussion by experimenting with an idea, by inviting the jurors to start imagining new possibilities, dreaming up different ways to analyze the questions at hand. They are negotiating over how they'll come to a decision *together.*

The momentum toward a guilty verdict has slowed, but they are still a long way from a unanimous choice.

HOW PERSUASION HAPPENS

What's This Really About? discussions tend to fall into one of two buckets. There are some conversations where people signal they are in a practical mindset: They want to solve a problem or think through an idea. They want to decide how much to bid for that house—and what does that mean about our life together?—or who to hire for the job they've been advertising—and do we actually need another employee? These discussions call for analysis and clearheaded reasoning. Psychologists refer to this kind of thinking as the *logic of costs and benefits.* When people embrace logical reasoning and practical calculations—when they agree that rational decision making is the most persuasive method for making a choice together—they're agreeing to contrast potential costs with hoped-for benefits.

But in some other *What's This Really About?* conversations, the aim is different. Sometimes people want to make choices together that might not align with logic and reason. They want to explore topics beyond cold rationality. They want to apply their compassion, talk about values, discuss matters of right and wrong in making joint decisions. They want to draw on their experiences, even if they don't completely overlap with the situation at hand.

In these kinds of conversations, facts are less persuasive. If someone says something about their feelings, their partner doesn't start debating with them. Instead, they sympathize, laugh, share a sense of outrage or pride. In general, in these kinds of discussions, we make decisions not by analyzing costs and benefits, but instead by looking to our past experiences and asking ourselves, "What does someone like me usually do in a situation like this?" We are applying what psychologists call the *logic of similarities.* This kind of logic is important because, without it, we wouldn't feel much compassion when someone describes sadness or disappointment, or know how to defuse a tense situation, or tell if someone is serious or kidding. This logic tells us when to empathize.

What kind of logic are we using?

{ The Logic of Costs and Benefits } { The Logic of Similarities }

These two kinds of logic exist, side by side, within our brains.* But they are often contradictory or mutually exclusive. So when we're negotiating over how a conversation will unfold—how we'll make choices together—one question we're asking is: What kind of logic does everyone find persuasive?

For Dr. Ehdaie, understanding the difference between the practical *logic of costs and benefits* and the empathetic *logic of similarities* was critical. Some patients came in with analytical questions and asked for data. They were clearly in a practical, analytical mindset—and so he knew they would be persuaded through evidence: studies and data.

Is this a practical discussion?

↓

Lean into data and reasoning.

But other patients told Ehdaie stories about their pasts and their anxieties. They talked about their values and beliefs. These patients were in an empathetic mindset. So Ehdaie knew he needed to persuade them through compassion and stories. He would tell them that he—a surgeon who loved surgery—would advise his own father to avoid this kind of operation. He told them what other patients had done, because in an empathetic mindset we are influenced by

* You may recognize similarities with the different kinds of cognition that Daniel Kahneman describes in his book *Thinking, Fast and Slow.* Kahneman describes the brain as containing two systems: System 1 is instinctual and can produce snap judgments, like the logic of similarities. System 2 is slower, more deliberate and rational, like the logic of costs and benefits.

narratives. "Stories bypass the brain's instinct to look for reasons to be suspicious," said Emily Falk, a professor at the University of Pennsylvania. We get drawn into stories because they *feel* right.

Is this an empathetic discussion?

↓

Lean into stories and compassion.

There's a lesson here: The first step of a quiet negotiation is figuring out what people want from a conversation. The second step is determining how we're going to make choices together—and that means deciding if this is a rational conversation or an empathetic one. Are we going to make decisions through analysis and reason, or through empathy and narratives?

Is this a practical discussion?	*Is this an empathetic discussion?*
↓	↓
Lean into data and reasoning.	Lean into stories and compassion.

It's easy to get this wrong. In fact, I have gotten it wrong many times. When one of my cousins started telling me about wild conspiracy theories ("Mattress stores are money-laundering fronts!"), I tried to convince him he was mistaken by using data and facts ("Actually, most of them are publicly traded, so you can see their finances online"). Then I was surprised when he said that *I* had been brainwashed. He was using a logic that drew on stories he had heard about elites taking advantage of other people, a *logic of similarities* that said we ought to be suspicious about corporations because they have lied before. My reasonable arguments, my *logic of costs and benefits,* wasn't persuasive to him in the slightest.

Or say you've telephoned a customer service representative with a complaint. You might assume they want to hear your story ("My son was playing with my phone and he somehow managed to order a thousand dollars' worth of Legos"), but you quickly discover they don't care ("Sir, please just give me the date of the transaction"). They don't need the backstory. They're in a practical mindset, and just want to find a solution and move on to the next call.

When John Boly heard his fellow jurors telling stories about their lives and talking about concepts like justice and ethics, he sensed that some of them were looking for a conversation that went beyond analysis and reasoning. They were in an empathetic frame of mind. Boly responded by talking about how it would *feel* to carry a gun, imagining what Leroy Reed was thinking. He started telling stories: "He handles it almost like it was this sacramental thing." These weren't profound or elaborate stories, just wisps of a narrative, but it's enough to prompt others to start imagining what it's like to be Reed, to start telling tales of their own. "We can't even say," one juror comments, "that he knew how to use a gun."

Boly has shifted, ever so slightly, how he is speaking and the logic he is using, and that is enough to convince his fellow jurors that this conversation isn't done.

THE NEGOTIATION CONCLUDES

The jurors have been in the room for a little over an hour when one suggests it's time for a formal vote. Each person scribbles their verdict on a piece of paper. The foreperson tallies them. Opinions have changed: They are now at nine votes to acquit, three to convict.

But a verdict, of course, must be unanimous. Anything else triggers a mistrial. Studies of jury deliberations indicate that moments such as this—when a small group has vocally committed to a specific verdict—are perilous. Once people like Karl and the foreperson stake a strong claim to guilt, it's difficult for them to change their minds. All it takes is one adamant juror, certain the accused should go to jail, for a mistrial to occur.

In this room, there are still three people who think Leroy Reed is guilty.

But the stories are whirring inside everyone's heads.

The foreperson clears his throat. "I have something to say," he announces.

He had voted guilty, he continues. But, as he listened to the other jurors, he started imagining himself in Leroy's shoes. In particular, he later told me, he remembered a moment when he had been pulled over for a speeding ticket, and "when the cop pulled me over, I told him it's not right to give me a ticket, it's not justice, because I wasn't putting anyone else at risk by going a few miles over the speed limit."

That logic had made sense to him at the time. And now, in the jury room, it occurs to him that Leroy Reed is in the same position, accused of a crime that didn't put anyone at risk. If you buy a gun and hide it in your closet, you may have technically broken the law, but does that mean you should be punished? Does that align with the stories we tell ourselves about justice and fairness?

"I can see a reason for somewhat of a doubt, however minor it might be," the foreperson tells the others. He's changing his mind.

Another juror has changed his mind, as well. Looking at the facts from Reed's perspective, he says, made him rethink things.

Sometimes, the stories we hear are enough to help us see a situation through someone else's eyes, to empathize and reconsider. At other times, dispassionate reason wins the day. But we can only make decisions together if we all agree on which *kind* of logic is most persuasive. Once we are aligned, our minds become more open to what others have to say.

• • •

There's only one guilty vote remaining now. One last negotiation, and the jury's job is done.

But that vote is Karl, and even after all this back-and-forth, he is still certain Reed should be convicted. "We're going way too deep into his psychological thoughts," he has told the other jurors. "We're guessing at what he was thinking, we're guessing at what he knew, we're guessing at what he didn't know." Leroy Reed was a felon who bought a handgun. That's all the story Karl needs.

Throughout this deliberation, Karl hasn't told any stories about himself. Other jurors have peppered their comments with asides—tales about their lives, revelations from their pasts—but not Karl. Karl's son told me that his father, who died in 2000, was the ideal fireman, "a real follow-the-checklist, respect-the-chain-of-command kind of guy." Karl taught himself to rely on the practical, analytical *logic of costs and benefits* because, during an emergency, that kind of thinking saves lives.

So Boly embarks on a different kind of negotiation.

It begins when a juror poses a question to Karl, an open-ended inquiry: "It appears to me that your decision that this man is guilty is very important and complete in your mind. Share more of that with us, if you will."

Karl shifts in his seat. "I can't . . ." He pauses. "I don't have the education and the training to put myself into your class as far as being able to understand the human mind and how it works and what people think," he says. "It sounds very cold and simplistic to look at three reasons and say, yes, they meet this and this," but, to Karl, that's the whole case.

"Lemme ask you one quick question," another juror says. "Do you think there's ever a case where exceptions can be made?"

"Sure," Karl replies. "When I get Mr. Reed out there, and I look at him, to me, he's not a person that's gonna harm anyone. I don't think he had any ill intent. I don't feel he's a threat to society."

But Karl explains that there's a bigger issue to consider here, a trade-off of costs and benefits. If juries stop enforcing laws, that's anarchy. Acquitting Leroy Reed could encourage other people to lawlessness.

If it would help public safety, Karl says, he could see himself make an exception and let someone go. But he can't see any such benefit in Leroy Reed's case.

Something important has just happened: Karl has revealed his deepest desire. He values public safety above all else. That's why he's pushing for a guilty verdict—in his practical mindset, a guilty verdict preserves law and order, keeps people protected.

Boly recognizes this as an opportunity to add something new to the table, to experiment with a different approach. For instance, what if an *innocent* verdict makes people even safer?

"You know," Boly says, addressing his words to the room, though his intended audience is Karl, "I think this is a good law, and I don't want to say or do anything that suggests that I don't take this law seriously." But still, he says, he's frustrated. "Part of what's motivating me is that I've got a lot of other things to do. This is finals week," and he has a lot of work at the university. What's more, "my students have been the victims of crime. A week ago, a woman in one of my classes was walking to my class, and she was assaulted. . . . Another woman in a class I was teaching at the time was assaulted. She was beaten and she was raped.

"So, I mean, I want to do my civic duty," he continues. "I've got a lot of other things to do. I come down here, to the courthouse, and the DA gives me this case, and in spite of this awesome room, and these very serious people, and in spite of their lovely dog and pony show and the legal rigamarole, I'm sort of sitting to myself, thinking, this is Mickey Mouse. I mean, I really don't feel that this is a justified expenditure of my time." They could be putting a thief behind bars, or a rapist, or a murderer. Instead, they're debating whether Leroy Reed—someone who poses no real threat to public safety—should go to jail. "I'm thinking of a message I'd like to send the DA's office. Believe me, I would love to send them a message and the message would be: Dammit to hell, I'm afraid to walk to my car in the parking lot! I've got women students who are being mugged, who are being beaten, who are being raped. The same thing is happening to my male students. They're being mugged. And you give me Leroy."

If they acquit Reed, Boly tells the room, they're sending a message to the police and the district attorney: Focus on the real criminals. Focus on keeping the public genuinely protected. By finding Reed innocent, they're actually *helping* public safety. It's a creative take on the situation, for sure, but he's applying reason, comparing potential drawbacks with expected gains. He's using practical, analytical logic to add new options to the conversation. He's aligning with Karl, and arguing that if they care about stopping crime, the rational choice is letting Reed go free.

"Definitely he shouldn't be here," Karl says. He still isn't completely convinced, though.

So Boly offers one last bargain: "I have an enormous amount of respect for your sense of the importance of the law," he tells Karl. "Your sense of the importance of getting it right and your dedication to the integrity of the judicial process."

There is a cost to changing one's mind, Boly knows, an expense paid by our ego. But there is a benefit, as well: The esteem and self-respect that come from doing the right thing.

As the conversation continues, it's unclear how Karl is processing all of this. But he's thinking.

"Let's say we take a vote on it?" the foreperson asks as they approach two and a half hours of deliberation.

Each juror takes a piece of paper and scribbles their verdict:

Not guilty. Not guilty. Not guilty. Not guilty. Not guilty. Not guilty. Not guilty. Not guilty. Not guilty. Not guilty. Not guilty. Not guilty.

Leroy Reed will go free.

• • •

How do we connect during a *What's This Really About?* conversation?

The first step is trying to figure out what each of us wants from a discussion, what we are seeking from this dialogue. That's how we get at the deeper questions beneath the surface.

Boly connected with his fellow jurors by understanding that each person wanted something different. Some wanted to talk about justice; others wanted to focus on law and order. Some wanted facts; others craved empathy. Dr. Ehdaie connected with his patients by asking about what mattered to them most. We unearth these kinds of desires by taking the time to ask *What's This Really About?*

When someone says, "Can we talk about the upcoming meeting?," or "That memo was crazy, right?," or worries aloud, "I'm not sure he can get the job done," they are inviting us into a *What's This Really About?* discussion, signaling there's something deeper they want to discuss. Boly knew how to listen for those signals, and Dr. Ehdaie learned how to look for them.

Then, once we know what people want from a conversation, we next need to work out how to give it to them—how to engage in a quiet negotiation—so that their needs are met, as well as our own. That requires conducting experiments to reveal how we'll make decisions together. This is the *matching principle* at work, recognizing what *kind* of conversation is occurring and then aligning with others, and inviting them to align with us. Boly and Ehdaie understood that matching isn't mimicry; it's not simply looking concerned and repeating back what others have said.

Rather, matching is understanding someone's *mindset*—what kind of logic they find persuasive, what tone and approach makes sense to them—and then speaking their language. And it requires explaining clearly how we, ourselves, are thinking and making choices, so that others can match us in return. When someone describes a personal problem by telling a story, they are signaling they want our compassion rather than a solution. When they lay out all the facts analytically, they are signaling they are more interested in a rational conversation than an emotional one. We can all learn to get better at noticing these clues and conducting the experiments that reveal them.

The most profound gift of the *What's This Really About?* conversation is a chance to learn what others want to talk about, what they need out of a discussion, and inviting everyone to make choices together. That is when we begin to understand one another, and start finding solutions that are better than anything we could dream up on our own.

A GUIDE TO USING THESE IDEAS

PART II

Asking Questions and Noticing Clues

In 2018, researchers at Harvard began recording hundreds of people having conversations with friends, strangers, and coworkers, hoping to shed light on a question: How do people signal what they want to talk about? How, in other words, do we determine *What's This Really About?*

The participants in the experiment spoke face-to-face and over video calls. They were provided with some suggested subjects to start—"What do you do for work?" "Are you a religious person?"—but were allowed to meander across topics. Afterward, they were asked if they enjoyed their discussion.

The answer, for many, was essentially "No." People had tried to change the subject, had hinted they wanted to talk about something new, had indicated when they were bored, had introduced new topics. They had experimented with different approaches. But their partners had failed to notice.

The clues that someone wanted something different from a conversation were obvious, the researchers found, once people knew what to look for. But in the rush of talking, those clues were also easy to miss. When someone says something and then laughs afterward—even if it wasn't funny—it's a hint they're enjoying the conversation. When someone makes noises as they listen ("Yeah," "Uh-huh," "Interesting"), it's a sign they're engaged, what linguists call *backchanneling.* When someone asks follow-up questions ("What do you mean?" "Why do you think he said that?"), it's a clue they're interested, whereas statements that change the subject ("Let me ask you about this other thing") are hints they're ready to move on.

"Although people filled their conversational speech with information about their topic preferences," the researchers later wrote, "their human partners failed to pick up on many of those cues (or ignored them), and they were slow to act on them. Taken together, our results suggest that there is ample room for improvement."

These findings aren't exactly shocking, of course. We've all experienced this before. Sometimes people don't notice the signals we're trying to send, because they haven't trained themselves to pay attention. They haven't learned to experiment with different topics and conversational approaches.

But learning to pick up on those clues and conduct these kinds of experiments is important because they get at the second rule of a learning conversation.

Second Rule:
Share your goals, and ask what others are seeking.

We achieve this in four ways: By preparing ourselves before a conversation; by asking questions; by noticing clues during a conversation; and by experimenting and adding items to the table.

PREPARING FOR A CONVERSATION

A *What's This Really About?* conversation often occurs at the start of a discussion, and so we're well served to do a bit of prep work before a dialogue begins.

Researchers at Harvard and other universities have looked at exactly which kind of prep work is helpful. Participants in one study were asked to jot down a few topics they would like to discuss before a conversation began. This exercise took only about thirty seconds; frequently the topics written down never came up once the discussion started.

But simply preparing a list, researchers found, made conversations go better. There were fewer awkward pauses, less anxiety, and, afterward, people said they felt more engaged. So, in the moments before a conversation starts, it's useful to describe for yourself:

- **What are two topics you might discuss?** (Being general is okay: *Last night's game* and *TV shows you like*)
- **What is one thing you hope to say?**
- **What is one question you will ask?**

Prepare for the conversation

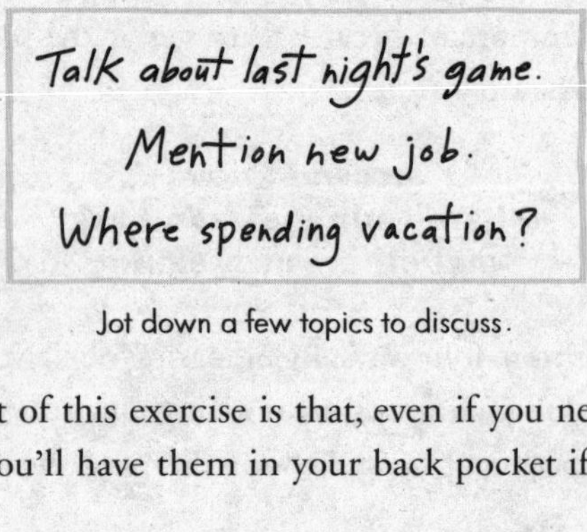

Jot down a few topics to discuss.

The benefit of this exercise is that, even if you never talk about these topics, you'll have them in your back pocket if you hit a lull.

And simply by anticipating what you'll discuss, you're likely to feel more confident.

Once this exercise becomes second nature—and it quickly will—you can make your preparation even more robust:

- **What are two topics *you most want* to discuss?**
- **What is one thing you hope to say *that shows what you want to talk about?***
- **What is one question you will ask *that reveals what others want?***

ASKING QUESTIONS

There is a quiet negotiation at the heart of the *What's This Really About?* conversation that emerges when we need to make a decision or set a plan. Sometimes it's quick—a friend says, "We gotta talk about the schedule for Saturday," and you reply, "Okay!"—and the negotiation is done.

For more meaningful and complex conversations, however, that negotiation is longer and more subtle. We might start with pleasantries, then move to an easy topic—the weather or a friend in common—and eventually arrive at what we actually want to discuss: "I was wondering if you might consider investing in my new company?"

Regardless of how this negotiation unfolds, there is a common format: Someone will make an *invitation,* and their partner will *accept* or make *counter-invitations.*

Sometimes, we want others to go first. The easiest way to do that is by asking open-ended questions, just as Dr. Ehdaie did with his patients. And open-ended questions are easy to find, if you focus on:

- **Asking about someone's beliefs or values** ("How'd you decide to become a teacher?")
- **Asking someone to make a judgment** ("Are you glad you went to law school?")
- **Asking about someone's experiences** ("What was it like to visit Europe?")

These kinds of questions don't feel intrusive—asking "How'd you decide to become a teacher?" doesn't seem overly personal—but it's an invitation for someone to share their beliefs about education, or what they value in a job. "Are you glad you went to law school?" invites someone to reflect on their choices, rather than simply describing their work. Open-ended questions can be shallow or deep. But, as the next chapter explains, questions about values, beliefs, judgments, and experiences are extremely powerful—and easier to ask than we think.

Ask questions

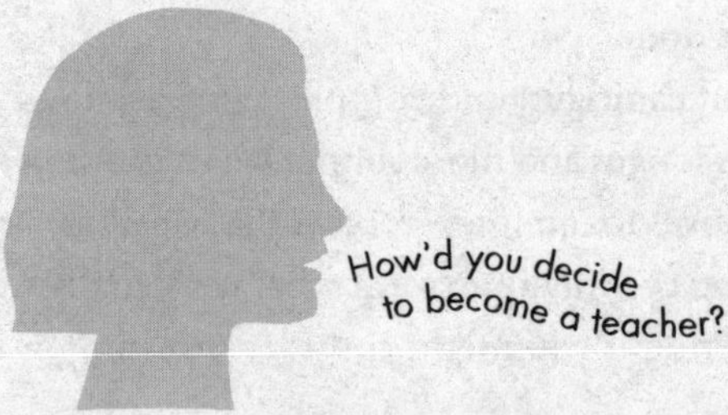

Ask about beliefs, values, judgments, and experiences.

NOTICE CLUES DURING CONVERSATIONS

In other conversations, rather than wait for our companions to express their needs and goals, we might seek first to express our own. At those moments, when we extend an invitation—"We need to talk about the schedule for Saturday," or "I was wondering if you might invest in my company?"—how the other person responds is important, and so we need to train ourselves to notice what might go unsaid.

Some important things to pay attention to:

- **Do your companions lean toward you, make eye contact, smile, backchannel ("Interesting," "Hmm"), or interrupt?**

Those are signals they want to accept your invitation. (Interruptions, contrary to expectations, usually mean people want to add something.)

- **Do they become quiet, their expressions passive, their eyes fixed somewhere besides your face? Do they seem overly contemplative? Do they take in your comments without adding thoughts of their own?**

People often misperceive these responses as listening. But they usually aren't. (In fact, as the next few chapters explain, listening is much more active.) These are signals that someone is declining our invitation and wants to talk about something else—in which case, you need to keep searching—and experimenting—to learn what everyone wants.

Notice clues

Are they leaning in and showing interest?
Or looking away and passive?

It's easy to miss these reactions, in part because speaking takes up so much of our mental bandwidth. But if we train ourselves to notice these clues, it helps us answer *What's This Really About*?

EXPERIMENT BY ADDING ITEMS TO THE TABLE

When someone declines our invitation, we might feel stuck. At such moments, it's useful to remember the lesson of interest-based bargaining: Get creative. Start experimenting with new topics and approaches until a path forward is revealed, the same way John Boly introduced a new way of thinking about public safety to draw in Karl.

We can figure out which new topics and approaches might be fruitful by paying attention to:

- **Has someone told a story or made a joke?** If so, they might be in an empathetic *logic of similarities* mindset. In this mindset, people aren't looking to debate or analyze choices; they want to share, relate, and empathize.
- **Or are they talking about plans and decisions, or evaluating options?** Have they brought up politics or finances or choosing a place for next year's vacation? ("Is Maine or Florida better in June?") If so, they might be in a more practical *logic of costs and benefits* mindset, and you're better off getting analytical yourself.
- **Listen for attempts to change the topic.** People tell us what they want to discuss through their non sequiturs, asides, and sudden shifts—or, put differently, through the experiments *they* conduct. If someone asks the same question in different ways, or if they abruptly introduce a new subject, it's a sign they want to add something to the table and we'd be wise to let them proceed.
- **Finally, experiment.** Tell a joke. Ask an unexpected question. Introduce a new idea. Try interrupting, and then not interrupting.

Watch to see if your companions play along. If they do, they're hinting at how they want to make decisions together, the rules and norms they accept. They are signaling how they'd like this conversation to unfold.

Add items to the table

Are people telling stories, or are they making plans? Are they changing the topic?

You likely already have these instincts, but they're easy to forget. And we don't have to embrace all these tactics at once. We can gradually make them part of our conversations until, eventually, negotiating over *What's This Really About?* feels natural.

THE *HOW DO WE FEEL?* CONVERSATION

AN OVERVIEW

Emotions shape every conversation. They guide what we say and how we hear, often in ways we don't realize. Every conversation is, in some respect, a discussion about *How Do We Feel?*

Because this kind of dialogue is so important, the next three chapters are devoted to emotional conversations. When it comes to discussing emotions, listening is essential. We need to listen for vulnerabilities, hear what is unsaid—and, just as important, we must *show* we are listening. Good listening, when it works, reveals new worlds beneath the surface of people's words.

Chapter 3 explains how to listen more deeply and what to do when we hear someone say something meaningful. Chapter 4 examines how we can get better at hearing emotions that are unspoken—how our bodies, our vocal tones, our gestures, and our expressions say as much as our words. Chapter 5 explores how emotions can fuel conflicts or help resolve them, and how to create safer environments for discussing disagreements, both online and off.

The *How Do We Feel?* conversation is essential to connection. These next three chapters explore how to express—and how to hear—what we feel.

3

THE LISTENING CURE

Touchy-Feely Hedge Funders

The men and women filling the auditorium of the Connecticut hedge fund all appeared to hail from the same, very expensive planet. Many wore bespoke suits, while others sported watches that cost more than some cars. As they waited for this invite-only event to begin, they discussed their recent art acquisitions and real estate projects, or groused about how the Seychelles and Vineyard had become overrun. A few, in an effort to demonstrate their uniqueness, wore kabbalah beads or limited-edition sneakers. One person had a soul patch.

But despite these attempts at distinctiveness, all of them—professional investors from dozens of Wall Street firms who oversaw billions of dollars—spent their days in much the same way: Talking to CEOs and chatting up investment bankers, poring over economic reports and working hallways at industry conferences, always hoping to find some nugget of information that might help them predict which stocks would go up and which would go down.

Today, however, was different. Today they were here to meet with a forty-three-year-old psychology professor from the University of Chicago, Nicholas Epley, who had flown in to give a presentation on how to listen. All the attendees knew, many from personal experience, that poor listening skills could be very, very costly. One person in the room had managed to lose $20 million in a single afternoon after he failed to register that a broker, who was usually cheerful and unflappable, had yelled at a waiter during a two-martini lunch and had repeatedly excused himself to answer phone calls. The man had offered a valid explanation each time he returned to the table, but the hedge funder later learned the man's firm had been failing, and he had missed the clues. One tiny mistake—not hearing the hesitation in someone's voice during a meeting, overlooking an evasive answer to a straightforward question—could spell the difference between victory and defeat.

So the organizers of this event had brought in Epley to help everyone get better at hearing what was easy to miss. Epley was just the person for the task because he had devoted most of his career to studying why we *mishear* one another. Why, for instance, were some people incapable of picking up on the emotions in others' voices? How was it that two people could attend the same meeting and then, afterward, completely disagree on what had been said?

Many in the audience assumed that Epley would launch into a PowerPoint with a series of listening tactics: Always maintain eye contact. Nod encouragingly to show you're paying attention. Smile a lot. In other words, the kinds of tips popular on late-night infomercials and social media accounts.

But Epley's research indicated that such methods, particularly when forced, undermine real communication. Nodding doesn't mean you're listening. Constant smiling and eye contact can be a little . . . intense. Besides, Epley believed, everyone already knows how to listen closely. "You don't need anyone to teach you how to listen to an interesting podcast or a good joke," he told me. "When you're in a great conversation, no one has a problem following along. When something is interesting, you listen without thinking about it."

Epley wanted to help this group tap into their natural listening abilities, which meant he needed to help them learn how to have more interesting and meaningful conversations. One way of doing that, he was convinced, was getting everyone to talk about more intimate things. In particular, he believed people should talk about their emotions. When we discuss our feelings, something magical happens: Other people can't help but listen to us. And then they start divulging emotions of their own, which causes us to listen closely in return. If the hedge funder who lost $20 million, for instance, had inquired how his lunch companion was feeling, had pressed him on emotional questions, he likely would have heard that the man was stressed. He would have noticed clues that something was amiss.

Epley wanted to nudge these hedge funders into a *How Do We Feel?* conversation. "When you open up to somebody," Epley told me, "they get drawn in."

However, Epley knew that many people shy away from discussing intimate or emotional topics because we think it will be awkward, or unprofessional, or we'll say the wrong thing, or the other person will respond poorly, or we're too busy thinking about what the other person thinks of us.

Epley believed he had found a way around these kinds of pitfalls. The key to starting a *How Do We Feel?* conversation was teaching people to ask specific kinds of questions, the kinds that don't, on the surface, *seem* emotional, but that make emotions easier to acknowledge. Epley had spent the previous decade teaching people to ask these kinds of questions, and now he wanted to see if his techniques would work with a group of hedge funders, people who are usually allergic to touchy-feely displays. So as he stood at the front of the room, he laid out what was going to happen: Everyone, he explained, would be assigned a partner, someone they didn't know. And for the next ten minutes, they would engage in a conversation.

Then Epley revealed the questions they would ask each other. There were three of them. The third one was: "Can you describe a time you cried in front of another person?"

"Oh, shit," said someone in the front row. "This is going to be awful."

• • •

There comes a moment, in many dialogues, when you must decide: Will I allow this conversation to turn emotional? Or will I keep it dry and aloof?

Perhaps you're discussing plans for the weekend with a friend and, during a lull, they say, "There's some stuff going on I might need to deal with." Maybe you're catching up with a coworker and you hear a sigh hinting at sadness and troubles. Perhaps it's a reference to a family emergency, or a mention of how proud someone is of their kids. At these moments, you face a choice: Are you going to let that comment go by without asking for elaboration? Or are you going to acknowledge the feelings that were expressed, and respond emotionally yourself? This is when the *How Do We Feel?* conversation begins—if we allow it to.

Regardless of your decision, it is certain that emotions are *already* influencing your discussion. Numerous studies show that emotions come into play nearly every time we open our mouths or listen to what someone says. They influence everything we say and hear. They've already entered your conversation through that sigh, or that flash of pride, or in a thousand other ways you hardly noticed. Emotions have been at work since you sat down, shaping how you react, how you think, why you're here in the first place. However, you can glide over the sigh, let the pride pass unacknowledged. You can minimize *How Do We Feel?* and stick to safer territory: The shallows of small talk.

Most of the time, that's the wrong choice. And it's wrong because it denies us access to a powerful neural process that has evolved over millions of years to help us bond. It's wrong because it will leave everyone less satisfied, and make a conversation feel incomplete. It's wrong because if we acknowledge someone else's vulnerability, and become vulnerable in return, we build trust, understanding, and connection. If you choose to embrace the *How Do We Feel?* conversation, you are harnessing a neurochemical process that powers our most important relationships.

How Do We Feel? is critical because it reveals what's happening inside our heads, and opens a path to connection.

THE POWER OF QUESTIONS

Once upon a time, Nick Epley had been a very bad listener. So bad, in fact, it almost ruined his life. He had grown up in a small town in Iowa, a high school football star, as strutting and self-assured as you might imagine. Then one night, during his junior year, he was driving home from a boozy party, weaving across lanes, when he was pulled over for drunk driving. The cop saw Epley's letterman's jacket, which seemed to trigger a pity for youthful stupidity. So instead of putting him in handcuffs, he delivered a lecture: If you don't turn your life around, you're going to end up somewhere ugly. Then he called Epley's parents and told them to come get their son.

Over the next few weeks, his mother and father lectured him relentlessly about the dangers of this path he was on. They told Epley they understood how hard it was to be a teenager; they realized he wanted to impress his friends and test his limits; they sympathized with his desire to experiment. After all, once upon a time, they had been teenagers themselves. But they were worried he was making bad choices. Epley hardly paid attention. "It kind of washed over me," he told me. They were just adults saying the things that adults are supposed to say.

A few months later, he was pulled over for drunk driving a second time. A different cop gave him another, similar lecture and, once again, let him off after calling his folks. At that point, his parents decided, it was time for professional help.

Epley started meeting with a counselor and braced himself for more lectures and criticisms. But the counselor was completely unlike his parents, not to mention most of the other adults he had met. She didn't give speeches or tell him he needed to turn his life around. She didn't say she understood where he was coming from or give him advice. Instead, she simply asked questions: "Why were you drinking?" "How would you have reacted if your car had hit someone?" "What would happen to your life if you had been arrested, or had injured yourself, or had killed another person?"

"I had to sit with that," Epley told me. "I couldn't pretend I didn't know the answers."

The questions themselves didn't ask about Epley's emotions, but, inevitably, he became emotional as he responded to them. They pushed Epley to talk about his beliefs and values, how he felt, what he was anxious about, what he feared. He came home from each session exhausted and ashamed, scared and angry, and most of all confused, a complicated mix of feelings that usually took days to untangle. These were some of the most emotionally intense conversations of his life, even though the therapist never asked him to describe his feelings.

These sessions also seemed to unlock something. Epley began talking to his parents about what he was feeling—and listening, for the first time, as they described their own emotional lives. Epley's dad mentioned a day, a few years earlier, when Epley had left the house early in the morning without telling his parents. They went into the basement looking for him and saw a rifle was missing. They panicked. Was he going to kill himself? His father described his grief and terror until Epley came home, unharmed and annoyed by his parents' worry, peevishly explaining that he had gone hunting with his friends. As his father recounted the day, Epley could remember that moment, could remember that his dad had been upset, how he had brushed off his parents' panic because it had seemed so ridiculous at the time. He hadn't been able to hear what they were trying to say: They had wanted him to understand that he was loved. But love carries obligations to be safe, to tell others when you leave or where you are going, not to dismiss a parent's worries. "That conversation changed our relationship," Epley told me. "I felt so lucky I was finally able to see him as this real, complex person."

After his second session with the counselor, Epley decided he wouldn't drink anymore. Then he decided to get serious about school. Eventually, he enrolled at St. Olaf College, where he discovered psychology. After getting his degree, he entered a PhD program at Cornell.

While there, Epley began thinking more deeply about why, after those near arrests, he had been so unwilling to listen at first. "Sometimes you look back, and you wonder, *Why was I so deaf?*" Why hadn't the police officers' lectures scared him straight? Why had it been so easy to ignore his parents when they had pleaded, cajoled, and tried so earnestly to help him?

By 2005, Epley was a professor at the University of Chicago. He was married, starting to have kids of his own, and terrified that, someday, they would become teenagers who shut him out and refused to listen. He wanted to understand how to convince them to hear him.

At the time, one prevailing theory within psychology said that, in order to understand others—and persuade them to listen to us—we should engage in what is known as *perspective taking*: We should try to see a situation from the other person's perspective and show them we empathize. Psychology journals noted that "to communicate effectively, we must adopt the perspective of another person both while speaking and listening." Textbooks taught that "perspective taking not only fosters greater interpersonal understanding" but also "constitutes a vital skill for very powerful negotiators."

When Epley looked back on his high school experiences, he realized that his parents, in their own way, had been trying to engage in perspective taking after his drunk driving near arrests. They had tried to put themselves in his shoes. They had tried to forge a connection by imagining the pressure he was under. They had hoped that demonstrating their empathy would convince him to listen to their advice.

But, if anything, his parents' perspective taking had made it clear to Epley, at that moment, how much they *didn't* understand about him. When they tried to commiserate, when they shared stories of their own adolescent mistakes, all Epley heard was adults who had no idea what it was like to be a teenager nowadays.

His parents had failed to connect with him because they hadn't understood how he *felt.* And they didn't understand because they had never asked. They had never inquired about his anger or uncertainty, had never asked why it had felt so necessary to prove himself by drinking all those beers. Even if they had asked, Epley wouldn't have known what to say. He hadn't understood, himself, what was going on inside his head, not until he had started talking to the counselor and she, instead of trying to put herself in his shoes, had simply asked him questions that elicited emotional replies: "Why are you making these choices?" "Is this who you want to be?" Then she had listened and had asked smart follow-up questions, and that, somehow, had inspired Epley to start listening to her, and then to himself, until he realized he needed to change.

Now, as an adult, Epley wondered if the psychology textbooks had it wrong. Perhaps the correct approach wasn't trying to put yourself in "someone else's shoes." That, after all, was impossible. Rather, maybe the best you can do is ask questions. Ask about people's lives, about what they're feeling, about their hopes and fears, and then listen for their struggles, disappointments, joys, and ambitions.

Hearing people describe their emotional lives is important because when we talk about our feelings, we're describing not just what has happened to us, but why we made certain choices and how we make sense of the world. "When you describe how you feel, you're giving someone a map of the things you care about," Epley said. "That's why I connected with my parents, because I finally understood what mattered to them. I understood they were scared and worried and just wanted me to be safe."

This is why the *How Do We Feel?* conversation is so crucial. Every discussion is shaped by our emotions, and when we bring those feelings to the surface—when we share them and ask others to share with us—we begin to see how we might align.

The Three Conversations

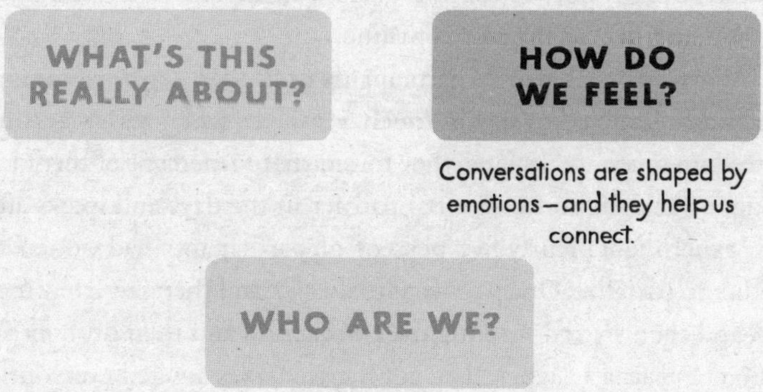

Epley began thinking there must be an alternative to perspective taking. Maybe there was a different technique to help people ask the

kinds of questions that nudge emotions into the open? Perhaps, instead of perspective *taking*, we ought to be focused on perspective *getting*, on asking people to describe their inner lives, their values and beliefs and feelings, the things they care about most. Epley sensed there was something about asking questions—the right questions—that contained the seeds of real understanding.

But which questions were the right ones?

THE RIGHT QUESTIONS

In 1995, Elaine and Arthur Aron, a husband-and-wife team of research psychologists at the State University of New York–Stony Brook, placed two chairs atop a bright orange rug in a windowless room and invited strangers, in pairs, to come in, sit down, and take turns asking each other a list of questions. None of the participants—who eventually numbered more than three hundred—knew one another prior to entering the room, and each session lasted only sixty minutes. The questions had been selected ahead of time by the researchers, and they ranged from the frivolous ("When did you last sing to yourself?") to the profound ("If you were to die this evening with no opportunity to communicate with anyone, what would you most regret not having told someone?").

Afterward, each pair of participants went their separate ways; no one was instructed to stay in touch. However, when researchers followed up seven weeks later, they found that 57 percent of them had sought out their conversational partner in the days and weeks after the experiment. Thirty-five percent of participants had gotten together to socialize. One pair went to dinner, and then saw a few movies, and then started meeting over weekends, and then on holidays. About a year later, when they got married, they invited everyone in the psych lab to the ceremony. "The impact exceeded everyone's expectations," Arthur Aron told me. "Even now I'm surprised by it. We had no idea what this would become."

The Arons had launched their study to see if there was "a practical methodology for creating closeness," a technique that might generate connection. In particular, they wanted to see if it was possible to make strangers into friends. Other experiments had revealed a long list of factors that had no impact whatsoever. Researchers had learned that simply because two people had experiences or beliefs in common—they both went to the same church and both smoked, or were both atheists who hated tobacco—these similarities, on their own, were not enough to foster camaraderie. Studies had shown that instructing people to make small talk, or do puzzles together, or tell each other jokes, were all ineffectual at creating a sense of closeness. Merely informing study participants "We have taken great care in matching partners" and "we expect that you and your partner will like one another" did not necessarily mean people would like each other at all.

In fact, there was only one method the Arons tested that could reliably help strangers form a connection: A series of thirty-six questions that, as Elaine and Arthur Aron later wrote, elicited "sustained, escalating, reciprocal, personalistic self-disclosure." These questions eventually became known as the *Fast Friends Procedure,* and grew famous among sociologists, psychologists, and readers of articles with headlines such as "The 36 Questions That Lead to Love."*

What's particularly interesting about the Fast Friends Procedure is that the thirty-six questions were chosen somewhat haphazardly, at least at first. Some of them came from a game named "The Ungame" that was popular among stoners and university students (a demo-

* A full list of the Fast Friends Procedure questions can be found in the endnotes.

graphic that included more than a few of the Arons' research assistants). Other questions were dreamed up during coffee breaks, or by whoever happened to be within earshot when everyone went to a bar. "There wasn't a lot of what you would call 'strict science' in how we initially found the questions," Ed Melinat, one of the Arons' grad students, told me. "We must have come up with, I don't know, two hundred of them, and then we would run tests until we figured out which ones worked best."

The researchers assumed the best approach was to start with shallow, safe questions ("Whom would you want as a dinner guest?") and then slowly get to the deeper stuff. "It felt weird to ask people to start baring their souls right away," Melinat said. "So we decided to start simple."

By question seven ("Do you have a secret hunch about how you will die?") people were being asked to reveal their deepest anxieties. By question twenty-four ("How do you feel about your relationship with your mother?") and twenty-nine ("Share with your partner an embarrassing moment") participants were being asked to describe their closest relationships and most painful memories. Question thirty-five ("Of all the people in your family, whose death would you find most disturbing?") felt so intimate that participants often asked, and answered it, in a near whisper. The last question was open-ended ("Share a personal problem and ask your partner's advice"), and by then, one or both participants were frequently crying.

THE IMPORTANCE OF VULNERABILITY

As the Stony Brook team tried to figure out the best questions to use, they found themselves stumped by a seemingly simple problem: How do you distinguish emotional questions from unemotional ones?

There were some questions—such as "Would you like to be

famous?"—that could go either way. For some people, the answer was a simple yes or no. For others, it opened the floodgates to soul-baring confessions of bygone dreams and failed ambitions. So is that question a reliable invitation to emotional self-disclosure, or an example of small talk?

Eventually, the researchers figured out how to gauge if a question was likely to spark an emotional reply: Questions that asked about everyday experiences or uncontroversial opinions—such as "How did you celebrate last Halloween?" or "What is the best gift you ever received?"—tended to yield answers that were reliably unemotional.

In contrast, questions that pushed people to describe their beliefs, values, or meaningful experiences tended to result in emotional replies, even if the questions themselves didn't seem all that emotional. These kinds of questions were powerful because they often prompted people to reveal vulnerabilities. When someone asks "What do you value most in a friendship?" (question sixteen), it might not seem particularly emotionally probing, but it frequently draws unexpectedly revealing replies about past incidents of hurt or betrayal, or expressions of love for friends, or other anxieties or pleasures. Such questions make ever-deepening follow-ups ("What did you say after he broke up with you?") easy to ask.

Put another way, the difference between a shallow question and one that sparks an opportunity for emotional connection is vulnerability. And vulnerability is what makes *How Do We Feel?* so powerful.

EMOTIONAL CONTAGION

To the Arons, the idea that vulnerability was important made perfect sense, in part because it lined up with a well-documented psychological phenomenon known as "emotional contagion." In the early 1990s, a series of experiments had shown that humans typically "synchronize their own emotions with the emotions expressed by those around them." This synchronization is sometimes deliberate, like when we choose to empathize with another person; more often it is automatic, happening outside of our consciousness, causing us to tear up or get angry or proud on someone else's behalf, whether we want to or not.

This contagion is at the root of the *How Do We Feel?* conversation, and it explains why emotions influence our dialogues, even when we don't recognize them. "Emotional contagion is a fairly primitive process," a study published in 2010 observed. "Men and women tend to 'catch' expressions of joy, love, anger, fear, and sadness." Emotional contagion, scholars believe, evolved because it helped humans form bonds with other people. It begins almost at birth: One study found that "10-week-old infants could and would imitate their mothers' facial expressions of happiness, sadness, and anger." This instinct has evolved within our brains so that we'll feel good when we connect with other people—and thus become more likely to build alliances and friendships, families and societies.

However, emotional contagion must be triggered by something, and one of the most reliable triggers is vulnerability. We become more prone to emotional contagion when we hear someone else express—or when we reveal our own—deeply held beliefs and values, or when we describe past experiences that were meaningful to us, or when we expose something else that opens us to others' judgments. These are the same factors the Arons used to distinguish deep questions from shallow ones.

In other words, we become more susceptible to emotional contagion, and more emotionally contagious ourselves, when we share something that feels raw, something that another person might judge. We might not care about their judgment, we might forget it as soon as we hear it, but the act of exposing ourselves to someone's scrutiny engenders a sense of intimacy. To get deep, we have to make an offering of our vulnerability. "The louder the emotion, the more likely that contagion will occur," Amit Goldenberg, a Harvard psychology researcher, told me. "And vulnerability is one of our loudest emotions. We're hardwired to notice it."

This explains why the Fast Friends Procedure is so effective, and it illuminates which kinds of questions are most likely to help people emotionally align. There is a cycle: Asking deep questions about feelings, values, beliefs, and experiences creates vulnerability. That vulnerability triggers emotional contagion. And that, in turn, helps us connect.

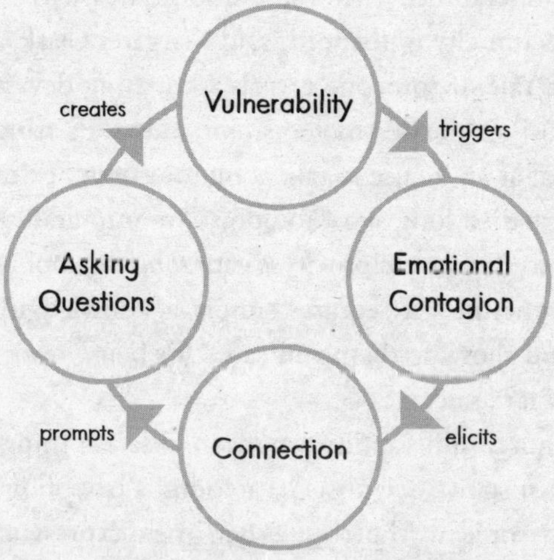

As the Arons continued exploring these kinds of phenomena, they discovered another interesting detail: The Fast Friends Procedure worked only if participants took turns asking each other questions. In a separate experiment, each participant was instructed to answer all thirty-six questions in a row while their partner listened, and then trade places. Volunteers said the experience was awkward and boring. No one felt close afterward. But when the Arons, in their experiment, told people to go back and forth and "share your answer with your partner, then let him or her share their answer to the same question with you," people started to bond. "Reciprocity is critical," Arthur Aron told me. "It's one of the most powerful forces in the world. If you don't have reciprocity, then people aren't matching each other's emotional ups and downs."

Once again, this is the *matching principle*—which says that communication requires recognizing what kind of conversation is occurring, and then matching it—at work. These thirty-six questions are effective because they help people match each other emotionally, and going back and forth encourages everyone to offer, and then reciprocate, vulnerability. This also demonstrates why mimicry isn't enough. "Reciprocity is nuanced," said Margaret Clark, a psychology professor at Yale. If someone reveals something devastating, like a scary diagnosis or the death of a parent, it doesn't bring us together if we use that as an excuse to talk about our own health, or a family member who died long ago. "You don't want to grab the spotlight," Clark told me. Rather, reciprocity means *thinking* about how to show empathy. Sometimes it requires simply acknowledging someone's emotions and showing them you care. "It's being responsive to others' needs," Clark said.

What's more, vulnerability can mean different things in different settings. For instance, scientists have found a troubling double standard within some workplaces: When men express emotions like anger or impatience, it is commonly viewed as a sign of self-confidence, even good leadership. When a man cries at work, it is evidence of how much he cares. But when women express emotions such as anger or sadness, "they are more likely to suffer negative social and professional consequences," found one study from 2016. "Women incur social and economic penalties for expressing masculine-typed emotions. . . . At the same time, when women express female-typed emotions, they are judged as overly emotional and lacking emotional control, which ultimately undermines women's competence and professional legitimacy." These kinds of unequal standards can make some displays of vulnerability feel unsafe.*

However, despite these complexities, the insights of the Fast Friends Procedure, paired with Epley's research, are useful because they provide us with a framework for emotional connection: If you want to connect with someone, ask them what they are feeling, and then reveal your own emotions. If others describe a painful memory or a moment of joy, and we reveal our own disappointments or what makes us proud, it provides a chance to harness the neurochemicals that have evolved to help us feel closer. It creates an opportunity for emotional contagion.

The *How Do We Feel?* conversation is a tool that functions by inviting others to reveal their vulnerabilities, and then being vulnerable in return.

EMOTIONAL CONNECTION
is triggered by asking deep questions
and reciprocating vulnerability.

These are useful insights, but that doesn't make them practical advice. It's easy, after all, to ask deep questions when you are inside a laboratory and a scientist has handed you a list to work from. But how do you get deep in the real world?

GETTING DEEP FAST

Imagine that you've just met someone. A friend of a friend, or a recently hired coworker, or maybe you're on a blind date. You both introduce yourselves, say a bit about your backgrounds. You get *What's This Really About?* out of the way. Then there's a pause, an expectant silence.

* The troubling discrepancies in who is allowed to show vulnerability in various settings have important implications. For more, please see the endnotes.

What should you say next?

The Fast Friends Procedure suggests asking a question. But you can't progress through all thirty-six of them, not here. So maybe you jump to question three: "Before making a telephone call, do you ever rehearse what you are going to say?" Or, given that time is short, go deeper with question eighteen: "What is your most terrible memory?"

You don't need a PhD in psychology to realize that's not a great plan. Asking a stranger these kinds of questions, outside of a psych lab, will ensure you'll spend the evening alone. In the real world, the thirty-six questions are of little real help.

What kinds of questions, then, should we ask?

In 2016, a group of scientists from Harvard began wondering the same thing. They scrutinized hundreds of conversations that had been recorded during events such as speed-dating meetups, and gauged which conversations were successful (as measured by people saying they wanted to go on a real date), and which weren't (people indicated they didn't want to follow up). They found that during successful conversations, people tended to ask each other the kinds of questions that drew out replies where people expressed their "needs, goals, beliefs [and] emotions," as the researchers later wrote. In unsuccessful conversations, people talked mostly about themselves, or they asked shallow questions, the kinds of inquiries that didn't reveal anything about how their partners felt.

Put another way, if you want to have a successful conversation with someone, you don't have to ask them about their worst memories or how they prepare for telephone calls. You just have to ask them to describe how they *feel* about their life—rather than the facts of their life—and then ask lots of follow-ups.

Questions about facts ("Where do you live?" "What college did you attend?") are often conversational dead-ends. They don't draw out values or experiences. They don't invite vulnerability.

However, those same inquiries, recast slightly ("What do you like about where you live?" "What was your favorite part of college?"), invite others to share their preferences, beliefs, and values, and to describe experiences that caused them to grow or change. Those questions make emotional replies easier, and they practically beg the questioner to reciprocate—to divulge, in return, why they live in this neighborhood, what they enjoyed about college—until everyone is drawn in, asking and answering back and forth.

"It might seem hard to reframe questions in a way that's vulnerable," Epley told me. "But it's actually pretty easy once you start looking for it. Like when I'm on a train, talking with people commuting to work, I might ask them, 'What do you do for a living?' And then I might say, 'Do you love that job?' or 'Do you have something else you dream of doing?' And right there, you're two questions in, and you've gotten to somebody's dreams."

SHALLOW QUESTIONS...
...CAN BECOME DEEP

Where do you live?
What do you like about your neighborhood?

Where do you work?
What was your favorite job?

Where did you go to college?
What was the best part of college?

Are you married?
Tell me about your family.

How long have you lived here?
What's the best place you've ever lived?

Do you have any hobbies?
If you could learn anything, what would it be?

Where did you go to high school?
What advice would you give a high schooler?

Where are you from?
What's the best thing about where you grew up?

What's more, these kinds of deeper questions can help fight the unfair discrepancies in how men and women, as well as other groups, are allowed to express emotions. In part, these kinds of questions succeed because they allow vulnerable replies without mandating them. They don't seem pushy or out of place within, say, an office. But they undermine double standards by nudging people to think a bit more about how to respond. "One reason women are penalized for talking about emotions is because it plays into stereotypes," said Madeline Heilman, a professor of psychology at NYU who studies gender and bias. Humans tend to be cognitively lazy: We rely on stereotypes and assumptions because they let us make judgments without thinking too hard. "So when a woman talks about her emotions, it can be damaging because it gives listeners permission to assume a stereotype—women are overly emotional—is true." But studies show that when women, as well as other underrepresented groups, ask deep questions, "it can cause people to reevaluate how they see you," said Heilman. When we ask a meaningful question such as "What's the best part of working here?," it pushes the listener to think before replying, and "that's sometimes enough to get them to start questioning their assumptions, and start listening more," Heilman said.

There was one other key finding in the Harvard study of speed daters: Follow-up questions are particularly powerful. "Follow-ups are a signal that you're listening, that you want to know more," one of the researchers, Michael Yeomans, told me. Follow-up questions make reciprocity easier ("Your favorite part of college was ultimate frisbee? Me too! Do you still love to play?"). "They allow self-disclosure without it seeming like self-obsession," said Yeomans. "It makes a conversation flow."

This is how to ask emotional questions in the real world: Ask someone how they *feel* about something, and then follow up with questions that reveal how you feel. It's the same framework for emotional connection described before, but in a slightly different guise: If we ask questions that push people to think and talk about their values, beliefs, and experiences, and then reciprocate with emotions of our own, we can't help but listen to one another. "The best listeners aren't just listening," said Margaret Clark, the Yale psychologist. "They're triggering emotions by asking questions, expressing their own emotions, doing things that prompt the other person to say something real."

THE JOY OF RECIPROCITY

"As I mentioned," Epley told the room of hedge funders, "you've been paired with someone you don't know for a ten-minute conversation." Many of the attendees had flown in for this event and had never met each other before. Epley explained that he was conducting an experiment, and each person would need to ask and answer a few specific questions with their partner: "If a crystal ball could tell you the future, would you want to know?" "For what do you feel most grateful?" And "Can you describe a time you cried in front of another person?"

Epley could have started out slow—with a question like "Where did you go on your last vacation?"—before going deep. The Arons, in creating the Fast Friends Procedure, had assumed they needed to start with shallower questions.

But Epley suspected that assumption was wrong. He hypothesized that deep, vulnerable questions were easier to ask—and more enjoyable to answer—than most people realized. Now he had a chance to test his theory out.

Before the conversations began, Epley asked everyone to take out their phones for a quick survey that would gauge how uncomfortable they anticipated this discussion would be. The data, as it flowed in, provided a clear answer: People were dreading this exercise. They thought "they wouldn't like their partner very much, wouldn't enjoy the experience much, and it would be pretty awkward," Epley told me.

Next, everyone paired off with their partners and began talking. Epley couldn't hear most of what was said, but after a few minutes, he saw someone wiping tears from his face. Not long after, a man and a woman hugged. After ten minutes, he asked everyone to stop. They ignored him. Epley tried again. "Excuse me," he said, louder this time. "Could you please end your conversations?" Finally, after twenty minutes, Epley managed to quiet the room.

At this point, the participants pulled out their phones and completed another survey about how uncomfortable the conversation had *actually* been. As the data was collected, Epley asked them to describe what had occurred.

"That was amazing," one participant said. He had been unenthusiastic about the exercise at first, he explained, but something had happened once the crying question was asked: He had replied as honestly as he could by describing the funeral of a close cousin. And then his partner had leaned in, gripped his shoulder, and begun comforting him, telling him it was okay, tearing up himself. Then, his partner had started revealing things about himself—intimate, personal things—without prompting. "This was the best conversation I've had in months," the man said.

When Epley later reported on this and other iterations of the experiment in the *Journal of Personality and Social Psychology* in 2021, he wrote that participants "consistently expected their conversations to be more awkward, and to lead to weaker connections and less happiness, than they actually did." He has conducted versions of this exercise with students, strangers in public parks, politicians, lawyers, tech employees, and people recruited online. Each time, the results are the same: The data shows people feel "significantly more connected to their deep conversation partner" after asking and answering just a few questions. The sense of vulnerability that comes from "sharing personal information about one's past experiences, preferences or beliefs," and saying things aloud that "leave people feeling more vulnerable to others' evaluations," causes participants to feel "more connected," "more caring," and "to listen attentively." When Epley looked to see if there were distinctions in the experiences of men and women, he found no meaningful gender differences, he told me. From the wealthiest financiers to the most distant online strangers, "we all crave real connections," Epley said. We all want to have meaningful conversations.

Dozens of other studies from the University of Utah, the University of Pennsylvania, Emory, and elsewhere have found that people who ask lots of questions during conversations—particularly questions that invite vulnerable responses—are more popular among their peers and more often seen as leaders. They have more social influence and are sought out more frequently for friendship and advice. Any of us can do this in nearly any setting or conversation, be it with a roommate, a coworker, or someone we just met. We simply need to ask people how they feel and reciprocate the vulnerability they share with us.

In one experiment, researchers instructed participants to ask strangers and friends questions such as "Have you ever committed a crime?" The researchers found that "questioners assumed that asking sensitive questions would make their conversation partners uncomfortable and would damage their relationships. But in fact, we consistently found that askers were wrong on both fronts." Asking deep questions is easier than most people realize, and more rewarding than we expect.

EMOTIONAL DIALOGUES ARE THE HARDEST TO MATCH

When I first telephoned Epley to interview him for this book, I had a long list of topics I wanted to cover, from his research to the last time that *he* had cried in front of another person. (The previous day, he told me. He had been talking about his kids at lunch.)

Within minutes, however, Epley redirected our conversation, steering it with question after question of his own. He asked me why I had decided to become a journalist, what had gotten me interested in this topic, my experiences living in California during the pandemic. I kept trying to get back to *my* list of questions, the straightforward, practical ones about his work. But he kept asking, and then following up with deeper and deeper inquiries, until I found myself telling him about my family, about a brother who had run into legal problems, about my hopes this book might help people understand one another a little better. I talked nonstop about myself—which is not what you're supposed to do as a journalist.

"I'm sorry I'm asking so many questions," Epley said at one point. "I don't mean to waste your time." But it didn't feel like a waste. The conversation felt important.

We know it is critical to understand what kind of conversation we're having, and that it's necessary, at a discussion's start, to establish ground rules and determine what kinds of logic we'll use to make choices together.

But that's not enough to create a real, lasting bond. For that, we need emotional connection. Emotional dialogues are vital because they help us figure out who we're talking to, what's going on inside their heads, what they value most. A *How Do We Feel?* conversation can seem anxiety producing. It can sometimes seem easier to pretend we don't hear the emotion in someone's voice, or to glide past a disclosure, rather than acknowledge a vulnerability and reveal ourselves in return. But emotions are how we connect.

When my father died a few years ago and I told people I had recently attended his funeral, some of them offered their condolences. But almost no one asked me any questions. Instead, they quickly moved on to other subjects. The truth was, I was desperate to talk about what I had been through, about my dad, about the eulogies that had made me so proud and sad, about how it feels to know I won't be able to call him with good news. His death was one of the most important—most emotional and profound—events in my life. I would have treasured someone asking, "What was your dad like?" But outside of my closest friends and family, no one asked anything, either because they didn't know how, or because it felt impolite, or they didn't know I wanted to talk, or because they worried that, if I answered, they wouldn't know what to say next.

"It is easier to judge a man by his questions rather than by his answers," the nineteenth-century thinker Pierre-Marc-Gaston de Lévis wrote, and yet he stayed silent on which questions, exactly, should be asked. Science has provided guidance: Ask others about their beliefs and values. Ask them about experiences and those moments that caused them to change. Ask how they feel, rather than about facts. Reframe your questions so they are deeper. Ask follow-ups. And as people expose their vulnerabilities, reveal something about yourself. It will be less uncomfortable than you imagine. It will be more fascinating than you think. And it might lead to a moment of true connection.

However, sometimes it is hard to find the language for our emotions, and so we express our feelings not through our words, but our bodies, vocal inflections, sighs, and laughs. How do we become emotionally intelligent listeners when people aren't speaking clearly? How do we hear vulnerabilities when we're talking about everything *except* how we feel?

4

HOW DO YOU HEAR EMOTIONS NO ONE SAYS ALOUD?

The Big Bang Theory

The original pitch for *The Big Bang Theory*—which would eventually become one of the most successful sitcoms in history—was fairly straightforward: Let's make a show about a group of awkward geniuses who have trouble connecting with other people unless they speak Klingon or enjoy quantum mechanics jokes.

The idea had come to the sitcom's creators, Bill Prady and Chuck Lorre, during a brainstorming session in 2005. Prady had taken a circuitous route to Hollywood, working as a software engineer before teaming up with Lorre, a TV veteran known as "the king of sitcoms." One day, the two men were dreaming up concepts for new shows when Prady began describing the strange and fascinating characters he had met when he was a computer programmer. There was one guy, he told Lorre, who was brilliant at writing code but terrible at human interactions. Whenever they went to lunch, the man would take forever figuring out how much to tip the server. "He would say things like 'Well, she smiled at me, so I guess I should increase her tip by two percent, but she only refilled our water once, which means I should deduct three percent, but I don't know how to account for the fact that she seemed a little flirty but she also forgot my name,'" Prady said. "It would take him twenty minutes to pay the bill. He couldn't wrap his mind around the people part of everything."

"I've never seen someone like that on TV," Lorre told him. "Maybe there's a show there?"

They began sketching out plots and characters. Computer programmers, they decided, were too boring—all they do is stare at screens—so they came up with a group of young physicists. They would be the kind of people who could easily explain the Born-Oppenheimer approximation and Schrödinger's cat, but were bewildered by dating, or fell apart if someone sat in their favorite chair during *Battlestar Galactica.*

Each physicist would have their own sort of awkwardness. The main character, Sheldon, would be uptight, analytical, and emotionally clueless, mostly incapable of reading others' feelings or expressing his own. Sheldon's roommate, Leonard, would pine for a girlfriend, but be so socially inept that he would invite a woman to join him in eating Indian food by explaining that "curry is a natural laxative." Another character, Raj, would become mute whenever a woman was present. A fourth, Howard, would be an engineer rather than a physicist—earning the others' disdain—but speak Klingon and a little Elvish, and boast a repertoire of outrageous pickup lines. Most of all, the characters would share a common trait: A general social incompetence, a tendency to misread others' emotions and miscommunicate their own feelings. It would be a show about how even the smartest people can struggle with the people part of everything.

Lorre and Prady pitched their idea to studio heads even before they had written the first script. Everyone loved it. These were such original characters! A pilot was ordered. However, when the writers started plotting out the initial episode, a problem emerged: "A sitcom only works if you know what the characters are feeling," Prady told me.

Sitcoms are so fast moving, joke after joke and twist after twist, that, to succeed, the audience needs to understand each character's emotional state as soon as they appear on screen. What's more, "the audience needs to see the emotional relationships between the characters," Prady said. "They have to know if two people are fighting because they hate each other, or because they love each other, or they're pretending to hate each other because they're actually in love." Emotions are everything in television. "They have to be obvious," he told me. Put differently, it's crucial for an audience to "hear" a character's feelings, even when those emotions aren't spoken aloud.

That created a problem, however, because the characters in *The Big Bang Theory* were *designed* to be bad at expressing their feelings. Sheldon, for instance, viewed emotions as a nuisance, and felt the best way to assuage a friend was to point out that "you have an entire lifetime of poor decisions ahead of you." Leonard could explain $E=mc^2$ but couldn't fathom why someone would get upset when he read their private diary. These kinds of misunderstandings were at the core of the show's humor. But how do you write a compelling script when your characters are incapable of showing how they feel?

One option was simply to have them announce their feelings—to tell, not show. There's a problem with this approach, though. "You can write dialogue like, 'I'm mad you're late for dinner!'" Prady told me. "But no one talks that way in real life." People don't announce their emotions. They perform them. "Someone screams, 'I cooked you dinner and you're welcome!,' and that's how you know they're angry," said Prady. Psychologists refer to this kind of communication as *nonlinguistic emotional expressions,* and they comprise a vast portion of how we convey our feelings in everyday life. "People's emotions are rarely put into words," wrote the psychologist Daniel Goleman. "The key to intuiting another's feelings is in the ability to read nonverbal channels: tone of voice, gesture, facial expressions and the like."

Lorre and Prady confronted a conundrum: They couldn't have their characters announce what they were feeling, because that was unrealistic and made for terrible television, and they couldn't have them show what they were feeling, because, by design, they were supposed to be bad at showing their emotions. So the writers tried juxtaposing the physicists with other, more emotionally nimble characters to establish contrasts. They created Katie, a jaded neighbor who is fresh from a breakup and whose bitter pessimism highlights the main characters' cheerfulness. To emphasize the characters' longing for companionship, they invented a female physicist named Gilda, whose sexual frankness—she once had sex at a *Star Trek* convention while in costume, she announces in the pilot—underscores the men's naïveté.

The writers finished their script, auditioned actors, shot the pilot, and delivered it to the studio bosses, who recruited test audiences to provide feedback. This was largely a formality, however. Everyone was certain viewers would love the show.

Audiences hated it. They disliked the characters, particularly Gilda and Katie, who struck them as toxic and threatening. But most of all, the audiences were confused. How were they supposed to *feel* about these characters? Were the physicists innocent children or sexualized adults? Were they lovable prodigies or gullible fools? None of the characters, viewers said, seemed to click with each other. The show was emotionally bewildering.

"You cannot make a sitcom where the audience doesn't know how to feel," Prady told me. "It can't be twenty-two minutes of jokes with nothing emotionally holding it together."

The Big Bang Theory had failed to ignite. However, the studio bosses offered Lorre and Prady a lifeline: If they reworked the script, they could reshoot the pilot and try again. When he got the news, Lorre turned to Prady. "I told Bill, 'We gotta dive into these wonderful, brilliant misfits and figure out how to make it clear who they really are.'"

FREEZE-DRIED ASTRONAUT FEELINGS

From infancy, even before we learn to speak, we absorb how to infer people's emotions from their behaviors: Their body language, vocal inflections, glances and grimaces, sighs and laughs. As we grow older, however, this capacity can atrophy. We start to pay increasing attention to what people say rather than what they do, to the point where we can fail to notice nonlinguistic clues. Spoken language is so information rich, so easy to rely upon, that it lulls us into ignoring hints that someone might be, say, upset—*crossed arms, creased brow, downcast eyes*—and instead focus on their words when they say, *It's nothing. I feel fine.*

Some people, however, have a talent for detecting emotions, even when they're unspoken. They exhibit an emotional intelligence that seems to help them hear what's unsaid. We all know people like this: Friends who seem to intuit when we're feeling down, even if we haven't said anything; managers who sense when a kind word is needed, or a bit of tough love, to help us get over a hump at work. It's natural to assume these people are unusually observant, or uncommonly sensitive. Sometimes they are. But years of research indicates this is a skill anyone can develop. We can learn to identify the nonverbal clues that indicate someone's true emotions and use these hints to understand what they are feeling.

In the 1980s, a NASA psychiatrist named Terence McGuire was thinking about this very thing, wondering if it was possible to test whether someone—like, say, a job applicant—possessed the skills to pick up on other people's feelings. In particular, McGuire wanted to identify which of NASA's astronaut candidates were talented at emotional communication. McGuire was NASA's lead psychiatrist for manned flight, in charge of screening the thousands of men and women applying to be astronauts each year. His job was to evaluate their psychological readiness for the stresses of space.

NASA, at that moment, was confronting a new kind of challenge. For most of the agency's history, manned space flights had been relatively brief, typically just a day or two, usually no longer than a week and a half. But in 1984, President Ronald Reagan ordered NASA to start work on an international space station where people could live for up to a year. To McGuire this meant NASA needed a new kind of astronaut—and new types of psychological evaluations. "The advent of the space station, with minimal tours of six months in a crowded environment from which there is no respite, suggests the need for greater attention to personality factors," McGuire wrote to his bosses in 1987.

NASA already had exceedingly high standards for potential astronauts: Applicants had to pass strenuous physicals; they needed a degree in science or engineering and experience in tasks like piloting fighter jets; they couldn't be too tall (anyone over six foot four wouldn't fit in a spacesuit) or too short (less than four foot eight and your feet wouldn't touch the floor and you might slip out of the shoulder belts); they had to show they could stay calm—one test sometimes used required them to keep their blood pressure steady during underwater maneuvers—and could handle the stresses (and, optimally, avoid vomiting) on an airplane simulating zero-g.

But now, McGuire was convinced that NASA needed to start screening for something else: Emotional intelligence. The concept was just then being defined by two psychologists at Yale, who argued that there was a form of "social intelligence that involves the ability to monitor one's own and others' feelings and emotions." People with emotional intelligence knew how to build relationships and empathize with colleagues, as well as regulate their own emotional-ity and the emotions of those around them. "These individuals," the Yale researchers wrote in the journal *Imagination, Cognition and Personality* in 1990, "are aware of their own feelings and those of others. They are open to positive and negative aspects of internal experience, are able to label them, and when appropriate, communicate them. . . . The emotionally intelligent person is often a pleasure to be around and leaves others feeling better. The emotionally intelligent person, however, does not mindlessly seek pleasure, but rather attends to emotion in the path toward growth."

Some recent events had made clear the importance of emotional intelligence while flying through space. In 1976, a Soviet space mission had been canceled midway through after the crew began experiencing shared delusions and complaining of a strange scent that was later determined to be imaginary. Both the United States and the Soviet Union had diagnosed depression among astronauts and cosmonauts during, and after, missions in space, and had found that this despondency could lead to bickering, paranoia, and defensiveness with colleagues.

But NASA's biggest worries focused on breakdowns in communication. The agency was still haunted by the events of 1968, when the crew of the Apollo 7 began arguing with mission control as they hurtled through the atmosphere. The disputes had specific causes at first: The three astronauts complained they were being rushed to complete tasks and given unclear commands. But the arguments gradually morphed into a formless anger and expressions of general discontent, until the astronauts were fighting about even minor issues: The quality of the food, NASA's orders to appear on an upcoming television broadcast, poor designs that made it difficult to use the bathroom, mission control's tone of voice. Spurring on these battles was the on-board commander, Wally Schirra, a former navy test pilot with an exemplary career up to that point. NASA psychologists later suggested that, due to the emotional stresses of the mission and his grief over the recent deaths of three other astronauts in a cockpit fire, Schirra had become combative and suspicious as the trip progressed. After they returned to earth, Schirra and his co-astronauts never flew into space again.

NASA needed people who could control their feelings, were sensitive to others' emotions, and could connect with colleagues, even when tensions were running high and they were stuck in a small can hundreds of miles above the earth. McGuire was brought into NASA around the same time as the Apollo 7 debacle, and for the next twenty years he screened astronaut candidates, looking for clues that they might be prone to depression or combativeness. But now, as space missions were set to get longer, he felt something more was needed: NASA had to find astronauts who were not only free of psychological weaknesses, but, in fact, the opposite: People with enough emotional intelligence to live alongside colleagues in space while navigating the tensions, boredom, arguments, and anxiety that come from being together in a small work area that doubles as living space, surrounded by vacuum, for months at a time.

However, McGuire also knew how hard it was to screen candidates for such traits. The biggest problem was that nearly every applicant's psychological evaluation looked basically the same. No matter what tests he used, which questions he asked, he couldn't get inside candidates' heads deep enough to figure out how they would act during a six-month mission, or a tense moment in space. Every applicant seemed to know what they were supposed to say during interviews. They had practiced describing their biggest weaknesses and greatest regrets, had perfected explaining how they managed stress. McGuire's psychological screenings couldn't differentiate the emotionally intelligent from those who faked it really well. "I, like my predecessors, utilized a formidable battery of psychological testing," McGuire wrote to his NASA bosses. "But I found myself disappointed with the yield."

So McGuire began rereviewing twenty years of audio recordings from past applicant interviews, looking for clues that he had missed, the kinds of signals that differentiate the emotionally intelligent from everyone else. He had access to personnel records, so he knew, among those who had been selected, which candidates had gone on to become strong leaders, and which others had eventually washed out because they couldn't play nice.

It was during these review sessions, as McGuire listened to old recordings of interviews, that he picked up on something he hadn't noticed before: Some of the candidates *laughed* differently.

LAUGHING AT WHAT'S NOT FUNNY

Laughter might seem like a strange place to look for emotional intelligence, but, in fact, it's an example of a basic truth of emotional communication: What's important is not just hearing another person's feelings but *showing* that we have heard them. Laughter is one way of proving that we hear how someone feels.

In the mid-1980s, a few years before McGuire began looking for new ways to test astronaut applicants, a psychologist at the University of Maryland named Robert Provine had started digging into when—and why—people laugh. Provine and a group of assistants had observed people at malls, eavesdropped in bars, and ridden buses while equipped with hidden audio recorders. Ultimately, they collected firsthand observations on 1,200 instances of "naturally occurring human laughter."

Provine's not-too-surprising hypothesis, at first, was that people laughed because they encountered something funny. He quickly realized this was wrong. "Contrary to our expectations," he reported in the journal *American Scientist*, "we found that most conversational laughter is not a response to structured attempts at humor, such as jokes or stories. Less than 20 percent of the laughter in our sample was a response to anything resembling a formal effort at humor."

Rather, people laughed because they wanted to connect with the person they were speaking with. The vast majority of laughs, Provine wrote, "seemed to follow rather banal remarks," such as "Does anyone have a rubber band?"; "It was nice meeting you too"; and "I think I'm done."

"Mutual playfulness, in-group feeling and positive emotional tone—not comedy—mark the social settings of most naturally occurring laughter," Provine concluded. Laughter is powerful, he wrote, because it is contagious, "immediate and involuntary, involving the most direct communication possible between people: Brain to brain."

We laugh, in other words, to show someone that we want to connect with them—and our companions laugh back to demonstrate they want to connect with us, as well. This is the same kind of reciprocity that powers the Fast Friends Procedure. It's an example of emotional contagion. And so it follows that we exhibit emotional intelligence not just by hearing another person's feelings, but by *showing* we have heard them. Laughter, and other nonlinguistic expressions such as gasps and sighs, or smiles and frowns, are embodiments of the *matching principle,* which says that we communicate by aligning our behaviors until our brains become entrained.

But *how* we match other people matters. While reviewing his recordings, Provine noticed something interesting: If two people were laughing at the same time, but one of them was caught up in a belly laugh, while the other was just chuckling, they usually didn't feel closer afterward. When we laugh together, it's not just the laughter that's important. It's similar intensities—the evidence of a desire to connect—that is critical. If someone gives a half-hearted chuckle while we are doubled over with laughter, we're likely to sense their

Emotional intelligence...

...comes from *showing* people we hear their emotions.

tepid enthusiasm and see it as a hint we're not aligned, "a signal of dominance/submission or acceptance/rejection," as Provine wrote. If we chuckle only slightly at someone's joke, while they laugh uproariously, we'll both see it as a sign that we're not in sync—or, worse, that one of us is trying too hard, or the other is not trying hard enough.

This observation—that laughter is useful because it helps us determine if others genuinely want to connect—is important, because it tells us something about how the *matching principle* works: The reason why simply mimicking another person's laughter, or the words they use, or their expressions doesn't bring us closer is because it doesn't really show anything. Simply mirroring someone doesn't prove that we genuinely want to understand them. If you laugh loudly, and I merely smile, it won't feel like I want to bond. It will feel like I'm uninterested, or patronizing. What matters isn't speaking and acting alike, but rather matching one another in ways that convey the *desire* to align.

In one study published in 2016, participants who listened to one-second recordings of people laughing could accurately distinguish between friends laughing together, and strangers trying to laugh alike. Laughter, like many nonlinguistic expressions, is useful because it's hard to fake. When someone isn't genuinely laughing, we can tell. The participants listening to the recordings in that study, based on just one second of decontextualized sound, could tell when people felt aligned and when they were likely forcing it. A joke might not be funny, but if we both agree to laugh in similar ways, we're signaling to each other that we want to connect.

MOOD AND ENERGY

So how do we signal to others that we're trying to connect? How do we show others we're listening to their feelings, and not just mimicking what they say and how they act?

The answer starts with a system that has evolved within our brains, a kind of quick-and-dirty method for gauging other people's emotional temperature that we usually rely upon without consciously noticing it. This system comes alive whenever we encounter another person, and it functions by pushing us to pay attention to their "mood," or what psychologists refer to as *valence,* and their "energy," or *arousal.**

When we see someone and they exhibit an emotional behavior—like a laugh, a scowl, or a smile—the first thing we usually notice is their mood (*is this person feeling positive or negative?*) and their energy level (*are they high energy or low energy?*). For instance, if you encounter someone who is frowning (*negative*) and quiet (*low energy*), you might assume they're sad or frustrated, but you won't assume they pose a threat. Your brain won't start issuing warnings to flee.

However, if they are frowning (*negative*) and shouting and glaring (*high energy*) you'll infer they're angry or violent, and you'll become wary. Your brain will generate a mild anxiety that prepares you to scurry away. All we need to make a prediction is to notice some-

* As anyone who has ever read a psychology journal knows, researchers can be very particular about terms like *mood* and *energy.* For more on the language used in this chapter, please see the endnotes.

one's mood and energy. That's enough to quickly evaluate what they are feeling.

You might not be fully aware that you have noticed someone's mood and energy when you encounter them. It might occur nonconsciously, and just feel like an instinct. But your brain has evolved to use information on mood and energy to gauge whether someone is a friend or a threat. One benefit of this capacity is that we can judge others' emotional states very rapidly, with little more than a glance and no prior knowledge of them. Noticing mood and energy allows us to immediately determine whether we should flee or stay, if they're a potential friend or foe. That's useful when, say, we're trying to decide if a stranger is lost and frustrated and needs our help, or is angry and unstable and likely to turn their fury on us.

ENERGY	MOOD: Positive	MOOD: Negative
High	*Upbeat, enthusiastic, joyful, and excited*	*Angry, indignant, insulted, and outraged*
Low	*Blissful, content, grateful, and satisfied*	*Frustrated, annoyed, grumpy, and discouraged*

Mood and energy often show themselves via nonverbal cues. These cues are important because, while it would be nice to know at a glance if someone is angry or frustrated, those kinds of specific emotions "are really, really hard to read with any accuracy," said Hillary Anger Elfenbein, a professor of organizational behavior at Washington University in St. Louis. Is someone's brow furrowed because they're anxious, or are they just concentrating? Are they smiling because they're pleased to see us, or are they smiling in a way that suggests they are *too* excited, and a little creepy? Even if we genuinely want to know and match someone's emotions, that's hard to do, because we don't know precisely what they are feeling.

So, instead, our brains have evolved this quick-acting system to examine mood and energy, which provides a general sense, in a split second, of someone's emotional state. That's usually enough to figure out how to align, and whether we should feel safe or alarmed.

As the laughter researchers conducted their studies, an interesting finding emerged: When people genuinely laughed together, their mood and energy almost always matched. If one person chuckled softly (*positive, low energy*), and their companion laughed in a similar way, they usually felt aligned. If another person exploded in laughter (*positive, high energy*), and their companion laughed back with the same basic volume, cadence, and forcefulness, they felt connected.

But when people were not connecting with each other—when one person was laughing and the other merely playing along—you could tell because, even if they sounded similar, their mood and energy levels *didn't* match. Yes, they were both laughing. But one person was laughing loudly while the other was responding with a light chuckle. To someone half listening, they might sound alike. But to anyone paying attention, it was clear their volume and cadence—their energy and mood—were out of sync. The laughs were somewhat similar, but if the valence and arousal didn't match, it was clear they weren't aligned.

We exhibit emotional intelligence by showing people that we've heard their emotions—and the way we do that is by noticing, and then matching, their mood and energy. Mood and energy are nonlinguistic tools for creating emotional connection. When we match someone's mood and energy, we are showing them that we want to align. Sometimes we might want to match someone exactly: If you are laughing joyfully, I'll laugh joyfully as well. At other moments, we might want to demonstrate that we see their emotions ("You seem sad") and, rather than match them precisely, offer our help ("What will cheer you up?"). But in each case, we're sending a message: I hear your feelings. This clear desire to connect is an essential step in helping us bond.

This same pattern shows up in other nonverbal behaviors, as well. When we're crying, or smiling, or scowling, we believe others hear us when they respond with a similar energy and mood. They don't need to cry with us—but they need to match our arousal and valence. That's what makes us believe they understand what we're feeling. If they seem to be behaving similarly to us on the surface, but their mood and energy is different, something feels off. "Your facial expressions might be the same, and the words you are saying might be almost exactly the same—nearly everything might be the same—but if your valence is different, you'll know you aren't feeling the same thing," said Elfenbein.

One of the reasons supercommunicators are so talented at picking up on how others feel is because they have a habit of noticing the energy in others' gestures, the volume of their voices, how fast they are speaking, their cadence and affect. They pay attention to whether someone's posture indicates they are feeling down, or if they are so excited they can barely contain it. Supercommunicators allow themselves to match that energy and mood, or at least acknowledge it, and thereby make it clear they *want* to align. They help us see and hear our feelings via their own bodies and voices. By matching our mood and energy, they make it obvious they are trying to connect.

WANNA HEAR A JOKE ABOUT ASTRONAUTS?

Terence McGuire was an avid reader of psychology journals, and as part of his work at NASA, he regularly attended academic conferences where scholars like Provine shared their latest work. So, as he reviewed his audio recordings from twenty years of interviews with potential astronauts, he was aware of the emerging research on nonlinguistic expressions and the importance of mood and energy. He began to wonder if there were any insights that might help him gauge applicants' emotional intelligence in their sighs and grunts, chuckles and tone of voice. As he listened, he started making lists of how applicants had conveyed their emotions beyond using words.

Eventually, he noticed something about the recorded interviews: Sometimes, McGuire would laugh during an interview and some of the candidates—the ones who, later, became great astronauts—would often match his mood and energy. They chuckled when he chuckled, even if what he said wasn't funny. They belly laughed when he did. These didn't seem to McGuire like attempts at manipulation. They were too natural and spontaneous. They sounded like honest reactions. And McGuire remembered how, in those moments, he had felt relaxed, understood, a little bit closer to the applicant.

Then there were other candidates—including many who turned out to be less successful choices for NASA—who, when McGuire laughed on the recordings, would laugh along, but with very different moods and energy levels. When McGuire laughed hard, they chuckled. When McGuire laughed slightly, they responded uproariously, which sounded, as McGuire relistened, like pandering. These candidates had understood they ought to laugh along—it was basic social politeness—but they didn't work too hard at it.

As McGuire made his lists, he found all kinds of other emotional expressions, besides laughter, where the same patterns emerged. In some of the tapes, when McGuire would mention an emotion, the applicant's nonlinguistic expressions—their vocal inflections, tone of voice and pacing, the noises they made—would either match him or diverge. These kinds of "words, tones, postures, gestures and facial expressions," McGuire later wrote to NASA's leaders, "can be a gold mine of information." The nonlinguistic clues were signals as to whether someone genuinely wanted to connect, and if they were adept at doing so, or if they didn't consider emotional bonding to be much of a priority. If someone could connect this way during an interview, McGuire suspected, they'd also be good at aligning with colleagues in space.

So, for his next round of interviews, McGuire decided to try something new. He would intentionally express more emotions during each interview, and then ask candidates to describe their own emotional lives. And he would vary his mood and energy levels and watch to see if the applicant matched him or not.

• • •

A few months later, McGuire walked into a room to interview a man in his midthirties with neatly trimmed hair and a sharply creased uniform. The applicant was physically fit, with a PhD in atmospheric chemistry and fifteen years of exemplary navy service. In other words, he was the perfect NASA candidate.

As McGuire entered the room, he spilled his papers all over the floor in what seemed like an accident (but was actually deliberate), and while collecting the documents, he mentioned that his tie—garish yellow, with colorful balloons—had been a gift from his son. The boy had insisted he wear it today, he explained. "And so now I look like a clown!" McGuire said, laughing loudly. The candidate smiled but didn't laugh back.

During the interview, McGuire asked the candidate to describe a difficult time in his life. The man said that his father had died in a car accident about a year earlier. It had devastated his family, he explained. He had spoken with a pastor about his grief and was slowly coming to grips with all the things he wished he had told his dad. It was a perfect answer, honest and vulnerable. It showed that the man was in touch with his emotions, but not beholden to them. It was exactly the response NASA sought in an astronaut candidate. In previous years, McGuire would have given him high marks.

This time, though, McGuire kept pushing: He told the candidate that his own sister had unexpectedly passed away, as well, and as he spoke, he let his voice waver. He described their childhood, how much she had meant to him. He made his own grief obvious.

After a few minutes, McGuire asked the candidate to describe his father.

"He was very kind," the man said. "Kind to everyone he met."

Then the man sat, waiting for the next question. He didn't elaborate or describe his father's qualities. He didn't ask any questions about McGuire's sister.

The man was not selected as an astronaut. "It was clear to me he wasn't in the top tier for empathy," McGuire told me. Perhaps he was the type of person who didn't enjoy talking about his personal life. Maybe his father's death was still too raw to discuss easily. Neither of those were character flaws—but they indicated he was someone who was less practiced at emotional connection. That alone wasn't the sole reason for his rejection, "but it was part of it," McGuire said. NASA had plenty of qualified applicants and could afford to be picky. "We needed the best of the best, and that meant people who were exceptional at emotional intelligence."

A few months later, another candidate came in for an interview with McGuire. Once again, McGuire spilled his papers as he entered the room and made the same joke about his tie. The candidate laughed with McGuire and leapt up to help him gather his documents. When McGuire asked the applicant to describe a difficult moment in his life, the man talked about a friend who had passed away, but said he was otherwise lucky: Both parents were still alive. He had gotten married at nineteen and still loved his wife. His kids were healthy. Then McGuire mentioned his own sister's death. The candidate began asking him questions: Were you close? How did it impact your mom? Do you think about her, even now? The candidate described how, for months after his friend's passing, he would talk to him in his dreams. McGuire told me that "it was clear he wanted to understand what I'd gone through and share something." That man was selected as an astronaut.

Eventually, McGuire developed a checklist of things to watch for during interviews: How did candidates react to praise? What about skepticism? How did they describe rejection and loneliness? He would ask questions designed to assess their emotional expressiveness: When had they been happiest? Had they ever been depressed? He would pay close attention to their body language and facial expressions as they responded, note when their postures seemed to tense up or relax. Did it seem like they were inviting him in? Were they *showing* him they wanted to connect?

Each time McGuire asked one of those questions, after the candidate had a chance to speak, McGuire would answer the same question himself—expressing happiness or regret, making sure to display his anger or joy or uncertainty. Then he would pay close attention to whether the candidates tried to match him. Did they smile back? Did they comfort him? "Virtually all astronaut selectees have strong cognitive bases," he later wrote. "But it is a minority that have great awareness or sensitivity at a feeling level."

The specific emotions a candidate displayed were less important than *how* they expressed them. Some were quick to show their passions; others were more sedate. What mattered most, though, was whether they paid attention to McGuire's emotional displays and then matched his energy and mood. For some candidates, matching seemed like an instinct; for others, a learned skill. And for some, it didn't happen at all. These distinctions helped McGuire differentiate between those who he suspected could easily bond emotionally with others, and those who, when stresses got high, were more likely to turn inward or become defensive or combative. "Long-term confinement in crowded quarters is generally less stressful for those whose sensitivity and empathy allow them to recognize human problems earlier and to engage them effectively," he wrote to NASA command.

By the time NASA selected the class of 1990—five women and eighteen men, including seven pilots, three physicists, and a physician—McGuire had worked out what he was looking for: Did candidates make clear they were *trying* to align with his mood and energy? If the answer was yes, it indicated they probably took emotional communication seriously.

This framework offers lessons for the rest of us. It's hard to tell exactly what someone is feeling, to know if they are angry or upset or frustrated or annoyed or some combination of all those emotions. The person, themself, might not know.

So instead of trying to decipher specific emotions, pay attention to someone's mood (*Do they seem negative or positive?*) and their energy level (*Are they high energy or low energy?*). Then, focus on matching those two attributes—or, if matching will only exacerbate tensions, show that you hear their emotions by acknowledging how they feel. Make it obvious you are working to understand their emotions. And when you, yourself, are expressing your own emotions, notice how others are responding. Are they trying to align with your energy and mood? This technique is so powerful that, at some call service centers, operators are trained to match a caller's volume and tone in order to help the customer feel heard. Software made by the company Cogito prompts operators, via pop-up windows on their screens, to speed up their speech or slow down, to put more energy into their voice or match the caller's calm. (Companies that use the software told me it makes customer service calls go much better—as long, that is, as callers don't know that a computer is telling the operator how to speak.)

When we match or acknowledge another person's mood and energy, we show them that we want to understand their emotional life. It's a form of generosity that becomes empathy. It makes it easier to discuss *How Do We Feel?*

THE BIG (EMOTIONAL) BANG

By the time Chuck Lorre and Bill Prady learned they had a second chance to rewrite and reshoot their pilot episode, months had passed since they had taped the first one. "I was so close to picking up the phone and saying, *I'm out,*" Lorre said.

But they felt they had to give it one more shot. The actors, by now, had started exploring other projects, so Prady and Lorre needed to move quickly. Right away, they made some big decisions: Katie, the jaded neighbor, was axed. So was Gilda, the sexually adventurous *Star Trek* fan. Instead, they would introduce a new character: Penny, a friendly aspiring actress who is waitressing while waiting to be discovered. "We went the other direction and made Penny light and bubbly," Prady told me. "Someone who, even though she's not book smart, is smart about people."

The question, though, was how to establish the relationship between Penny and the awkward physicists. The same conundrum still existed: The show needed to make clear to the audience what emotions the characters were feeling, while staying true to Sheldon's and Leonard's incompetence at emotional communication.

As Lorre and Prady worked on the new pilot, they considered the scene where the physicists meet Penny for the first time. They had decided it would happen as she is moving into the apartment across the hall. But would Sheldon and Leonard be frantic and nervous? Or subdued and aloof? Neither seemed right.

Finally, a different approach emerged: What if, rather than focusing on Sheldon's and Leonard's specific emotions, each actor simply said the same word—"Hi!"—over and over with the same basic energy and the same basic mood? If nothing else, it would be funny. And maybe it would show the audience that everyone is trying to connect, even if they're too bumbling to know how. The writers didn't conceive of the scene specifically in terms of mood and energy, of course—television writers "don't think like that," Prady told me, "and most of what we know about psychology comes from sitting on a shrink's couch"—but their approach aligns with what we know about emotional communication: As long as the characters unmistakably showed they *wanted* to connect, the audience would intuit what they were feeling—even if the characters were terrible at expressing those feelings themselves.

The final version, when it was filmed, went like this:

SHELDON AND LEONARD SEE A BEAUTIFUL GIRL, PENNY, THROUGH THE OPEN DOORWAY.

LEONARD

(TO SHELDON)

New neighbor?

SHELDON

(TO LEONARD)

Evidently.

LEONARD

Significant improvement over the old neighbor.

PENNY SEES THEM IN THE HALLWAY AND SMILES.

PENNY

(BRIGHT AND CHEERFUL)

Oh hi!

LEONARD

(SAME VOLUME AND SPEED, BUT ANXIOUS)

Hi.

SHELDON

(SAME VOLUME AND SPEED, BUT UNCERTAIN)

Hi.

LEONARD

(NOW PANICKED)

Hi.

SHELDON

(CONFUSED)

Hi.

PENNY

(WONDERING WHAT'S GOING ON)

Hi?

A minute later, Sheldon and Leonard prepare to return to Penny's door to ask her to lunch:

LEONARD

I'm going to invite her over. We'll have a nice meal and chat.

SHELDON

Chat? We don't chat, at least not offline.

LEONARD KNOCKS ON PENNY'S DOOR.

LEONARD

(UNCERTAIN)

Hi . . . again.

PENNY

(SAME VOLUME AND SPEED, BUT BUBBLY)

Hi!

SHELDON

(REGRETFUL)

Hi.

LEONARD

(PANICKED)

Hi.

PENNY

(EXASPERATED)

Hiiii.

When they filmed the scene a few months later in front of a live audience, it killed. The actors imbued each "hi" with a series of vocal inflections, gestures, and tics that made clear their confusion and uncertainty and eagerness, while also making it obvious how desperately they wanted to become friends. As long as the actors aligned their energy and moods, the audience understood: Everyone was trying to bond with each other, but they were too emotionally clumsy to figure out how. "It sounded like a real conversation," Prady told me. They ended up shooting the scene multiple times and the audience laughed louder with each one. "We just knew, this is working. The audience understood exactly what they were supposed to feel."

The secret, according to the episode's director, James Burrows, was that "if they had the same intonation, and they were saying the same word, they could do it with totally different attitudes and you'd still know they liked each other. If one of them had said 'hello' instead of 'hi,' or if one of them had been loud and then Penny got soft, the whole scene would've fallen apart." It would have become confusing: Is she scared of them and wants to get away? Or is she disdainful?

It also worked in reverse. Just a couple of minutes after Sheldon and Leonard meet Penny, the opposite tactic is used to make it obvious when the characters *fail* to connect:

PENNY SITS ON THE COUCH IN SHELDON AND LEONARD'S APARTMENT.

SHELDON

(LOUD AND BRUSQUE)

Um, Penny. That's where I sit.

PENNY

(QUIET AND COQUETTISH)

So sit next to me.

SHELDON

(LOUD AND FAST, AND GESTURING TO THE SEAT)

No, I sit there.

PENNY

(SLOW AND QUIET)

What's the difference?

SHELDON

(VERY FAST)

What's the difference? In the winter that seat is close enough to the radiator to remain warm and yet not so close as to cause perspiration. In the summer it's directly in the path of a cross breeze created by opening windows there and there. It faces the television at an angle that is neither direct, thus discouraging conversation, nor so far wide as to create a parallax distortion. I could go on, but I think I've made my point.

PENNY

(RESERVED)

Do you want me to move?

SHELDON

(STILL WORKED UP)

Well . . .

LEONARD

(EXASPERATED)

Just sit somewhere else!

When they filmed that scene, "the audience went wild," Lorre said. "They were in love with Sheldon's neuroses. I'm standing on the stage, and I look at Jimmy Burrows, who directed both of our pilots, and Jimmy looks at me, and we both look at each other with these big grins. We knew this was working. It was one of those goose bump moments."

The writers had finally cracked the code: The characters could be bumbling and graceless and socially incompetent—and as long as they obviously tried to match one another's mood and energy (or deliberately didn't match), it would be clear when they were connecting or at odds. The audience would understand what they were feeling and could root for them, celebrate when they bonded, feel good when everything worked out in the end (including when—spoiler alert!—Leonard and Penny got married a few seasons later).

AFTER THE BOOM

The Big Bang Theory premiered on CBS on September 24, 2007, with more than nine million viewers. Critics, who are usually dismissive of these kinds of shows, were unusually enthusiastic. *The Washington Post* called it "the funniest new sitcom of the season." Another critic told the Associated Press that the show worked because of "characters you like and believe, who can be hilarious without being heartless, and consistent without being formulaic."

By its third season, fourteen million viewers were tuning in for every episode. By season nine, twenty million. The show would eventually earn fifty-five Emmy nominations and become one of the longest-running programs in history, lasting longer than *Cheers, Friends, M*A*S*H,* and *Modern Family.* Twenty-five million people watched the final episode in 2019.

Chuck Lorre and Bill Prady remained involved the entire time.

When I asked Lorre if he ever talked to the actors about the importance of matching one another's energy and moods, he said he didn't have to. Good actors already understand that, he said. They know how to deliver their lines while using their bodies, inflections, gestures, and expressions to convey what's unsaid. They know how to make sure the audience hears everything, including unspoken emotions. It's the same reason why, in improv, players are instructed to match each other by responding with "Yes, and . . ." It's what good politicians do when they tell a crowd, "I feel your pain."

"The show was a success, I think, because the characters are lovable," Lorre told me. "The writers loved them. The audience loved them. They made it okay to show that love."

When we make it clear to others that we are trying to hear their emotions, when we genuinely try to match or acknowledge their moods and energy, we begin to reciprocate and entrain. We bond.

But what about when you're in a fight with someone, or you believe in very different values? What if we're ideologically opposed? How do we discuss *How Do We Feel?* when talking about our emotions is the last thing we want to do?

Paradoxically, as the next chapter explains, revealing our feelings in these moments is even more important.

5

CONNECTING AMID CONFLICT

Talking to the Enemy About Guns

Melanie Jeffcoat was standing in the hallway of her high school in Las Vegas, Nevada, during the middle of her junior year, when she heard the noise, *pop-pop*, from inside a nearby classroom. *Did someone drop some books?* she wondered. Then she saw a student running. Then another. Then a third, sprinting past her, wide-eyed with fear.

At that moment she began hearing screams. Suddenly everyone was rushing into the hallway and shouting, running toward the auditorium without any real understanding of what was going on beyond overheard snippets: *A gun. Mr. Piggott shot. Blood on my sneakers.* It was 1982, years before the tragedies of Columbine and so many other places, before phrases like *active shooter* and *lockdown drill* would become common inside schools.

For years afterward, Jeffcoat would struggle to wrap her head around what had happened: A disgruntled student had used a handgun to shoot a history teacher and two of Jeffcoat's classmates. The teacher had died; the students survived. In retrospect, it seemed unbelievable, a story she had heard rather than lived through. But over the next few decades, as the list of schools with similar cataclysms grew and grew and grew—Heritage High, Buell Elementary, Virginia Tech, Sandy Hook—she began to realize that she had merely been early, rather than unique.

Then, in 2014, after Jeffcoat had become a parent herself, her eleven-year-old daughter sent a text in the middle of the day. There was a lockdown at her school because of a suspected shooter, she wrote. She was in gym class and students were grabbing baseball bats to defend themselves. "All I got was a golf club," she texted her mom.

Jeffcoat was at the doctor's office and all those old feelings—the terror and panic and helplessness—came rushing back. She jumped in her car and drove to the school. By then, the lockdown was over—it turned out to be a false alarm—but Jeffcoat found her daughter and drove her and three of her friends home. In the car, she listened to their chatter: "We would have totally died because my teacher said we should stay in the classroom." "My teacher opened the window and told us to jump out." "We went into the closet." Jeffcoat was horrified. "It broke my heart to hear them talking like this was a normal part of life," she told me. "How is this acceptable?"

A few months later, when she took her daughters to a movie, Jeffcoat spent the entire time eyeing the theater's exits, envisioning escape routes if a gunman came in. Afterward, she realized she couldn't remember the movie's plot.

She decided she had to do something. "I couldn't just sit there," she said. "If I didn't act, the fear would eat me up." So she joined a local group protesting gun violence. She was aware this wouldn't be popular. "We live in the South," she told me. "Most of my neighbors have guns." But she attended meetings and rallies on weekends, and then took a leadership role in her local group, and then became active within regional organizations, and eventually national associations. She became a public figure in the fight for gun control, quoted in the media and sent to lobby lawmakers. "It was my life," she said.

So it wasn't a complete surprise when she received an invitation from a group of civic-minded organizations asking her to join a discussion about guns in Washington, D.C. The event would include advocates from both sides of the issue. The goal, the invitation explained, was not to debate. It wasn't even, necessarily, to find common ground. Rather, it was an experiment to see if people who abhorred each other's beliefs could have a civil conversation.

Jeffcoat was dubious. How could any conversation with these people—these gun-loving fanatics she was devoted to defeating—be civil? But then again, she had been working on this issue for years and the school shootings hadn't stopped; in fact, they'd become more common. If nothing else, this might help her understand the other side's arguments a little better, which she could use in lobbying. She wrote back and agreed to attend.

CONVERSATIONS AMID CONFLICT

Sometime in the past few months, there's a good chance you've had a tough conversation. Perhaps it was a difficult performance review with a coworker or a squabble with your partner. It could have been a debate about politics, or a quarrel with siblings over who should host Mom during the holidays. Possibly it occurred online, with someone you've never met before and never will, where you traded barbs about vaccines, or sports, or parenting, or religion, or whether the final season of *Lost* was great or the worst. In each case, there was a conflict—opposing beliefs, values, opinions—and you and others attempted to air your disputes and, possibly, find a resolution (or, perhaps, just troll each other out of spite).

How did that conversation unfold? Did you and your spouse take turns calmly presenting facts and proposals, and then listening attentively? Did your coworker acknowledge their shortcomings and you graciously did the same? Did you dispassionately consider your siblings' opinions when they implied you were abandoning your mother? After trading insults on Twitter, did everyone change their minds?

Or—and this, of course, is more likely—was the conversation a messy battle from start to finish, with bruised feelings, anger, defensiveness, and misunderstandings galore?

It's not breaking news to suggest we are living through a time of profound polarization. Over the last decade, the number of Americans who say they are "deeply angry" at the other political party has increased sharply, to almost 70 percent of the electorate. Roughly half the nation believes those with differing political beliefs are "immoral," "lazy," "dishonest," and "unintelligent." Roughly four in ten self-described liberals, and three in ten conservatives, have unfriended or blocked someone on social media because of something they said. Over 80 percent of U.S. workers say they experience conflicts in the workplace.

Conflict, of course, has always been part of life. We argue in our marriages and friendships, at work and with our kids. Debate and dissent are part of democracy, domesticity, and every meaningful relationship. As the human rights activist Dorothy Thomas once wrote, "Peace is not the absence of conflict, but the ability to cope with it."

Today, however, it can feel like we have forgotten how to connect with each other amid our disputes. We seem, at times, unable to see beyond our anger and polarization. One way out of this morass, as previous chapters have shown, is by asking questions and listening to emotions. But sometimes, when it comes to discussing serious conflicts, asking and listening isn't enough.

So how do we connect when our differences seem so unbridgeable?

• • •

The event Jeffcoat had agreed to attend in Washington, D.C., was sponsored by one of the nation's biggest media companies, Advance Local, which had partnered with a group of journalists and civic-advocacy groups to see if there was a better way to have hard conversations.

The event's organizers wanted to conduct an experiment: If they brought together people with different opinions, and then taught them specific communication skills, would they be able to discuss their differences without rancor and bitterness? Could the right conversation, conducted the right way, help overcome the divide?

But what hot-button topic would provide the best fodder for the experiment? As the organizers were trying to decide, there was yet another school shooting: A nineteen-year-old former student at Marjory Stoneman Douglas High School in Parkland, Florida, walked onto campus with an AR-15-style rifle and opened fire, killing fourteen students and three adults. In the wake of that attack, the organizers of the experiment decided to focus on a discussion about guns, "a classically broken conversation," as John Sarrouf, who helped design the project, put it to me. Sarrouf runs an organization devoted to reducing polarization, Essential Partners, and has followed the firearms debate for years. "There's lots of data showing that everyone shares so many opinions about guns," he said. For instance, the vast majority of Americans support background checks for gun purchases. Large majorities support bans on high-capacity magazines and assault-style weapons. But despite this consensus, it's almost impossible to get Democrats and Republicans, let alone groups such as the National Rifle Association and Everytown for Gun Safety, to work—or even sit down—together. "Everyone is so focused on defending their positions," Sarrouf said. "We thought, if we could bring these two sides together and teach them to have a different kind of conversation, maybe it would demonstrate something."

The organizers posted invitations on websites and reached out to gun-control activists such as Melanie Jeffcoat, as well as gun-rights advocates. More than a thousand people responded. Dozens of them were invited to Washington, D.C., to participate in training sessions and dialogues. Afterward, the conversation moved online, and over a hundred more people were invited to participate on Facebook.

"It seemed crazy to me at first," said Jon Godfrey, who learned about the experiment via an online ad. Godfrey served twenty years in the army and then spent a career in law enforcement. He owns between thirty and forty guns (he hasn't counted lately, he told me). When he spoke to the experiment's organizers, he informed them that they probably wouldn't be interested in having him join the conversation, because he wasn't much interested in giving up his weapons. What's more, he suspected they were a bunch of liberals hoping to embarrass conservatives.

The organizers replied that they hoped he would come to D.C., all expenses paid. "I didn't expect much, to be honest," he told me. "But I didn't have anything else going on that weekend, so I said yes, and it ended up being one of the most powerful things I've ever done."

BUILDING EXCEPTIONAL COMMUNICATORS

As the organizers were designing their experiment, they were guided, in part, by the work of researchers such as Sheila Heen, a professor at Harvard Law School who has spent her life trying to understand how people connect amid conflict.

Heen's father, a lawyer, had tutored her in the fine art of argument from a young age. Sometimes it felt as though she had to negotiate for everything: An ice cream cone, a horse, a late curfew, forgiveness when she violated that curfew. Consequently, by the time she got to college, she was a fearsome dorm-room debater. Then she enrolled at Harvard Law School and sought out Roger Fisher, who had recently written *Getting to Yes*, and began studying everything from the rivalries that spark civil wars to battles within companies. Eventually, she joined the Harvard faculty herself.

Heen was soon facilitating dialogues in Cyprus and among indigenous Alaskan populations. She trained appointees at the White House and justices of the Singapore Supreme Court, and advised Pixar, the National Basketball Association, and the Federal Reserve. As she moved among these different worlds, she realized that she had made a common mistake in her more youthful days: She had assumed that the goal of discussing a conflict and engaging in debate was achieving victory, defeating the other side. But that's not right. Rather, the real goal is figuring out *why* a conflict exists in the first place.

Combatants—be they arguing spouses or battling coworkers—have to determine why this fight has emerged and what is fueling it, as well as the stories they are all telling themselves about why this conflict persists. They need to work together to determine if there are any "zones of possible agreement," and have to arrive at a mutual understanding about why this dispute matters, and what's needed for it to end. This kind of understanding, alone, won't guarantee peace. But without it, peace is impossible.

So how do we achieve this kind of mutual understanding? The first step is recognizing that within each fight is not just one conflict, but, at a minimum, two: There's the surface issue causing us to disagree with each other, and then the *emotional conflict* underneath. "Say you have a couple fighting with each other about having another kid," Heen told me. "There's the top-level conflict—*you want another child, and I don't*—that seems, at first glance, to explain why they're fighting. But there's also a deeper emotional issue: *I'm angry because you're prioritizing a kid over my career* or *I'm scared another child will bankrupt us* or *I'm frustrated because you don't seem to care what I want.*" Those emotional conflicts are sometimes nebulous, difficult to pin down, but they're also incredibly powerful—because they contain so much of the anger and disappointment driving this argument beyond the possibility of compromise. "And we know those emotions are there," said Heen, "because whenever the couple fights, no matter how many sensible things they say, they never seem to get closer to a resolution."

Heen sometimes would go into negotiations among politicians, or disputes within companies, and listen to people describe problems with relatively simple fixes. Then she would watch people's emotions hijack the conversation until those fixes became impossible. People were furious, distrustful, they felt betrayed—but they rarely admitted that to the other person or, sometimes, even themselves. They stopped trying to understand why this conflict had emerged and, instead, started plotting revenge. And most of all, everyone wanted to win, to beat the other side, to feel vindicated.

This is all normal, of course. Every confrontation involves a range of feelings—anxiety, distress, a desire for retribution—that are natural. But these passions can make it impossible to discuss problems in a productive manner. "And if you don't acknowledge the emotions, then you'll never understand why you're fighting," said Heen. "You'll never know what this fight is actually about."

The key, Heen found, entailed getting people to express their emotions, to have a version of the *How Do We Feel?* conversation that allowed both sides to express the hurt and suspicion fueling the fight. The problem, however, is that we often hate talking about our feelings during a disagreement. "People love to pretend that they can become analytical robots," Heen said. "But, of course, no one can do that. All that happens is your emotions leak out in other ways." Or people might recognize their own emotions, but they are loath to reveal them. They think it will give the other side an advantage or will be viewed as a weakness. They worry about revealing a vulnerability that will be weaponized by their foes. Not to mention, when we're fighting, we usually feel stressed, which isn't a great environment for discussing our feelings.

This is the real reason why so many conflicts persist: Not because of a lack of solutions or because people are unwilling to compromise, but because combatants don't understand *why* they are fighting in the first place. They haven't discussed the deeper topics—the emotional issues—that are inflaming the dispute. And they've avoided that emotional discussion because they don't want to admit they are furious and sad and worried. In other words, they don't want to talk about *How Do We Feel?*, even though it's the most important conversation to have.

IN A CONFLICT
We learn why we are fighting
by ***discussing emotions***.

Discussing emotions won't solve everything, of course. Sometimes, one person wants a baby and the other doesn't, and no amount of emotional sharing is going to make them agree. "But if you don't at least talk about your emotions," Heen said, "you'll just keep having the same argument over and over."

So how, exactly, do we make people feel safe enough to talk about their feelings? It's a hard task, particularly if people are discussing something—like guns—they've been fighting about for decades, and everyone is certain they, alone, represent righteousness, while the other side is immoral and wrong.

TALKING GUNS IN WASHINGTON, D.C.

Melanie Jeffcoat and her fellow gun-control activists, as well as an equal number of gun-rights enthusiasts, arrived in Washington,

D.C., on a warm day in March 2018, and gathered in the lobby of the Newseum on Capitol Hill. It was the same weekend as the "March for Our Lives" rally organized by the survivors of the Marjory Stoneman Douglas school shooting. Right outside the doors—and in more than eight hundred cities and towns across the United States—students and parents were marching against gun violence. In response, hundreds of gun-rights groups were staging counterprotests. In all, an estimated two million people were in the streets that day to decry, or support, how easy it is to buy firearms in America.

As the participants walked into the Newseum, they could hear a hundred thousand people chanting outside. "It was beautiful," Jeffcoat told me. "Just really inspiring, all those people fighting for a better world. And then I went into a meeting room and sat down with someone who owned forty guns and said he needed an AR-15 for deer hunting."

Once everyone was assembled, the organizers explained their goal: "Whether you agree or disagree with what's going on outside, I think everyone can recognize this is a moment when our country is trying to have one of our most difficult conversations," John Sarrouf told the group. "This is a conversation about guns and safety that America has been trying to have for over two hundred years, and, for almost as long, it hasn't gone very well." Discussions about guns, he said, often devolve into shouting matches and accusations. Or, even worse, they never occur because people self-select into like-minded groups. "That's dangerous in a democracy," Sarrouf told the participants. "If we can't talk across our differences, we can't make decisions together." So the goal of this gathering was to have an honest discussion about guns and to "demonstrate that we can do this conversation differently. We think we can prove it's possible to discuss this issue with thoughtfulness and civility, and learn from each other, even if we disagree."

But first, Sarrouf continued, a bit of training was needed.

The training was important, because the organizers had a second, no less important goal. They knew almost everyone in the room was practiced at talking about guns. Everyone had facts memorized and talking points readily at hand. They all knew each argument and counterargument, how to frustrate their adversaries and lay rhetorical traps.

But the organizers wanted this conversation to be different. They wanted to see if they could get everyone to start sharing personal stories about guns and gun control, the emotions and values underlying their beliefs, and then see if that might change the tenor of the debate. In other words, they wanted to foster a *How Do We Feel?* conversation, in the hopes it might neutralize the poison that usually contaminates these discussions.

But the organizers couldn't simply command participants to reveal their innermost feelings. That was too odd a request, especially among people who believed the other side was an enemy. So, instead, the organizers focused on a different approach: Teaching everyone a technique for listening that makes it safer for emotional disclosures to occur. The secret was *proving* you were listening to each other.

Emotional intelligence comes from showing someone we have heard their emotions. But when we're in a conflict or a fight, simply showing often isn't enough. In those moments, everyone is skeptical and untrusting: *Are they listening, or just preparing their rebuttal?* Something more is needed, an extra step. To convince others we are genuinely listening during an argument, we must prove to them that we have heard them, prove we are working hard to understand, prove we want to see things from their perspective.

As one 2018 study put it, when someone proves they're listening it creates "a sense of psychological safety because [the listener] instills a confidence in the speaker that at least their arguments will receive full consideration and will, thus, be evaluated based on their real worth." When people believe that others are trying to understand their perspectives, they become more trusting, more willing "to express their thoughts and ideas." The "sense of safety, value and acceptance" that comes from believing a partner is genuinely listening makes us more willing to reveal our own vulnerabilities and uncertainties. If you want someone to expose their emotions, the most important step is convincing them you are listening closely to what they say.

IN A CONFLICT
We draw out emotions by
proving we are listening.

The problem, however, is that most people don't know how to prove they're listening. They try things like making eye contact with the speaker, or nodding their head to show agreement, and hope the speaker will pay attention. But speakers usually don't. "We have trouble noticing other people while we're talking," said Michael Yeomans, a professor at Imperial College London. When we're speaking, we're frequently so focused on what we are saying that we don't pick up on how our listeners are behaving. We miss the signals that listeners are trying to send to show they are following along.

So if a listener wants to prove they're listening, they need to demonstrate it *after* the speaker finishes talking. If we want to show someone we're paying attention, we need to prove, once that person has stopped speaking, that we have absorbed what they said.

And the best way to do that is by repeating, in our own words, what we just heard them say—and then asking if we got it right.

It's a fairly simple technique—prove you are listening by asking the speaker questions, reflecting back what you just heard, and then seeking confirmation you understand—but studies show it is the single most effective technique for proving to someone that we want to hear them. It's a formula sometimes called *looping for understand-*

*ing.** The goal is not to repeat what someone has said verbatim, but rather to distill the other person's thoughts in your own words, prove you are working hard to understand and see their perspective—and then repeat the process, again and again, until everyone is satisfied. Using techniques like *looping* "at the beginning of a conversation forestalls conflict escalation at the end," one 2020 study found. People who engage in it are seen as "better teammates, advisors" and "more desirable partners for future collaboration."

IN A CONFLICT

We prove we are listening by ***looping for understanding.***

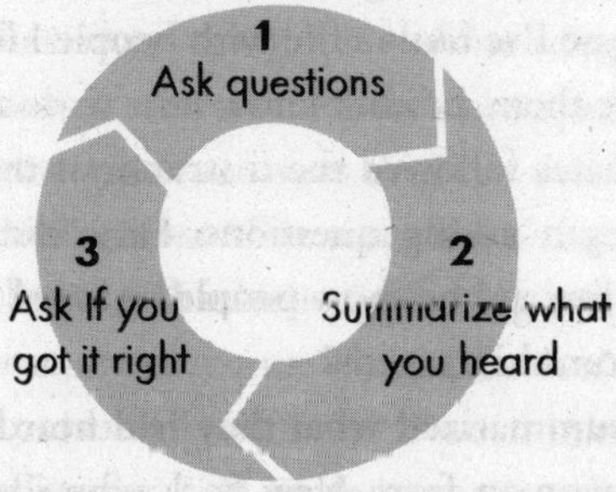

Repeat until everyone agrees we understand.

In the lobby of the Newseum, John Sarrouf divided the crowd into small groups with instructions: One person—the speaker—should describe "a time when they took on a challenge where they were not sure they could succeed, but eventually tried and overcame the challenge and were proud of themselves." Then, those listening should ask questions. And, once the questions were done, the listen-

* For more on this wonderful technique, allow me to recommend *High Conflict* by Amanda Ripley.

feelings, and perceptions. As for the listeners, they could ask questions, but they had to be open ended and curious. No rebuttals disguised as inquiries; no asking a question when you think you already know the answer.

Jeffcoat listened as one woman described how a relative had been assaulted within her own home. The next day, the woman said, she went to a firing range for the first time and has slept with a handgun in her bedstand ever since. "That's how I know I'll never let that happen," she told the group. "I'll never let myself be a victim." Jeffcoat asked if she worried the gun might be stolen or misused. No, the woman said, she had taken precautions. There was a trigger lock, and there were no kids in the house. "That gun is my peace of mind," she said, "and when people say they want to take it away, what they're saying is they want me to feel powerless again."

Someone in the group stepped in to summarize what they had heard: "You see your gun as a symbol that you won't let anyone hurt you. Did I get that right?"

"It's proof that I deserve to feel safe," the woman said. "I belong here as much as anyone else."

Another participant described his pride in teaching his children about ecology and their family's history while hunting together. Another lived near the border, in an area where people sometimes smuggled drugs, and said he once ran off an intruder by brandishing a rifle. Jeffcoat told her own story about the school shooting and her fears for her daughters. They all asked each other questions and summarized what they had heard, until everyone agreed they had all gotten it right.

"It shook me to hear everyone's stories like that," Jeffcoat told me. "It made me feel naïve, like I had just assumed all gun owners were the same angry white guys I saw at rallies."

By the end of two days, both of the organizers' goals had been satisfied: Participants had engaged in honest conversations about guns without those discussions becoming shouting matches. And people had learned how to *show* they were listening, ask honest questions, and become vulnerable enough to reveal feelings that, if they were lucky, led to finding common emotional ground.

"The whole weekend was exhilarating," Jeffcoat told me. "I walked away from it thinking, if we can do this on a large scale, we can change the world." As everyone left Washington, D.C., they promised to stay in touch. The organizers had established a private Facebook group so participants could keep the discussion going. There were moderators to guide the digital dialogue, and the organizers had invited over a hundred additional people to participate in the online conversation. These new people hadn't had the benefit of the training in D.C., but the organizers hoped they would absorb the new communication techniques from the moderators, as well as the participants who had been trained at the Newseum.

It didn't work out like that.

"I went home and went online, and it only took, maybe, forty-five minutes for someone to call me a jack-booted Nazi," said Jon Godfrey, the former cop. For Jeffcoat, the change seemed even swifter: "I flew back, got onto Facebook, and everything fell apart."

THE LOVE SHRINKS

Why do some conversations change so abruptly? Why, at times, can it feel like we've made a real connection with another person—and then our environment shifts, or a small conflict gets bigger, and suddenly we find ourselves so far apart?

In the 1970s, a group of young research psychologists began wondering about these kinds of questions. In particular, they were interested in studying how spouses navigate their relationships when conflicts emerge. Marriage, until then, had received surprisingly little academic scrutiny. Couples' problems were "something that pastors and friends usually dealt with," said Scott Stanley, a professor of psychology at the University of Denver. "Marriage hadn't been much of a priority."

The young psychologists came from the University of North Carolina–Chapel Hill, Texas A&M, the University of Wisconsin, the University of Washington, and over a dozen other schools, and they had come of age amid the cultural shifts of the 1960s, when divorce, the pill, and gender equality went mainstream. The idea of marriage—and what people expected from their spouses—was changing. All of which caused the researchers to wonder: Why do some married couples stay happy for decades, even as society shifts around them, while others, who had once been so certain they were soulmates, descend into bickering and misery?

This group of psychologists never had a formal name, nor an official membership list, but some referred to them as "the Love Shrinks." Their early research consisted primarily of videotaped interviews. Husbands and wives were brought into laboratories and asked to describe their marriages, sex lives, conversations, and fights. Arguments, in particular, interested the researchers. Spouses squabbled while scientists ran their video cameras. Within a few years, more than a thousand arguments had been recorded.

These early studies revealed interesting patterns: Many couples were quite good at listening to each other and even proving they were listening. "That's kind of the minimum for a marriage," said Stanley. "If you can't show the other person you're listening, you probably won't get married in the first place." Couples might not have been *looping* each other, but, either through intuition or advice they had received, they had figured out how to show they wanted to understand one another.

And yet, despite all that listening, America's divorce rate was skyrocketing: In 1979, more than a million couples—triple the number from just a decade earlier—had chosen to end their marriages. The scientists wondered: If couples were so good at hearing each other and proving they heard one another, why were they still splitting up?

The researchers started digging into their data. Eventually, two findings emerged. First, unsurprisingly, they confirmed that nearly every couple fought. Some couples argued frequently—about 8 percent of married Americans fight at least once a day—while others bickered only occasionally. But regardless of frequency, nearly every marriage contained some degree of conflict.

The second discovery was that, for some couples, those conflicts and arguments didn't seem to have much lasting impact. Regardless of how frequently some people battled, they said they were still fulfilled by their marriages, happy with their choice of spouse, and reported no thoughts of divorce or lingering rancor after a fight. Their conflicts were storms that appeared and then dissipated, leaving behind only blue skies.

For other couples, however, things were very different. In these relationships, even small conflicts often turned poisonous. Mild arguments became screaming battles. Reconciliations were mere pauses in ongoing wars, the hurt and anger just waiting for another spark. Unhappy couples said they thought about divorce frequently, threatened it regularly, imagined what they would tell the kids when it finally occurred.

The researchers looked for differences between the happy and unhappy couples. In particular, they wanted to know if the two groups fought in different ways. Their first hypothesis was that these groups were fighting over different things. The scientists suspected that unhappy couples were battling about more serious concerns—money problems, health crises, drug and alcohol use—while happy couples fought about trivial matters, such as where to spend their vacations.

However, they found that hypothesis was wrong. Happy and unhappy couples, it turned out, generally fought about similar issues.

Both groups had money tensions, health problems, and silly vacation disputes.

The next hypothesis was that happy couples were better at resolving their disagreements. Maybe they compromised faster? Perhaps they grew bored with fighting more quickly?

Wrong again. One group wasn't significantly more practiced at resolving conflict, nor more amenable to compromise. What's more, when researchers looked closely at the happy couples, they found that some of them were *terrible* at solving their problems. They would argue and argue and never come to any resolution. Yet they still enjoyed being married.

And then there were other couples who would fight the "right" way, who read all the relationship books and got lots of advice, but still ended up resenting each other. Some of them would do everything correctly, but "still end up divorced," said Benjamin Karney, who helps lead the Marriage and Close Relationships Lab at UCLA.

So the researchers began looking for other variables that might explain what separated happy couples from unhappy marriages. One thing they had noticed was that many couples—both happy and unhappy—sometimes mentioned tussles over "control" when asked to describe their fights. "He always wants to *control* me," one woman told scientists during an interview. "He wants to trap me, get me to say things I don't want to say." That's usually why they started fighting, she explained, "because I want to make decisions for myself, and he wants to be in charge."

Couples' anxieties about control showed up in other ways, as well. Researchers noticed that many divorces happened after major life changes, in part because these changes had triggered a sense of losing control. Sometimes, it was the arrival of children or a stressful new job, which made it harder for people to control their time and anxiety. Or it might be an illness—control over our health—or a big upheaval such as retirement or kids leaving for college, which makes the future seem less predictable. These shifts made people exhausted, lonely, anxious, as if they had lost agency over their days and bodies and minds.

We all crave control, of course. And while there are many factors that determine if a romantic relationship succeeds or flounders, one is whether the relationship makes us feel more in control of our happiness, or less. It is natural for couples to wrestle over control in a relationship; it's part of working out how to balance each person's needs, wants, roles, and responsibilities. But as the researchers watched their videotapes, they noticed a previously overlooked dynamic: During fights, happy and unhappy couples seemed to approach control very differently.

Both happy and unhappy couples, as they argued, struggled over who was in control. Sometimes a husband would limit the topics he was willing to discuss—"I'm not going to talk about that!"—or a wife would put an arbitrary timeline on the conversation—"I'll give this five minutes and then I'm done!"

But happy and unhappy couples, the scientists saw, sought to assert control in very different ways. Among unhappy couples, the impulse for control often expressed itself as an attempt to control the other person. "You need to stop talking, right now!" one man shouted at his wife during a session taped by researchers. She yelled back: "Well, you need to stop working all the time, and ignoring your children, and treating us like shit just because you had a bad day!" Then she began detailing her demands, each of which took the form of an attempt to control his behavior: "You have to show up for dinner, and stop criticizing me, and ask about my day once in a goddamn while." Over the next forty-five minutes, both tried to control each other's language ("Don't use that tone with me!"), what topics they were allowed to discuss ("Don't even go there"), and which gestures should be allowed ("If you roll your eyes one more time, I'm leaving").

They divorced nine months later.

Among happy couples, however, the desire for control emerged

IN A CONFLICT

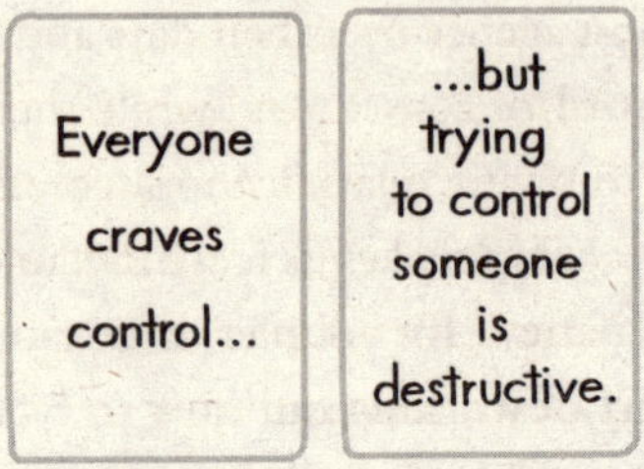

quite differently. Rather than trying to control the other person, happy couples tended to focus, instead, on controlling themselves, their environment, and the conflict itself.

Happy couples, for instance, spent a lot of time controlling their own emotions. They would take breaks when they felt themselves growing angry. They worked hard to calm down through deep breathing, or by writing down how they were feeling rather than shouting it, or by falling back on habits—using "I statements"; reciting a list of what they loved about each other; bringing up happy memories—that they had practiced during less angry times. They tended to speak more slowly, so they could stop, midsentence, if something came out harsher than they intended. They were more likely to defuse tensions by changing the subject or making jokes. "Happy couples slow down the fight," said Karney. "They exert a lot more self-control and self-awareness."

Happy couples also focused on controlling their environment. Rather than starting a fight at the moment a conflict arose, they would put off a tough discussion until they were in a safer setting. An argument might begin at two A.M., when everyone is exhausted and the baby is screaming, but rather than let it continue, happy couples tended to postpone the discussion until the morning, when they were better rested and the baby was quiet.

Finally, happy couples seemed to concentrate more on controlling the boundaries of the conflict itself. "Happy couples, when they fight, usually try to make the fight as small as possible, not let it bleed into other fights," said Karney. But unhappy couples let one area of disagreement spill into everything else. "They start arguing about, 'Are we spending the holidays with my family or yours?' and pretty soon it becomes, 'You're so selfish, you never do the laundry, this is why we don't have enough money.'" (In marriage therapy, this is called *kitchen-sinking,* a particularly destructive pattern.)

IN A CONFLICT

Focus on controlling:

1 Yourself
2 Your environment
3 The conflict's boundaries

One advantage of focusing on these three things—controlling oneself, the environment, and the boundaries of the conflict—is that it allowed happy spouses to find things they could control *together.* They were still fighting. They still disagreed. But, when it came to control, they were on the same side of the table.

Differences in how couples seek control are only one factor that helps explain why some marriages succeed while others stumble. But if, during moments of tension, we focus on things we can control together, conflicts are less likely to emerge. If we focus on controlling ourselves, our environment, and the conflict itself, then a fight often morphs into a conversation, where the goal is understanding, rather than winning points or wounding our foes. Control isn't the only thing that matters, of course, but if spouses don't feel like they share control, it's difficult for an argument to end, or a relationship to flourish.

This insight also has significance in other realms: During any conflict—a workplace debate, an online disagreement—it's natural to crave control. And sometimes that craving pushes us to want to control the most obvious target: The person we're arguing with. If we can just force them to listen, they'll finally hear what we're saying. If we can force them to see things from our point of view, they'll agree we're right. The fact is, though, that approach almost never works. Trying to force someone to listen, or see our side, only inflames the battle.

Instead, it is far better to harness our craving for control so that we're working together, cooperating to find ways to lower the temperature and make this fight smaller. Often, that cooperation spills into other parts of our dialogue, until we find ourselves looking at solutions, side by side.

This explains why *looping for understanding* is so powerful: When you prove to someone you are listening, you are, in effect, giving them some control over the conversation. This is also why the *matching principle* is so effective: When we follow someone else's lead and become emotional when they are emotional, or practical when they have signaled a practical mindset, we are sharing control over how a dialogue flows.

Once the Love Shrinks arrived at this realization—in addition to proving we are listening, we must seek to control the right things—and a host of other insights, they began overhauling how marriage therapy is done. New approaches, such as integrative behavioral couples therapy, which focuses on accepting a partner's flaws rather than trying to change them, began to spread. Within a decade, thousands of therapists were using the Love Shrinks' techniques. "Marriage therapists originally thought their goal was to help couples solve their problems," said Stanley, the University of Denver researcher. Today, though, marriage counseling sessions are more focused on teaching couples communication skills.

"There're lots of conflicts that don't have solutions," Stanley told me. "But when everyone feels in control, the conflict sometimes just fades away. You spoke your mind, your partner heard you, and you find something to work on together, and the issue stops feeling like such a big deal."

THE GUN CONVERSATION GOES ONLINE

When Melanie Jeffcoat, Jon Godfrey, and the other gun-control and gun-rights activists got home and went online, things got heated fast. There were about 150 people in the private Facebook group, many of them sending messages day and night, fifteen thousand posts in four weeks. The majority of participants were new to the group and hadn't attended the training session in Washington, D.C. They hadn't learned any of the organizers' communication skills, nor gotten a chance to bond in real life.

On Facebook, there were moments of real connection, but also plenty of ugliness. "I don't know what's more insulting, your assumptions or your dismissiveness," one participant wrote to another. "So you are good with brainwashing children about the dangers of freedom?" another asked. People called each other idiots, Nazis, and fascists, while writing that some people were "too dumb to understand my arguments because, I guess, you were busy doing drugs and having sex in college rather than learning to think."

The group's moderators had been trained to serve as "models of curiosity, civility and careful listening" and to work to "establish conversational norms." But online, the moderators discovered, those approaches sometimes fell short. They tried to emphasize various listening techniques. They tried to train people to speak with civility. But it proved less useful online than it had in person in D.C.

There were all the normal problems of online communication: Comments intended as sarcasm but read the wrong way; garbled phrasing that implied an offense the writer never intended; posts that seemed innocent to some but like fighting words to others. And one problem, in particular, that kept popping up was the same issue that marriage researchers had found was derailing spouses: On Facebook, people kept trying to control one another. These struggles for control weren't the only thing disrupting conversations—but when they emerged, they tore dialogues apart.

Some Facebook participants, for instance, tried to control what others were allowed to say, which opinions were permitted, what emotions could be expressed: "It's ridiculous to say you're scared because your neighbor owns a gun," one person told another. "There's no way you should feel that way."

Attempts at control popped up in more subtle ways, as well. Someone would introduce an issue, and another person would immediately suggest a solution or offer a long monologue, which struck the original poster as an attempt to police the conversation's direction and tone. Sometimes people downplayed issues—"I wouldn't have seen the big deal in a situation like this," one person wrote to another who described a troubling gun-training course—which felt like an attempt to control which kinds of concerns were legitimate and which ones were foolish.

Sometimes people didn't even seem to realize they were trying to exert control. "I'm seeing the same dudes posting over and over again with the same long drawn-out gun rhetoric and it's really off-putting," one woman wrote. Her intent was to express her frustration, but it came off like an attempt to restrain who was allowed to speak: "I'm most interested in hearing from other women," she wrote. "I am not at all interested in hearing from men." Sometimes, when we try to exert control, we don't realize we're doing it. We think we're simply stating our opinion, or offering advice, and don't understand that others will perceive it as attempting to strong-arm a conversation's direction.

"It's getting pretty tribal," one participant wrote. So the moderators, like the marriage counselors, started nudging people to focus on controlling things together. When it seemed as though a fight was about to break out, the moderators sent messages urging everyone to focus on their own needs and emotions—a polite way of asking people to exert self-control. "When you feel triggered or angry, take a breath," one moderator posted. "If you find yourself feeling defensive, step back." The moderators pushed people to think about the environment they created via the words they used. When hot-button phrases were posted—*police state, freedom warriors, assault weapons*—they asked participants to use less polarizing language, such as *rule of law, gun-rights advocate,* and *tactical rifles.* Moderators encouraged participants to control the boundaries of their conflicts by staying focused on one topic at a time. "I want to remind people that this is not a debate with a goal of scoring points," a moderator wrote to the group. "I am wondering if you can take the heat down a bit. . . . It might be best if we all take a pause."

This approach—nudging people to control themselves, their environments, and the boundaries of their conflicts—had an impact. The conversations got better, more human. People attacked each other less. "My stance on guns hasn't changed since joining this group," one person wrote, "but my approach to the gun conversation definitely has. I want to sit and talk and have these difficult conversations."

Then something surprising occurred. Godfrey, the former cop, sent a private message to Jeffcoat, saying he had noticed she kept getting shouted down in online chats. He wanted to help, and so they hatched a plan. The next morning, Jeffcoat posted in support of a polarizing issue: Red flag laws, which allow police to remove guns from people's homes. Jeffcoat knew her post would spark angry replies.

Godfrey, however, was ready. He responded before anyone else to say that, as a police officer and gun-rights supporter, there had been many times he had wished he could take a firearm from someone who posed a danger to themselves or others. Then he wrote that he hoped to hear about people's experiences with this one specific sliver of the gun debate. He worked to shape the environment and the conflict's boundaries. People began sharing stories about taking guns from relatives, or having their own guns taken away. Jeffcoat, rather than arguing her position, started *looping,* with posts summarizing what others had said. Soon, dozens of people were telling stories, admitting how complicated and nuanced this issue was. "Sometimes people don't know how to listen," Brittany Walker Pettigrew, a moderator, told me. "They think listening means debating, and if you let someone else make a good point, you're doing something wrong. But listening means letting someone else tell their story and then, even if you don't agree with them, trying to understand why they feel that way."

While those dialogues were occurring, another gun-control activist from the Facebook discussion, Helene Cohen Bludman from Bryn Mawr, Pennsylvania, went to a local planning session for an upcoming march in her city against guns. When she showed up, volunteers were making signs reading THE NRA IS EVIL. That upset Bludman. "Just a few months earlier, I would have carried that sign," she told me. "But the NRA is made up of people like Jon Godfrey, and he's a good person. We can't say that about him."

Conflicts don't usually resolve quickly. "It's hard to metabolize another person's perspective in just one conversation," Sheila Heen told me. "It takes a while, and so we usually have to revisit the conversation, again and again, until we can hear everything each person is saying." But this iterative process can easily go off the rails if we feel unsafe, or if it seems other people aren't listening, or if they're trying to control what we're allowed to say. That's when hurt and anger seep in, resentment builds, the conflict starts to spiral. But when we look for things we can control together, a path forward becomes easier to see.

• • •

The experiment to foster a civil conversation about guns concluded about six weeks after it began, as planned, when the organizers concluded the Facebook group. The results were, in a sense, mixed: Not everyone rose above their animosities. Not everyone found ways to connect. Some people were ejected by moderators, others opted out. "I am beginning to lose interest in this group," one person wrote a few weeks in. "Nobody is interested in changing their mind. You either believe in the most fundamental human right there is—the right to defend oneself, family, community, and country—or you believe in the denial of that most fundamental right. . . . I know that my mind is set on the issue, and that yours probably is too. . . . I guess in the end I will see you at the ballot box." Even those who found meaning in the conversations sometimes felt conflicted about their peers. "There's one guy who, if I never talk to him for the rest of my life, that's fine," Jeffcoat told me.

But there were also people who found real connections across vast divides. For them, the experience was profound. "I've used these skills in other arenas of my life," one participant wrote when the organizers polled people six months after the project ended. "I'm more tolerant when I'm talking to people with different points of view. I used to be intolerant of people with extreme positions, [but] now I'm able to have conversations with these people, and listen to them, while also getting my point through," another added.

For Jon Godfrey, the project was transformative. He still owns dozens of guns, he told me, and he's twice voted for Donald Trump in part because he believes Trump will protect the Second Amendment. Prior to participating in the experiment, Godfrey had generally put gun protesters in the same category as, say, communists, or perhaps vegans: People who don't understand how the real world works.

But he's rethought some things. Since the project ended, he has gotten into the habit of calling Jeffcoat, every few months, just to catch up and hear her take on what's going on in the news.

"It's a complicated world, you know?" Godfrey said. "You need friends who are different if you want to figure it out."

A GUIDE TO USING THESE IDEAS

PART III

Emotional Conversations, in Life and Online

Emotions impact every conversation, whether we realize it or not. Even when we don't acknowledge those feelings, they're still there—and when they are ignored, they're likely to become obstacles to connection.

So a critical goal, in any meaningful discussion, is bringing emotions to the surface, which is the third rule of a learning conversation.

> ***Third Rule:***
> **Ask about others' feelings, and share your own.**

There is a moment, in many conversations, when someone says something emotional, or we reveal our own feelings, or we want to understand why we keep fighting, or we hope to get closer to someone who feels distant. That is when a *How Do We Feel?* conversation might begin, if we allow it to. And one of the best ways to start is to **ask a deep question.**

Deep questions are particularly good at creating intimacy because they ask people to describe their beliefs, values, feelings, and experiences in ways that can reveal something vulnerable. And vulnerability sparks emotional contagion, which makes us more aligned.

Deep questions can be as light as "What would be your perfect day?" or as heavy as "What do you regret most?" Deep questions don't always seem deep at first: "Tell me about your family" or "Why do you look so happy today?" are easy to ask—and can be deep because they invite others to explain what makes them proud or worried, joyful or excited.

Nearly any question can be remade into a deep question. The key is understanding three characteristics:

1. **A deep question asks about someone's values, beliefs, judgments, or experiences—rather than just facts.** Don't ask "Where do you work?" Instead, draw out feelings or experiences: "What's the best part of your job?" (One 2021 study found a simple approach to generating deep questions: Before speaking, imagine you're talking to a close friend. What question would you ask?)
2. **A deep question asks people to talk about how they feel.** Sometimes this is easy: "How do you feel about . . . ?" Or, we can prompt people to describe specific emotions: "Did it make you happy when . . . ?" Or ask someone to analyze a situation's emotions: "Why do you think he got angry?" Or empathize: "How would you feel if that happened to you?"
3. **Asking a deep question should feel like sharing.** It should feel, a bit, like we're revealing something about ourselves when we ask a deep question. This feeling might give us pause. But studies show people are nearly always happy to have been asked, and to have answered, a deep question.

Once we ask a deep question, we need to listen closely to how others reply. Listening requires paying attention to more than just the words they say. To hear what a person is saying, we also need to pay attention to their **nonlinguistic emotional expressions**—the sounds they make, their gestures, tone of voice and cadence, how they hold their bodies and their expressions.

The last guide laid out some clues that are useful in determining what people want from a conversation. We can also learn to look for what they are feeling. But since it's easy to mistake, say, frustration for anger, or quiet for sadness, it is critical to be attuned to two things:

- **Mood:** Do they seem upbeat or glum? How would you describe their expressions? Are they laughing, or shouting? Are they up or down?
- **Energy:** Are they high energy, or low energy? Quiet and withdrawn or talkative and expressive? If they seem happy, is it calm and content (*low energy*) or excited and outgoing (*high energy*)? If they are unhappy, are they sad (*low energy*) or agitated (*high energy*)?

Look to *mood and energy* to gauge emotions...

ENERGY \ MOOD	Positive	Negative
High	*Upbeat*	*Angry*
Low	*Blissful*	*Frustrated*

...and then match to show you are listening.

Mood and energy levels often tell us all we need to know in order to align emotionally. Sometimes, we might not want to match emotions: If someone is angry, and we become angry, it may drive us apart. But if we acknowledge their mood and energy—"You seem upset. What's wrong?"—we can start to align.

RESPONDING TO EMOTIONS

Once we've brought our emotions to the surface, what do we do next?

One of the most important aspects of emotional communication is **showing** others we hear their emotions, which helps us **reciprocate.**

There's a technique for this—**looping for understanding.** Here's how it works:

- Ask questions, to make sure you understand what someone has said.
- Repeat back, in your own words, what you heard.
- Ask if you got it right.
- Continue until everyone agrees we understand.

We prove we are listening by
looping for understanding.

Repeat until everyone agrees we understand.

The goal of *looping* isn't parroting someone's words, but rather distilling another person's thoughts in your own language, showing them that you are working hard to see their perspective, and then repeating the process until everyone is aligned.

There are two benefits to *looping*:

First, it helps us make sure we're hearing others.

Second, it demonstrates we *want* to hear.

This second benefit is important because it helps establish **reciprocal vulnerability.** Emotional reciprocity doesn't come from simply describing our own feelings but, rather, providing "empathetic support." Reciprocity is nuanced. If someone reveals they've gotten a cancer diagnosis, we shouldn't reciprocate by talking about our own aches and pains. That's not support—it's an attempt to turn the spotlight on ourselves.

But if we say, "I know how scary that is. Tell me what you're feeling," we show we empathize and are trying to understand.

We reciprocate vulnerability by . . .

- **Looping for understanding,** until you understand what someone is feeling.
- **Looking for what someone needs:** Do they want comfort? Empathy? Advice? Tough love? (If you don't know the answer, *loop* more.)
- **Asking permission.** "Would it be okay if I told you how your words affect me?" or "Would you mind if I shared something from my own life?" or "Can I share how I've seen others handle this?"
- **Giving something in return.** This can be as simple as describing how you feel: "It makes me sad to hear you're in pain," or "I'm so happy for you," or "I'm proud to be your friend."

Reciprocity isn't about matching vulnerability to vulnerability, or sorrow to sorrow. Rather, it is being emotionally available, listening to how someone feels and what they need, and sharing our own emotional reactions.

HOW DOES THIS CHANGE IN A CONFLICT?

Sharing feelings can be difficult amid conflict. If we're in a fight, or talking to someone with different values and goals, connection can seem difficult—even impossible.

But because emotions drive so many conflicts, during fights it's even more important to discuss *How Do We Feel?* It can reveal how to bridge the gulf.

Researchers have found that in a conflict, **proving we are listening** and **sharing vulnerabilities** can be particularly powerful—and we can prove we are listening through specific techniques.

When we are in conflict with someone . . .

- **First, acknowledge understanding.** We do this through looping and statements such as "Let me make sure I understand."
- **Second, find specific points of agreement.** Look for places where you can say "I agree with you" or "I think you're right that . . ." These remind everyone that, though we may have differences, we *want* to be aligned.
- **Finally, temper your claims.** Don't make sweeping statements such as "Everyone knows that's not true" or "Your side always gets this wrong." Rather, use words like *somewhat* or "It might be . . ." and speak about specific experiences ("I want to talk about why you left dishes in the sink last night") rather than broad generalities ("I want to talk about how you never do your part around the house").

The goal is showing that the aim of this conversation is not winning, but understanding. You don't need to avoid disagreements or downplay your own opinions. You can offer thoughts, advocate for your beliefs, even make arguments and challenge each other—as long as your goal is to understand, and be understood, rather than to win.

HOW DOES THIS CHANGE WHEN WE GO ONLINE?

Humans have been speaking to each other for more than a million years and communicating via written language for more than five millennia. Over that time, we've developed norms and nearly unconscious behaviors—the lilt in our voice when we answer a phone; the sign-off in a letter signaling our fondness for the reader—that make communication easier.

In contrast, we've only been communicating online since 1983. Relatively speaking, the norms and behaviors for talking over the internet are still in their infancy.

One of the biggest problems with online discussions, of course, is they lack the information usually provided by our voices and bodies: Our vocal tones, gestures, expressions, and the cadence and energy we bring to our speech. Even when we write letters, we tend to include nuances and subtleties that come from editing ourselves and thinking about what we want to say.

Online, however, communication tends to be fast and unthinking, unedited and sometimes garbled, without any of the clues that our voices provide, or the thoughtfulness that formal correspondence allows.

But online communication is here to stay. So what do we need to know?

There are four things that studies show make online conversations better.

When talking online, remember to . . .

- **Overemphasize politeness.** Numerous studies have shown that online tensions are lessened if at least one person is consistently polite. In one study, all it took was adding *thanks* and *please* to a series of online arguments—while everything else stayed the same—to reduce tensions.
- **Underemphasize sarcasm.** When we say something in a wry tone, it signals an irony our audience usually understands. When we type something sarcastic online, we typically hear these same inflections within our heads—but the people reading our comments do not.
- **Express more gratitude, deference, greetings, apologies, and hedges.** Studies demonstrate that when we are grateful ("That comment taught me a lot"), or solicitous ("I would love to hear your thoughts"), or preface comments with a greeting ("Hey!"), or apologize in advance ("I hope you don't mind . . .") or hedge our comments ("I think . . ."), online communication gets better.
- **Avoid criticism in public forums.** In another study, researchers found that giving negative feedback online backfires much more than in real life. It pushes people to write more negative things, and to start criticizing others more frequently. When we criticize others publicly online, we make bad behavior into a digital norm.

All of these, of course, are also useful tactics when we're speaking face-to-face. Many of them are obvious, things we learned as kids. But online, they're easy to forget because we're typing fast, texting between meetings, hitting SEND or POST without rereading our words to see how they might land. Online, a bit more care and thought can yield outsized rewards.

THE *WHO ARE WE?* CONVERSATION

AN OVERVIEW

In a meaningful conversation, we bring not just ourselves to the discussion, but everything that brought us to this moment: Our histories and backgrounds, our families and friendships, the causes we believe in and the groups we love or deplore. We bring, in other words, our social identities. Many conversations focus explicitly on these identities: Who we know in common, how we relate to each other amid our communities, what we think about our relationships and how they influence our lives.

The social justice movements and tragic examples of violence of the past decade have made it painfully clear that inequality and prejudice touch many lives—and some more than others. Talking about our differences is important if we are to begin to move beyond these blights.

The next two chapters explore social conversations and how they can succeed, even amid discomfort. Chapter 6 examines how to take hold of an evolutionary instinct—to trust those who are like us, and distrust those who aren't—and use it to connect even when our backgrounds and beliefs set us apart. Chapter 7 studies how the most difficult conversations—about systemic forms of injustice, for example—can be elevated if we think more intentionally about *how* they ought to occur.

"It is not our differences that divide us," wrote the poet and activist Audre Lorde. "It is our ability to recognize, accept and celebrate those differences." The *Who Are We?* conversation explores how our social identities make us, and the world, a richer place.

6

OUR SOCIAL IDENTITIES SHAPE OUR WORLDS

Vaccinating the Anti-Vaxxers

When Jay Rosenbloom graduated from medical school in 1996 and started a pediatrics residency at the University of Arizona, he knew, as the new guy, he would get the jobs no one else wanted. He had earned an MD and a PhD from Oregon Health and Science University, but once he became an actual, practicing doctor, he spent much of his first year doing run-of-the-mill "well-baby" exams. Each day, anxious parents streamed through the clinic's doors, and Rosenbloom asked them about feeding schedules and diaper rashes, and then demonstrated swaddling techniques and burping methods.

It wasn't glamorous work, but toward the end of each appointment, he finally got a chance to deploy his medical skills: He prepared, and then administered, a series of immunizations. The American Academy of Pediatrics recommended starting vaccinations against diseases such as polio and whooping cough within three months of birth, and most parents were enthusiastic for their infants to get the shots.

Some parents, though, were skeptical. They had heard these vaccines caused autism, or physical deformities, or infertility. They worried vaccines were a profit-making ploy and made kids *more* susceptible to disease, so that companies could sell them more drugs. Some parents objected simply because they didn't like anything recommended by the government. Rosenbloom knew these concerns were misguided and irrational, but that didn't make them any less common.

"So I went to one of the senior physicians, and I asked him, what should I say to parents who refuse vaccines?" Rosenbloom told me. "And he said, just tell them: *I'm the doctor and I know better than you.*"

Even though he was the clinic's most junior employee, Rosenbloom realized that wasn't a winning strategy. So instead, in his off-hours, he designed handouts for parents documenting how many lives had been saved by vaccines. He photocopied medical studies and tracked down educational videos to show during exams. He told parents about the sadness he felt when unvaccinated children came in with easily preventable, life-threatening diseases. He tried everything he could think of—usually to no avail. "The more information I provided, the more they'd dig in their heels," he said. "Sometimes, I would share my research, send them home with all these charts and handouts, and the parents would thank me, and then a week later I'd find out they'd switched to another clinic."

One morning, a father and his twelve-year-old daughter came in and Rosenbloom asked if he might administer a vaccine. "Hell, no," the man said. "We're not going to put that poison in our bodies. You trying to kill us?" Rosenbloom didn't push it. "You're not going to convince a guy like that," he told me. "His whole self-image is built around the idea that vaccines are for suckers and doctors are either idiots or part of the plot."

This dynamic persisted as Rosenbloom finished his residency and joined a practice in Portland, Oregon. Over the next two decades, he became accustomed to recommending vaccines and then listening as some portion of his patients explained why the injections were dangerous or a conspiracy. It got to the point where these theories, no matter how outlandish, no longer surprised him. What did strike him as odd, however, was the sheer diversity of the anti-vaxxers. "You've got liberals who refuse vaccinations because they only eat organic, and conservatives who think it's government tyranny, and libertarians who say Bill Gates wants to put microchips in our bodies, and all those people normally hate each other. But when it comes to vaccines, it's like everyone's reading from the same hymnal."

This struck researchers as odd, as well. People who refused vaccines didn't seem to have much in common with the typical conspiracy theorists who go down rabbit holes after visiting fringe websites or talking to eccentric relatives. Rather, anti-vaxxers' refusals seemed to focus on how society embraced these drugs without question. As academics began studying the psychology of vaccine resistance, many came to believe the anti-vaxxers' antipathy had something to do with their "social identities": The self-images we all form based on the groups we belong to, the people we befriend, the organizations we join, and the histories we embrace or shun.

• • •

The last chapter looked at a hard conversation—the debate over guns—where people were divided by ideologies and politics. But there is another, different kind of division that can make it equally difficult for people to connect. This kind of division stems from our social identities, how society sees us and how we see ourselves as social creatures. These are the differences—and the conflicts—that can emerge because I am Black and you are white, or I am trans and you are cis, or I am an immigrant and you are not. In these situations, if we hope to connect, a different kind of approach is needed, something more than *looping for understanding* or proving we want to understand.

Social identities, as one psychology textbook explains, are "that part of our self-concept that comes from our membership in social groups, the value we place on this membership, and what it means to us emotionally." Our social identities emerge from a blend of influences: The pride or defensiveness we feel based on the friends we've chosen, the schools we've attended, the workplaces we've joined. It's the obligations we feel because of our family legacies, how we grew up, or where we worship. All of us have a personal identity, how we think of ourselves apart from society. And all of us have a social identity, how we see ourselves—and believe others see us—as members of various tribes.

Numerous studies have shown that social identities influence our thoughts and behaviors in profound ways. One famous experiment conducted in 1954 found that arbitrarily dividing eleven-year-old boys into two groups at a summer camp—they called themselves the Rattlers and the Eagles—was enough to cause them to start bonding intensely with their own faction, and then demonizing the other group until they were ripping down each other's flags and throwing rocks at one another's heads. Other experiments have demonstrated that, in social settings, people will lie about their pasts, willingly pay too much for a product, or pretend not to see a crime as it occurs simply to fit in.

We all possess numerous social identities—Democrat/Republican, Christian/Muslim, Black/white, self-made millionaire/working-class—that intersect in complicated ways: *I'm a gay Hindu computer engineer from the South who votes libertarian.* These identities nudge us and others to make assumptions. They can subtly cause us to "exaggerate the differences between groups" and overemphasize "the similarities of things in the same group," as one researcher from the University of Manchester wrote in 2019. Our social identities push us unthinkingly to see people like us—what psychologists call our in-group—as more virtuous and intelligent, while those who are different—the out-group—as suspicious, unethical, and possibly threatening. Social identities help us relate to others, but they can also perpetuate stereotypes and prejudice.

The Three Conversations

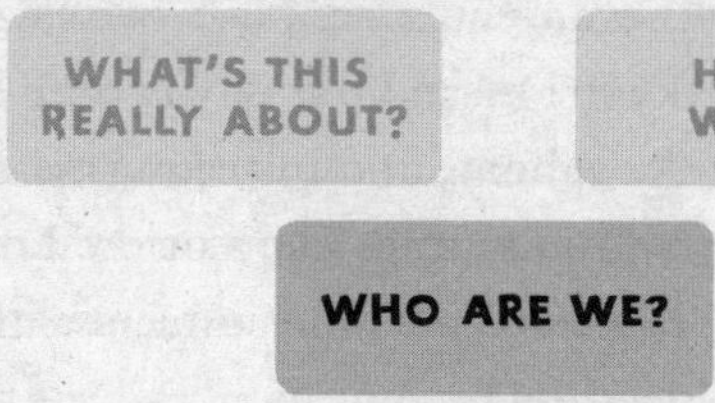

We all possess social identities that shape how we speak and hear.

These social impulses, good and bad, are likely rooted in our evolution. "If we hadn't developed a deep need for belonging and social interaction a long time ago, our species would have been toast," Joshua Aronson, a professor of psychology at NYU, told me. "If a baby doesn't have a social instinct, or its mother doesn't care about her offspring, the baby dies. So the traits that get passed down are caring about your in-group and wanting to defend your people and finding ways to belong."

The desire for belonging is at the core of the *Who Are We?* conversation, which occurs whenever we talk about our connections within society. When we discuss the latest organizational gossip ("I hear everyone in accounting is going to get laid off") or signal an affiliation ("We're Knicks fans in this family") or figure out social linkages ("You went to Berkeley? Do you know Troy?") or emphasize social dissimilarities ("As a Black woman, I see this differently than you"), we're engaging in a *Who Are We?* conversation.

These kinds of discussions often help us bond: When we discover we both played high school basketball or both attend *Star Trek* conventions, we're more likely to trust each other. And though these tribal declarations might present downsides—we might look down upon people who weren't athletes, or who don't appreciate Spock—there are also clear benefits: When we discover overlapping social identities, we're more prone to connect.

But not all social identities are equal. Simply because we both root for the same sports team doesn't mean I'll trust you once I learn that you have sixteen assault rifles at home or think eating meat should be criminalized. Particularly within settings like a medical clinic, some identities—such as being a doctor—are more influential than others.

Put differently, social identities become more and less powerful—or more and less *salient*—as our surroundings change. If I'm attending a neighborhood BBQ where everyone voted for Barack Obama, my pro-Obama T-shirt probably won't spark strong feelings of kinship. But if I'm wearing that shirt at an NRA rally, and meet another person in the same shirt, we might feel a sense of comradery. The meaningfulness of various identities—the importance of gender versus race versus politics versus who we support in the Super Bowl—becomes more and less salient based on our environment and what's happening around us.

• • •

Over the years, as Dr. Rosenbloom encountered more and more parents who refused to vaccinate their children, it began to seem to him that their refusals were related to their social identities: *We are skeptical about the medical establishment* or *We don't like the government telling us what to do.* Part of it, he suspected, had to do with the environment where these discussions occurred: These patients were in *his* exam room, where he had been cast as the expert, and they were forced into the role of supplicants seeking advice, a dynamic that could easily trigger resentment. One study published in 2021 found that such power imbalances and other factors have caused "nearly one-fifth of Americans [to] self-identify as anti-vaxxers at least some of the time, and that many of these individuals view the label as central to their sense of social identity." Studies indicate that the vaccine resistant see themselves as smarter than the average person, better at critical thinking, and more devoted to natural health. Being anti-vaccine provides "psychological benefits," the 2021 study reads, including "increased self-esteem and a sense of community." Those who self-identify as skeptical about vaccines are "more likely to view mainstream scientific and medical experts—who advocate widespread vaccination efforts—as threatening outgroups."

Breaking through these attitudes is difficult because "you're asking someone to give up the values and beliefs at the core of how they see themselves," one author of that study, Matt Motta of Boston University, told me. You'll never succeed at getting someone to change their behavior "if, as a prerequisite, you force them to say: Everything I've believed until now is wrong," said Motta.

But to Rosenbloom, it felt like the problem wasn't just his patients. Doctors were influenced by social identities, as well. When Rosenbloom thought back to his mentors—such as the physician who told him to say *I know better than you*—he recognized this as arrogance caused by a social identity gone awry. That doctor thought he was superior because he belonged to a tribe of experts. No matter how much that physician had in common with his patients, no matter if they lived in the same neighborhood and sent their kids to the same school, once the patients had refused his advice, he saw them as part of an ignorant group, a tribe that deserved disdain. Rosenbloom hated to admit it, but sometimes he saw this same impulse in himself, as well. "You put on this white coat, and you start to think of yourself as the team with all the answers," he told me. "And then, when a patient disagrees with you, you start thinking of them as backwards or wrong."

If Rosenbloom hoped to talk about vaccines with the vaccine resistant, he would need to get better at speaking their language and showing he understood their concerns. In other words, he needed to start having *Who Are We?* conversations.

But that required two things:

- First, he needed to figure out how to address the stereotypes inside his own head—and the heads of other physicians—that made them see the vaccine resistant as ignorant and irresponsible.
- Second, he needed to have conversations where patients felt respected, and everyone saw one another as members of a common tribe.

Then, in early 2020, Rosenbloom started hearing about a new, aggressive coronavirus in Wuhan, China. Soon, the virus was rocketing around the world, and nations were closing their borders and initiating lockdowns. In June of that year, when the number of COVID-19 cases in the United States topped two million, the federal government announced that vaccines would eventually be provided to everyone. The National Institutes of Health estimated that roughly 85 percent of Americans would need to get an injection for the nation to achieve herd immunity.

Rosenbloom's first thought? *That's ludicrous. There's no chance that many people will agree to get a shot.*

"But I knew we had to try," he told me. "If we couldn't figure out how to connect with anti-vaxxers, millions of people were going to die." That's when he started wondering about a potential way forward: "What if we got everyone to start reimagining these conversations? What if we got them to start reimagining themselves?"

QUIETING THE PREJUDICES INSIDE OUR HEADS

The women entering the laboratory for the experiment all had at least one thing in common: They were exceptionally good at math.

They were mostly freshmen and sophomores at the University of Michigan, had all scored in the top 15 percent on the math portion of the SATs, had earned high grades in at least two college-level calculus classes, and had told the researchers that "math was important to their personal and professional goals." There were men mixed into the crowd, as well, but the researchers were focused on the women because, the researchers suspected, these women were at a disadvantage that almost no one, including the students themselves, completely understood.

The seeds of the experiment had been planted a few years earlier when a psychology professor at the University of Washington named Claude Steele had started looking at patterns in the grades of college students. In general, what he saw matched his expectations: Students who did well in high school were more likely to do well in college. Students who scored high on the SAT, which is designed to predict college performance, tended to get slightly better grades than students who scored poorly.

But there was one pattern that didn't make sense: If Steele took a group of Black and white students who had scored similarly on the SAT—who, according to that standardized test, at least, were equally prepared for college—and then compared their university transcripts, the Black students consistently got lower grades. "I couldn't figure out why it was happening," Steele told me. As he later described in his book, *Whistling Vivaldi,* "at every level of entering SATs, even the highest level, Black students got lower grades than other students. . . . It was everywhere, from English to math to psychology." What's more, he wrote, "it happens to more groups than just Blacks. It happens to Latinos, Native Americans, and to women in advanced college math classes, law schools, medical schools, and business schools."

At first, Steele wondered if it might be the instructors' fault. Perhaps professors were racist or sexist? Or unconsciously influenced by stereotypes?

But as Steele looked deeper, he began to wonder if something else was going on. The data indicated that Black students and women in advanced math classes were getting lower grades due to one primary factor: Because they were doing worse on timed assignments. They seemed to know just as much as their fellow students, they worked just as hard, but when it came to exams with a time limit—an hour-long test, say—they seemed to second-guess their answers at the cost of precious minutes.

So, rather than focus on the teachers, Steele looked at the students themselves. Did they suffer from low self-esteem? They didn't seem to. Had they assumed, at the outset of the exam, that they wouldn't do well, and so their poor performances were self-fulfilling? There was no evidence of that. In fact, just the opposite: These students knew that they were ready for these exams and eager to prove themselves. Something else was happening, and Steele suspected he knew what it was. These students were being hobbled by social identities: The groups—women, Black students—they belonged to, and the prejudices they knew existed about those groups.

Steele understood, from personal experience, how much social identities can impact people's lives. He had been born to a Black father and a white mother in Chicago during a time when interracial marriage was illegal in many states, and he had experienced racism firsthand. His parents were involved in the civil rights movement, fighting against school and housing segregation and voting discrimination. Steele's activism, as he grew up, took a different form: He left Chicago to earn a PhD in psychology from Ohio State and began focusing on the psychology of prejudice. He ascended through the nation's most prestigious universities with unusual swiftness, with stints at the University of Utah, the University of Washington, Stanford, and Columbia. When he arrived, mid-career, at the University of Michigan, he began designing experiments to examine the confusing patterns he had found in students' grades.

The first study, conducted with a colleague named Steven Spencer and published in 1999, involved those women who were good at math. Steele knew, from surveys, that female math majors felt "that they have to prove themselves constantly, that their career commitment is questioned." Women were acutely aware of the stereotyped view that they were naturally less skilled at math than men—it was something, as Steele put it, "they knew they had to deal with." The fact that it had no basis in reality didn't make the stereotype any less pervasive.

For his experiment, Steele gave half the participants a challenging math exam, and the other half a difficult English test—English being a subject where, in general, women's aptitudes were not disparaged by stereotypes. The tests were relatively short—thirty minutes—and difficult, based on the GRE, the graduate school entrance exam.

On the English tests, the men and women, on average, scored equally. On the math exams, however, men outscored women by an average of twenty points. During the English tests, both women and men budgeted their time wisely. On the math exam women seemed to work less efficiently. "They would double-check their answers more often and re-do calculations," Steele said. They ran out of time "because they were multitasking, with part of their brains trying to answer the questions, and part thinking, *I need to double-check, I need to be careful, because I know there's this stereotype.*"

To Steele, it seemed as if female test takers had been undermined simply by the knowledge that a damaging prejudice existed, even if they also knew it wasn't true. As he later wrote, "on the basis of negative stereotypes of women's math ability, simply taking a difficult math test puts a woman at risk of stigmatization, of being seen as limited at math *because she is a woman.*" The existence of this stereotype generated just enough anxiety and distraction to slow them down, which translated into lower scores.

Next, Steele recruited Black and white students who were equally well prepared and asked them to complete the verbal reasoning section of the GRE. On this kind of test, Steele wrote, there was, for Black students, an ugly "stereotype of their group's lesser intellectual ability." When the results came back, "white students did a lot better on this difficult test than Black students" with "a large difference that, if sustained over the whole GRE exam, would be very substantial." Steele concluded this disparity was because Black students were aware of the stereotype suggesting they couldn't do well on the exam, which had generated just enough stress and demanded just enough mental energy to undermine their scores. (In contrast, when Black students were told that the test *didn't* evaluate intellectual ability, reducing the salience of the stereotype, they scored similarly to white students.)

Steele and his colleagues called this undermining effect *stereotype threat,* and since those first experiments in the late 1990s, hundreds of other studies have both confirmed its existence and examined its pernicious effect. Simply knowing that a stereotype exists can influence how we behave. For Black students, or women in advanced math courses, or many others, "it is the mere existence of the stereotype about their identity's abilities in society that threatens them, not necessarily the racism of the people around them," Steele said. Even if no one in the student's orbit is prejudiced, the student can still be undermined by the knowledge that a stereotype exists, and that their performance "could be taken, because of the stereotype and its effect on people's thinking, as confirmation of the stereotype."

Stereotypes, of course, surround all of us. In fact, it was stereotypes—of a very different sort—that influenced Jay Rosenbloom and so many other doctors to think poorly of patients who refused their advice. There was a social stereotype—doctors are experts—that pushed physicians to think of themselves as enlightened. Another stereotype—doctors are know-it-alls beholden to corrupt government recommendations—pushed patients to view their physicians with suspicion. Social identities can change how we act, even if we don't intend them to, even if we wish they didn't. These identities can push us to double-check our answers or arrogantly tell a patient "I know better than you."

Steele and other researchers have found some methods for counteracting stereotype threats. When, in one experiment, they told female participants that a test had been specially designed to sidestep perceived gender differences, and, in another, told Black students that a test "did not measure a person's intellectual ability" but rather "problem solving in general," it lessened the impact of stereotype threat. "With this instruction we freed these Black participants of the stigma threat they might otherwise have experienced," Steele wrote in his book.

Put differently, when researchers changed the environment, it made stereotypes less salient and therefore less threatening. "You can do that in a classroom, which is good," Steele told me. "But it's hard to do that in society, where everyone knows these stereotypes exist."

• • •

In 2005, another group of female and male math students were invited to participate in another experiment. This time, however, the study was occurring on the campus of Texas Christian University, under a different group of researchers who had changed the protocol slightly. To make sure a threatening stereotype was at the forefront of everyone's minds, the lead researcher, Dana Gresky, told the participants at the start of the experiment, "I'm studying the GRE because of the well-known stereotype that men usually outperform women on math tests." This kind of overt manipulation, previous studies had shown, would ensure that a number of women would be thinking of this stereotype, and would score worse on the exam as a result.

Then the participants were divided into three groups and taken to separate rooms.

One group started on the math portion of the GRE right away with no preamble or further instructions.

Members of the second group, before starting the test, were asked to briefly describe how they saw themselves. An easy way to do this, Gresky told them, was to sketch out a chart describing a few of their identities and roles. But time was short, she warned, so they should include only the most basic information. She showed them an example she had sketched:

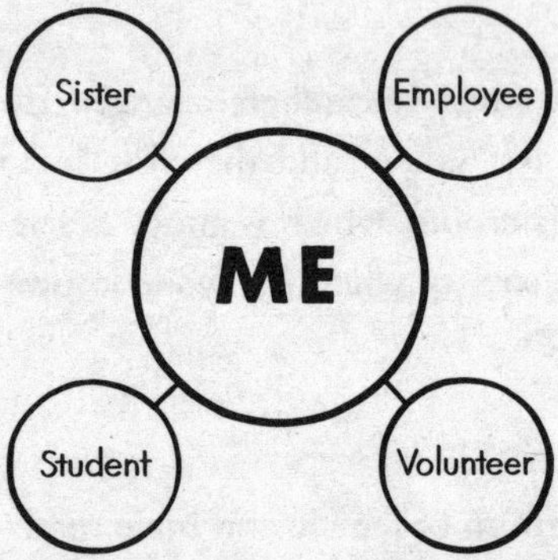

The third group was also told to describe how they saw themselves before starting the exam. This time, however, they were instructed to "write as much as you can" and make detailed sketches that provided plenty of information about the various clubs they belonged to, their hobbies, and the numerous identities and roles they occupied in different parts of their lives. They were also given an example.

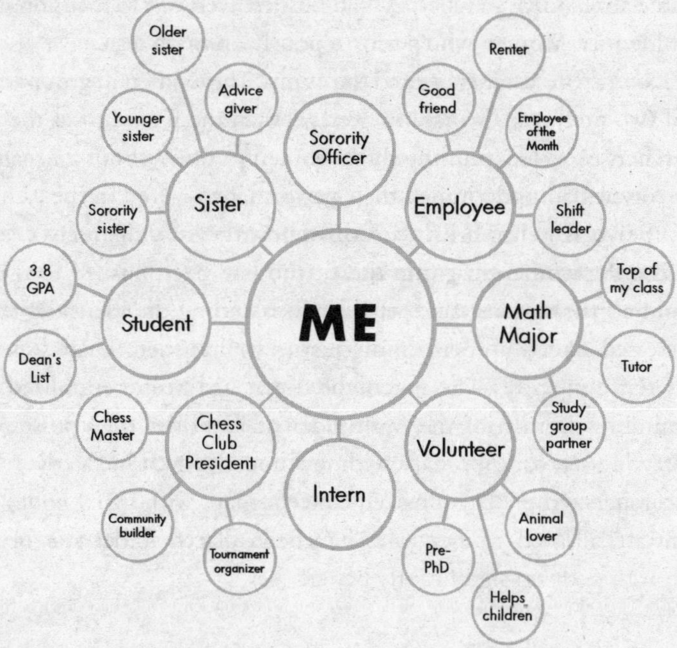

After making their sketches, participants in groups two and three started the math test.

The researchers wanted to see if "stereotype threat might be alleviated by reminding individual women of their multiple roles and identities," they later wrote. "A typical college woman might identify herself by her sex, race, ethnicity, social class, religion, sorority, class in school, job, athletic team, club membership, family. . . . Would it help the average woman's math performance to think about social identities other than being a woman, even if those other identities suggested no extraordinary math talent?" The researchers' hypothesis was that by prompting a test taker to remember all her complex identities, they could change the environment, just enough, to diminish the anxiety that had been triggered when Gresky, in her preamble about GRE stereotypes, had pushed everyone to focus on just *one* identity: Women who perform poorly on math tests.

Later, the researchers scored the exams. The women in groups one and two performed worse, on average, than the men. Just as the researchers expected, priming these women to think about a negative stereotype had undermined their performance—even in the case of group two, who had briefly described how they saw themselves.

But the women in group three, who had been pushed to think about all the various facets of their lives and all the identities they possessed, ended up performing just as well as men. There was no difference in scores. The stereotype threat had been neutralized by reminding women of the multitudes of identities they possessed. "Drawing self-concept maps with few nodes proved ineffective," the researchers wrote. "Drawing self-concept maps with many nodes, in contrast, allowed women who had been placed under stereotype threat to perform significantly better."

• • •

As Dr. Rosenbloom learned about these kinds of studies, they seemed to suggest a solution to one of his problems: How to counteract the "physician knows best" stereotypes inside so many doctors' heads. Rosenbloom knew how easy it was, once he put on the white coat, to start feeling one-dimensional, to become "The Doctor." "But if you can remember that you're a parent, then you know how scary it is to make health choices for your kids, and that sparks a little bit of sympathy," he told me. "If you can remember that you're a neighbor, then you know neighbors don't say things like *I know better than you.*"

In a *Who Are We?* conversation, we sometimes latch on to a single identity: *I am your parent* or *I am the teacher* or *I am the boss.* In doing so, though, we hobble ourselves, because we start to see the world solely through that one lens. We forget that we are all complex and that, if we were thinking like parents instead of doctors, we might also ask skeptical questions about the drugs a stranger wants to inject into our kids. We might remember that asking questions is what good parents are *supposed* to do.

With this lesson in mind, Rosenbloom began a new routine: Whenever he met the parents of a patient, he spent a few minutes finding an identity they had in common. "If they talked about other family members, then I would mention my own family, or if they said they lived nearby, then I would say where I lived," he told me. "Doctors aren't supposed to discuss their personal lives, but I thought it was important to prove that we had a link."

It might have seemed, to the patients, like he was trying to put them at ease. But he was also doing it for himself. "It reminded me I was more than a doctor," he said. "Then, when someone would say something irrational—like vaccines are a big plot—instead of getting annoyed, I felt some connection, because I know what it feels like to get pushed around by experts. I've experienced that."

It's crucial, in a *Who Are We?* conversation, to remind ourselves that we all possess multiple identities: We are parents but also siblings; experts in some topics and novices in others; friends and coworkers and people who love dogs but hate to jog. We are all of these simultaneously, so no one stereotype describes us fully. We all contain multitudes that are just waiting to be expressed.

This means that a *Who Are We?* discussion might need to be more meandering and exploratory. Or it might need to go deep and invite others to talk about where they come from, how they see themselves, how the prejudices they confront—racism, sexism, the expectations of parents and communities—have impacted their lives. "When my son goes to school, I tell him, remember, that test may be hard today, but think about who else you are," said Gresky, the researcher at Texas Christian University. "We can make the bad voices in our head less powerful by remembering all the other voices in there, too."

The process for drawing out those voices is relatively straightforward: In a *Who Are We?* conversation, invite people to talk about their backgrounds, allegiances, how their communities have shaped them. ("Where are you from? Oh, really? What was it like growing up there?") Then, reciprocate by describing how you see yourself. ("You know, as a southerner, I think that . . .") Finally, avoid the trap of one-dimensionality by evoking all the many identities we all possess as a conversation unfolds: "I hear you saying that, as a lawyer, you support the police, but as a parent, do you worry about cops pulling over your kid?"

This, of course, is only one part of a *Who Are We?* conversation. Remembering that we all contain multitudes can help us see each other more clearly—but it won't necessarily convince, say, a vaccine-resistant parent to trust a doctor.

To do that, we need to find an identity we can share.

ENEMIES PLAYING SOCCER

In the spring of 2018, flyers began appearing in Qaraqosh, Iraq, announcing the formation of a new soccer league. This was a bit surprising because Qaraqosh was, at that moment, only just recovering from a brutal war. Over the previous few years, the city's Christian population had been relentlessly attacked by the Islamic State of Iraq and Syria, or ISIS. Hundreds of Christians had been killed and some fifty thousand forced to flee their homes. ISIS combatants had ransacked churches, torched Christian-owned businesses and assaulted Christian women. When ISIS finally withdrew from Qaraqosh in 2016 and Christian refugees began returning, many felt betrayed by their Muslim neighbors. "When I bump into them now, they turn their faces and walk away," a sixty-year-old Christian man told a reporter in 2017. "They know what they did. They know they're guilty."

Before the ISIS invasion, there had been a number of amateur soccer teams for adults in Qaraqosh, but most of them were only for

Christian players. Christians and Muslims almost never played together. In fact, Christians and Muslims hardly ever intermingled, even off the field: There had always been Christian restaurants and Muslim restaurants, Christian grocery stores and Muslim grocery stores, each with bouncers checking IDs that listed people's religion.

When Qaraqosh's Christian refugees started coming home, their soccer teams gradually began playing again. Then came the day when the flyers appeared in Christian neighborhoods announcing a new league and inviting players to an informational meeting. Inside a church half-destroyed by fire, the league's organizers explained that they were sponsoring a tournament. It would be free of charge, open to any existing team, and everyone who participated would get a jersey with their name emblazoned on the back. There would be professional referees at each game, fresh nets and balls, and trophies for the winners. There was a catch, however: Only teams that already existed could participate, and though it was customary, in Qaraqosh, for teams to have nine players, each team in the league would need twelve players. What's more, while half the teams would be permitted to add any players they wanted—and they would, presumably, all be Christian—on the other half of teams, the three additional players would be Muslims selected by league officials.

The league had been dreamed up by Salma Mousa, a PhD candidate at Stanford who was interested in testing what's known as the *contact hypothesis*—the theory that, if you bring people with clashing social identities together under specific conditions, you can overcome old hatreds. The idea that a soccer league might overcome deep enmities in Qaraqosh, where a vast majority of Christian residents, when polled, said their Muslim neighbors had betrayed them, seemed preposterous. And, in fact, at the informational meeting, when coaches and players learned that half the teams would need to accept Muslim players, many walked out. "They told us this would ruin the teams," Mousa told me. "They said we were going to cause another war."

However, the lure of professional referees and large trophies convinced a few teams to sign up. Then the new jerseys arrived, and soon everyone wanted in. Eventually, forty-two teams joined the league. Mousa and her assistants assigned Muslim players to half of them, handed out schedules, and sat back to watch.

Practices, at first, were tense. Some Christian players refused to introduce themselves to their Muslim teammates, and they sat as far from each other as possible on the sidelines. "The Muslim players tried to fit in," Mousa said, but the Christians were openly hostile. However, Mousa had instituted a rule that every teammate needed equal playing time, so although the Christians and Muslims didn't mingle on the benches, they were forced to cooperate during practices and games.

That alone was sufficient to cause a shift. Some teams had initially insisted on speaking Syriac—the language spoken by Christians in the Middle East, but essentially no one else, including most Muslims—and, not surprisingly, it had caused on-field communication problems. So coaches on two teams instituted a new rule for their players: Everyone must speak Arabic, which both Muslims and Christians understood. When those teams began winning, other coaches started copying the rule.

About a week later, a group of Christian players complained that their Muslim teammates were habitually late, costing them precious practice time. The Muslim players explained they were coming from across town and had to pass through multiple checkpoints on slow-moving buses. So the Christian players pooled donations to pay for taxis to speed the Muslims across the city.

Eventually, Mousa had trouble telling the Christian and Muslim players apart. They sat together on benches. They celebrated together after goals. One team chose a Muslim as their captain. Some all-Christian teams began complaining they were at an unfair disadvantage because they didn't have any Muslims. When Mousa surveyed the players, she found those on mixed teams "were 13 percentage points more likely to report that they would not mind being assigned to a mixed team next season, 26 percentage points more likely to vote for a Muslim player (not on their team) to receive a sportsmanship prize, and 49 percentage points more likely to train with Muslims six months after the intervention ended." Prejudices didn't disappear, of course. Christian players admitted they still felt uncertain about *other* Muslims, those who weren't their teammates. But the shift was striking: One day, as Mousa and her colleagues walked through Qaraqosh, they saw a few Christian players inside a bar watching Barcelona play Real Madrid. Next to them were their Muslim teammates, who the Christians had somehow gotten in.

Before the Qaraqosh tournament's championship game, featuring the Qaramlesh Youth versus the Guards of the Nineveh Plains, the players posed for a group photo. Both teams were a mix of Muslims and Christians, and some players carried portraits of family members who had been killed, "these huge photos of uncles and cousins who had died," said Mousa. "And right next to them is a Muslim, and their arms are around each other." After the Guards of the Nineveh Plains won, all the teams voted on player of the year. A Muslim was chosen. Polls conducted five months later showed that the Christians continued playing with Muslims, and that, as one player put it, "when the game is over, we hug, kiss, congratulate each other even when we lose. . . . We see each other in the neighborhood, call each other, invite each other for a glass of tea or coffee at home." Muslim players told pollsters "there isn't this idea of which community you're from" and they "proposed to league staff that they invite all-Muslim teams from the area to participate in the future."

The results exceeded even Mousa's expectations. "Maybe some people will say, well, that's because sports breaks down barriers," Mousa told me. "But it's not just that. It's how we structured everything that made the difference."

In fact, there were three decisions in designing the league that changed the environment so that players could bond. These are the same choices at the core of any successful *Who Are We?* conversation.

The first decision drew on the same psychology that helped boost the scores of female math students by reminding them of their non-mathematical identities: The soccer teams were deliberately structured to give players roles that nudged them to think about identities beyond religion. One player might be Muslim, but he was also the goalkeeper, and he led stretches during halftime. Another player was Christian, but was also in charge of bringing sports drinks, was the team captain, and always gave an inspiring speech before games. "There was an effort, by the teams themselves, to give everyone different identities," said Mousa. "And those identities became more important than religion because they were related to winning."

The second crucial decision was to make sure that, on the field, all the players were equal. Within Qaraqosh, there were hierarchies: Christians, historically, had been wealthier than Muslims and better educated. The invasion had temporarily upended things by expelling much of the town's upper class, but as Christians returned, the old social order reasserted itself. "But on the field, because everyone had to play the same amount, all the players were the same," said Mousa. "There weren't power differentials." That meant that old rivalries and grudges—social identities that put one group above another—were put aside, at least for the duration of a game.

The final reason this experiment worked is the same reason a *Who Are We?* conversation, if it goes well, succeeds: It allowed the players to form new in-groups, to establish social identities they had in common. And those in-groups were powerful because they built on identities that players already possessed. It might seem surprising, to an outsider, that Muslim and Christian players would bond so quickly. But it didn't wholly shock Mousa because she wasn't asking them to redefine themselves. She was simply making an identity they already carried—soccer teammates—more salient, and as a result their religious identities were a little less loud.

These kinds of environmental shifts point to what is needed for a successful *Who Are We?* conversation:

First, try to draw out your conversational partners' multiple identities. It's important to remind everyone that we all contain multitudes; none of us is one-dimensional. Acknowledging those complexities during a conversation helps disrupt the stereotypes within our heads.

Second, try to ensure everyone is on equal footing. Don't offer unsolicited advice or trumpet your wealth or connections. Seek out topics where everyone has some experience and knowledge, or everyone is a novice. Encourage the quiet to speak and the talkative to listen, so everyone is participating.

Finally, look for social similarities that already exist. We do this naturally when we meet someone new and start searching for people we know in common. But it is important to take those connections a step further and make our commonalities more salient. Our similarities become powerful when they are rooted in something meaningful: We may both be friends with Jim, but that's not much of a connection—until we start talking about what his friendship means to us, how Jim is an important part of both our lives. We may all be Lakers fans, but that only becomes powerful when we share what it felt like, for each of us, to go to games with our parents and watch Magic score, how we share the memory of that thrill.

How to Talk About Who We Are

1. Draw out multiple identities.
2. Put everyone on equal footing.
3. Create new groups by building on existing identities.

Social dialogues—*Who Are We?* conversations—are gateways to deeper understanding and more meaningful connections. But we need to allow these discussions to become deep, to evoke our many identities and express our shared experiences and beliefs. The *Who Are We?* conversation is powerful not only because we bond over what we have in common, but because it lets us share who we really are.

ADDRESSING THE COVID CONUNDRUM

By the spring of 2021, Jay Rosenbloom was frantic. COVID had already killed more than two million people globally, and had pushed billions more into lockdowns. Inoculation campaigns had begun, but Rosenbloom was convinced they would fall short of their goals. "Lots of experts were saying, well, if we just educate people that the vaccines are safe, if we give them the data, they'll come around," he told me. "But anyone who's worked with these patients knows that won't work. They already have lots of data! They've spent hours doing online research! You're not going to convince them they're wrong."

Rosenbloom had started volunteering with a group named Boost Oregon to search for new approaches. Hundreds of similar groups had sprung up around the planet, a loose network of physicians and social scientists focused on persuading people to get the shot. Many of these groups had already spent years studying vaccine hesitancy and had concluded that the most effective approach was something known as *motivational interviewing,* a method originally developed in the 1980s to help problem drinkers. In motivational interviewing, a 2012 paper explains, "counselors rarely attempt to convince or persuade. Instead, the counselor subtly guides the client to think about and verbally express their own reasons for and against change." Motivational interviewing seeks to draw out a person's beliefs, values, and social identities, in the hopes that, once all these complexities and complicated beliefs are on the table, unexpected opportunities for change might appear.

For more than a decade, the Centers for Disease Control and Prevention had been urging physicians to use motivational interviewing techniques with patients who resist vaccines. For Rosenbloom and his colleagues, that meant speaking with people who were skeptical about COVID vaccines in very specific ways. When an elderly patient came into the clinic of Dr. Rima Chamie in Portland, for instance, and the patient said he didn't want a COVID vaccine because he'd heard rumors the science was untested, the physician didn't argue with him. Instead, she began asking open-ended questions about how he saw himself. He said he had three grandchildren and was a retired police officer. He was also deeply religious. His church was the most important place in his life. "That's why I don't need the shot," he told her. "God will take care of me. I wash my hands, I wear the mask. God will provide. He knows my path."

Chamie is the kind of doctor everyone hopes for: Confident and warm, someone who can quiet a wailing infant with a caress or their overwrought parents with a sympathetic laugh. She's a mom herself, and her children know they ignore her advice at their peril. She's spent her career serving migrants and kids, the poor and the homeless. She knows what her membership in the tribe of medical experts means. "The white coat, it's got some power," she told me.

But, with this particular patient, she also knew that no amount of data showing that the COVID vaccine was safe, no amount of mentioning that the pope had said people should get vaccinated, was going to change his mind. "All it would have done is make him stop listening," she said. So Chamie took a different approach. She didn't mention COVID again. "It's wonderful your faith gives you so much strength," she told him. "You clearly have a really close relationship with God."

Then, almost as an aside, Chamie brought up another identity. "I imagine your grandchildren's health is probably very important to you," she said. Yes, he agreed, he loved being a grandfather.

"Then we went on to other topics," Chamie said. "But towards the end of the appointment, as a way to wrap things up, I said, 'You know, I don't usually talk about religion with patients, but I'm so thankful that God gave us these brains, and these laboratories, and the ability to make vaccines. Maybe He gave us vaccines to keep us safe?'" Then she left the room.

She didn't do anything except acknowledge that they both contained numerous identities, and that some of them—religious devotion, caring about children—overlapped and offered different perspectives on what constitutes "safety." With that, the appointment was over.

Thirty minutes later, the man was still in the exam room. Chamie pulled a nurse aside. "Why's he still here?" she asked.

"He wanted the vaccine," the nurse said.

Chamie and Rosenbloom have used motivational interviewing with hundreds of patients. "It's different every time, of course," Chamie said. "Sometimes we talk about religion, sometimes our kids. Sometimes I just ask: On a scale of one to ten, how do you feel about this vaccine? And when they say 'three,' I ask: Why not two? Why not four? Like, I'm genuinely curious why you're a three, what that says about you."

In the same manner as Salma Mousa's soccer league, Chamie's conversations put everyone on equal footing—no one is an expert on parenting or God's will. And they build on existing social identities to construct a new in-group: We are all people who want to do the right thing for our families. Regardless of other differences, we have that in common.

"I had a family that came to my practice with two kids," Rosenbloom told me. "They had just moved to town and were upper-middle-class, well educated, but both children were completely unvaccinated. The parents told me they'd heard some scary information about vaccines, but when they brought up questions with their previous doctor, he'd kind of dismissed them."

So Rosenbloom spoke to the couple for a while. He asked where they lived, where they planned to send their kids to school, what they enjoyed doing on weekends. He told them about himself, and they discovered a few restaurants and parks they both liked. He asked them to describe their concerns about vaccines, but also inquired about other worries: Were they anxious about their kids starting school? How did they feel about things like sugar and soda pop? He never pushed the vaccines. Instead, he just asked questions, and after they answered, he shared his own thoughts. At the end of the conversation, the parents said they wanted to start a vaccination schedule for their kids that day. "It worked because they felt listened to," Rosenbloom told me. "You have to find some way to connect if you want people to hear what you're saying."

The *Who Are We?* conversation is crucial because our social identities exert such a powerful influence on what we say, how we hear, and what we think, even when we don't want them to. Our identities can help us find values we share or can push us into stereotypes. Sometimes, simply reminding ourselves that we all contain multitudes can shift how we speak and listen. The *Who Are We?* conversation can help us understand how the identities we choose, and the identities imposed on us by society, make us who we are.*

But what happens when simply talking about our identities feels threatening? How, at moments like that, do we learn to speak and hear?

* It is tempting to suggest that simply finding commonalities is sufficient in helping us communicate. But, as the next chapter explores, connection also often comes from understanding how differences shape us.

7

HOW DO WE MAKE THE HARDEST CONVERSATIONS SAFER?

The Problem Netflix Lives With

If you were to ask Netflix employees when things started going wrong inside the company, many would point to an afternoon in February 2018. Netflix's publicity department—about thirty people—were gathered in a conference room inside the firm's Los Angeles headquarters. At that moment, the company was on track for its most successful year ever, with more than $15 billion in revenue and 124 million subscribers. Everyone was there for a weekly staff meeting, and people chatted and caught up with one another as their boss, communications chief officer Jonathan Friedland, stood to speak.

Friedland began by telling the group that Netflix had recently released a comedy special titled *Tom Segura: Disgraceful.* Most of the people in the room had never heard of the program—nor, for that matter, had many viewers. At any given moment, Netflix hosts tens of thousands of shows; subscribers spend an estimated 70 billion hours per year on the platform. This one comedy special, like so many others, would likely come and go. But Friedland was mentioning the program, he explained, because it featured a comedian being unusually offensive: Waxing nostalgic for a time when people could use terms such as *retarded,* making fun of people with Down syndrome, complaining because he can't say *midget* anymore.

A few disability advocacy groups had already raised objections, and the company needed to be prepared for more criticisms. It was important, Friedland stressed, that they treat these complaints seriously. Everyone needed to appreciate how hurtful the word *retarded* could be. Hearing it was a "gut-punch" to any parent whose child is cognitively different, Friedland said. Then, to drive his point home, he offered an analogy: It would be "as if an African-American person had heard" and here he said the n-word.

Everyone in the room went silent. The mood changed instantly. *Did he really just say that?*

Friedland did not seem to notice the shift. He moved on to other topics. When the meeting ended, employees returned to their desks. Some seemed not to give the incident another thought. Others mentioned to colleagues what had occurred, and they, in turn, told other people, who told others. Two employees approached Friedland to complain about his language and said that using that word, in any setting, was unacceptable. It was particularly offensive coming from one of the company's highest-ranking executives. Friedland agreed with them, apologized, and notified human resources of what had occurred.

"And that," one employee told me, "is when the civil war began."

• • •

Netflix had been founded in 1997 by Reed Hastings, an entrepreneur with an unusual business philosophy: The fewer rules, the better. Hastings believed companies were hobbled by meddlesome managers; bureaucracy was the road to ruin. He eventually memorialized his beliefs in a 125-page PowerPoint that was shared with every employee and became required reading for new hires. When it was posted on the internet, the "Netflix Culture Deck" was downloaded millions of times.

At Netflix, the culture deck explained, "we seek excellence," and in return, employees were granted unusual freedoms. Workers could take as much vacation as they wanted, work whichever days or hours they desired, authorize almost any kind of purchase—a first-class plane ticket, a new computer, millions of dollars to acquire a film—without prior permission, as long as they could justify their choice.

Whereas it was treasonous at most firms to apply for jobs with competitors, at Netflix employees were encouraged to submit applications to other companies—and if they were offered a higher salary, Netflix would either match it or encourage them to leave. The company expected "amazing amounts of important work," the culture deck decreed, and to achieve that, employees had permission to try nearly anything, as long as it delivered higher profits or revealed new insights.

Employees who couldn't consistently deliver top-tier excellence were warned that a merely "adequate performance gets a generous severance package." And whenever someone was dismissed—which happened frequently—another Netflix ritual kicked in: A note was sent to that person's team, or department, or sometimes the entire company, explaining why the person had been let go. The departing employee's disappointing work habits, their questionable decisions and mistakes—all of it was spelled out in detail for everyone who remained. One current Netflix worker told me, "When I got to Netflix, I got a 'why Jim was fired' email on my second day, and I freaked out. It was *very* candid." He wondered, *Did I make a mistake coming here? Is this place a snake pit?* "But eventually I realized, it's actually helpful to get emails like that because, if you've read a few of them, you know what the company expects. It takes the mystery out of everything."

As the company expanded, there were growing pains. In 2011, Hastings, without much internal debate, announced that he intended to split the firm in two: One company would handle DVDs by mail, and the other would provide online streaming services. The announcement was not well received. The stock plunged by 77 percent, forcing Hastings to backtrack almost immediately.

Top executives later blamed this misstep, and the resulting crisis, on an insufficient amount of internal skepticism. Executives should have told Hastings they disagreed with him, should have pushed back more forcefully. In fact, as a rule, all employees needed to challenge one another's decision making more aggressively. The culture deck was amended to note that "silent disagreement is unacceptable." Hastings went so far as to tell workers that "it is disloyal to Netflix when you disagree with an idea and do *not* express that disagreement" and that they ought to "farm for dissent" among their peers. Before long, meetings were filled with people tearing apart one another's proposals. Teams would schedule "feedback dinners" where everyone would go around the table offering something they appreciated—and the five or six things they did *not* appreciate about each of their coworkers.

For some, this atmosphere was exhilarating. "All that anxiety you normally feel trying to figure out what your manager thinks, and what their manager thinks, and wondering what's actually going on, that's all gone," one employee told me. For others, the radical candor could feel cruel. "It gave people permission to be savage," another employee, Parker Sanchez, said. "Some days I'd cry for an hour."

One advantage of this culture, though, was that it made it easy to discuss nearly anything. "Nothing is off the table," a high-ranking executive told me. "You think your boss is making a mistake? Tell them. You don't like how someone runs meetings? Say it. You're more likely to get promoted than punished." Employees would regularly send Hastings emails critiquing his strategies or what he had said during meetings, or they would openly criticize him on internal message boards, "and Reed would publicly thank them," said the executive. "I've never worked in a culture like this before. It's amazing."

It was also effective. Netflix's stock recovered, and the company got larger every year. Its unusual culture enabled it to hire some of the best software engineers, television producers, tech executives, and filmmakers in the world. It quickly became one of the most admired and successful firms in both Silicon Valley and Hollywood. *Fortune* magazine named Hastings Businessperson of the Year.

Then came the meeting where Jonathan Friedland uttered the n-word.

WHY CONVERSATIONS ABOUT IDENTITY MATTER

Over the past half decade—in the wake of reports of racism and sexism within numerous companies, evidence of ignored sexual assaults inside organizations, and the growth of social movements devoted to equality and inclusion—there has been a renewed focus on making workplaces fairer and more just. Thousands of firms have hired "inclusion coaches," or have purchased diversity, equity, and inclusion curriculums, in the hopes of fostering meaningful, long-overdue conversations about how to combat racism, sexism, and other prejudices. Today, nearly every *Fortune* 1000 company has at least one high-ranking executive focused on undoing the biases and structural inequities that unfairly disadvantage some employees and customers.

These programs are necessary correctives for real problems, reminders that there are injustices that make it hard for some people to get the jobs they want, the salaries they deserve, or the respect they merit simply because of the color of their skin, their country of origin, or some other aspect of their identity that shouldn't have any impact on their careers.

However, many of these well-intentioned programs don't seem

particularly effective. When a team of researchers from Princeton, Columbia, and Hebrew University examined more than four hundred studies of attempts to reduce prejudice, they found that in 76 percent of cases, the best that could be said was that the long-term impact "remains unclear." A 2021 *Harvard Business Review* article regarding eighty thousand people who had undergone unconscious bias training found that such "training did not change biased behavior." Another examination of three decades of data concluded that "the positive effects of diversity training rarely last beyond a day or two, and . . . can activate bias or spark a backlash." A fourth study found that after unconscious bias training, "the likelihood that Black men and women would advance in organizations often *decreased*," because the trainings made race and gender stereotypes more salient. A summary in the 2021 *Annual Review of Psychology* found that while, "by many metrics, the study of interventions designed to reduce prejudice is thriving," the authors "conclude that much research effort is theoretically and empirically misguided if the aim is to provide actionable, robust, evidence-based recommendations for reducing prejudice in the world."

This does not, by any means, suggest that efforts at addressing inequity or rooting out prejudice should be abandoned. It does not mean that reducing bias and structural injustice is impossible. There are real insights—as we saw with *stereotype threat*—that can help historically marginalized people succeed. There are interventions—such as those that took place on the soccer fields in Qaraqosh, Iraq—that have bridged differences.

However, figuring out precisely *how* to confront inequality and prejudice is more complicated than hiring a diversity consultant or asking workers to attend an afternoon training session. And these complications are heightened by the fact that many people feel that discussing *Who Are We?* poses real risks. Though we all hopefully recognize that using a racial slur is unacceptable, when it comes to other kinds of dialogues, it can be hard to know what's out of bounds. How much can we ask a coworker about their background, their life beyond work, their beliefs, their identity, without running the risk of overstepping? How do we overcome the worry that saying the wrong thing, or asking a naïve question, might destroy friendships or careers?

Who Are We? conversations have a place beyond discussions of race, ethnicity, and gender, of course. Many of our toughest conversations are hard precisely because they touch on social identities that have nothing to do with our ancestry. When we critique an underperforming employee, criticize a spouse, or tell a boss they aren't giving us what we need, it can easily come off as a denunciation of who they are, a swipe at their abilities and judgments, or an attack on their sense of identity.

So how do we get better at talking about *Who Are We?* when we're discussing the most sensitive subjects? How do we nudge people to discuss differences in ways that bring us together rather than drive us apart? How do we have these vital conversations in settings, such as the workplace, where they can seem so perilous?

• • •

Within just a few days of Friedland's use of the n-word, it seemed as if every one of Netflix's 5,500 employees had heard about the incident—and most of them had strong opinions about what ought to happen next.

Human resources opened an investigation. Friedland apologized to the meeting's participants, his entire team, and then the company's other divisions. He attended an off-site with senior staff to explain what had occurred and what he had learned from it. He met with human resources to express his contrition—but, during that meeting, while recounting the incident, he said the n-word again. Soon everyone knew about that as well.

Within the wider Netflix community, some employees began posting angry missives on internal message boards arguing that the company had been ignoring racial tensions for years. Critics of those posts responded by saying that the issue wasn't racism, but rather oversensitivity by some people who were not cut out for Netflix's hard-charging culture. There were worker surveys showing that Netflix's employees of color felt excluded, marginalized, and disadvantaged when promotions were handed out. Others, abiding by the maxim that "silent disagreement is unacceptable," argued that these people had missed out on advancements not because of prejudice, but because they hadn't worked hard enough.

In between these extremes were many employees who acknowledged that Friedland had done something offensive and inappropriate but felt he should be forgiven. "Yes, Jonathan made a mistake, but he admitted the mistake, apologized, and tried to make amends," a high-ranking executive told me. "That's what we're supposed to do. We're supposed to screw up, give and accept feedback, learn from it, and move on. But some people wouldn't let it go."

Complicating matters further was the fact that all of Netflix's top executives were white, and nearly all were male. "There was this feeling, like, if the head of communications can use the n-word and there's no consequences, why shouldn't every Black employee feel like a second-class citizen?" one employee told me. "I think that was a watershed moment—oh wait, some people thought this was a perfect place, but, actually, there're some things that 'farming for dissent' can't fix."

The controversy seemed to get bigger each week. Finally, months after the initial incident, Hastings told Friedland he had to leave. He then sent a "why Jonathan was fired" email to the entire company explaining that Friedland's "use of the n-word on at least two occasions at work showed unacceptably low racial awareness and sensitivity. . . . There is not a way to neutralize the emotion and history behind the word in any context." Hastings said that he regretted not acting sooner.*

The move was cheered by some employees and resented by others. More than anything, though, it created confusion: Netflix prided itself on a culture where employees could say nearly anything to one another. Racial insults, clearly, were out of bounds. But what about if you're discussing a show that, itself, uses a racial slur? Is it okay to specify what a character says, if your goal is to figure out what's appropriate and what isn't? Netflix hosted a popular comedy special named *Private School Negro.* Was it okay to say the title in meetings? What was forbidden and what was allowed? "It was genuinely confusing," one executive told me. "And Reed's email didn't make things clearer, which is the whole point of sending emails like that."

The previous year, Netflix had added an "Inclusion" section to the culture deck, asking employees to be "curious about how our different backgrounds affect us at work, rather than pretending they don't," and to "recognize we all have biases, and work to grow past them." The company pushed employees to discuss biases and "intervene if someone else is being marginalized." One thing everyone could agree on was that, by these standards, the company wasn't doing great. So Netflix began hiring new executives, including a woman named Vernā Myers, to oversee a newly created division that was devoted to equity and diversity. The goal was to foster dialogues, confront biases, and make Netflix a shining example of inclusivity.

* Friedland, who had a long career before joining Netflix, in an interview with me expressed contrition: "I understand why I was fired," he told me. "Was I tone-deaf? Yeah. I didn't understand how that word would be heard, and I shouldn't have said it. But what's painful is that this is one small moment in a long career, and I'm not sure it's fair to judge anyone by one mistake."

But how do you discuss the most sensitive topics, the kinds of subjects where an ill-phrased question or an awkward comment might draw anger or hurt, in a culture where relentless debate and scathing disagreement are the norm?

WHY SOME CONVERSATIONS ARE SO HARD

In 2019, two researchers from Columbia and UC Berkeley asked more than 1,500 people to describe their toughest conversations from the previous week.

Their goal was to figure out the specifics of why some topics—such as race, gender, and ethnicity—can be so hard to discuss. To get a cross section of perspectives, they recruited people from all walks of life. Their ages ranged from eighteen to seventy-three; some were rich, others poor. The researchers had found them through online ads—and so, in some respects, the group represented the same kinds of diversity one might find inside a large company.

The researchers asked each participant a series of questions: *Have you been in a recent discussion where you felt like you didn't fit in? Have you been in a conversation where someone expressed prejudiced beliefs? Have you heard someone make jokes about "people like you," or pretend to talk like you, or assume you were friends with someone because you were the same ethnicity or gender?*

It quickly became clear from participants' answers that some of their recent conversations had been challenging because of the topics they had discussed—they had talked about subjects like politics or religion, where some degree of tension is normal. But many other discussions had started out relatively benign—about, say, sports or work or what's on television—until someone had said something that made someone else feel uncomfortable or upset.

It was these moments of discomfort the researchers wanted to explore. What exactly had been said, and how had someone said it, that caused another person to grow anxious or angry? What had prompted the listener to withdraw, to grow defensive, to want to fight back?

The researchers—Michael Slepian and Drew Jacoby-Senghor—found there were lots of things that might make a conversation go bad. Someone might say something offensive, or they might say something ignorant, or cruel. They might alienate their companions intentionally, or it might occur by accident. But there was one behavior, in particular, that consistently made people uncomfortable and upset: If a speaker said something that lumped a listener into a group against her or his will, the discussion would likely go south.

Sometimes speakers would assign listeners membership in a group they didn't like—"You're rich, so you know most rich people are snobs"—and the listener would be offended by the insinuation they were snobbish. Sometimes a speaker would deny someone membership in a group they esteemed—"You didn't go to law school, so you don't understand how the law actually works"—and the listener would be insulted by the accusation that they were uninformed.

Sometimes, when speakers made such comments, they were indirect: "You're one of the good Republicans, but most of them only care about themselves" or "You got into that college because you're smart, but some people like you get in because of affirmative action." Occasionally the person making the comment seemed to have no idea they were offending: "Since you don't have kids, you might not understand how a parent feels seeing a child treated that way." Regardless of the phrasing, the result was consistent: Anger and alienation, a conversation that fell apart.

These kinds of comments sparked irritation because the listeners had been assigned to a group (the wealthy snobs, the selfish Republicans, the undeserving college students) they didn't identify with. Or, they were denied membership in a group (people who understand how the law works, people who sympathize with children) where they felt they rightfully belonged. So the listener, offended, would become defensive as their sense of self—their identity—was attacked.

In psychology, this is known as *identity threat,* and it is deeply corrosive to communication. "When someone says you don't belong, or they put you in a group you don't appreciate, it can cause extreme psychological discomfort," Slepian told me. Studies have shown that when people confront identity threats, their blood pressure can rise, their bodies can become flooded with stress hormones, they begin looking for ways to escape or fight back.

Identity threats are one reason why conversations about *Who Are We?* can be so difficult. When some Netflix employees accused their coworkers of being "oversensitive" or "not Netflix material," it felt to the accused as if they were being forced into a group—*petulant complainers*—they abhorred, or were being excluded from a group—*those prepared to succeed at Netflix*—to which everyone wanted to belong. And when those who had been criticized responded by arguing that their critics' comments came from a place of privilege and were themselves evidence of racial insensitivity, it felt to the critics like they had been lumped in with racists and bigots, which made them defensive in response.

Identity threat isn't unique to the workplace, of course. It can occur anywhere: At a party, inside a bar, during a conversation with a stranger while waiting for the bus. Nor is it uncommon, as Slepian and Jacoby-Senghor found. Of the more than 1,500 participants who took part in their study, only 1 percent had *not* encountered a recent identity threat. "Participants on average had experienced 11.38 identity threats in the past week," they wrote in their 2021 paper in *Social Psychology and Personality Science.* "Across 40 percent of our observations, participants felt threatened on a single identity, and 60 percent represent perceiving a threat on multiple identities."

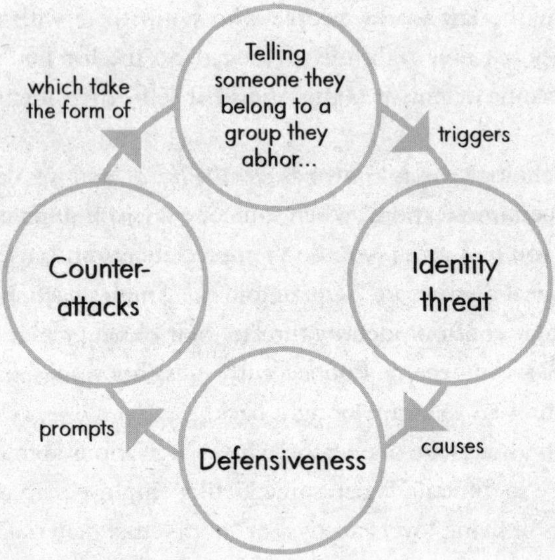

The study's participants reported experiencing identity threats due to where they lived, where they worked, who they were married to, who they were dating, where they had been born, how they spoke, how much money they earned, and dozens of other reasons. Being rich or white or straight—or socially advantaged in any other way—didn't protect them. And being poor or Black or part of another minoritized group meant they likely confronted identity threats as often as every day.

We've all felt the sting of identity threat at some point, or have said something we didn't intend as offensive but which came off as insensitive. The mere *possibility* of identity threat frequently stops people from talking about *Who Are We?* In a 2021 study, 70 percent of participants said they saw real risks to participating in a dialogue about race, even with friends. "Black friends worry their white friends will say something racist, maybe unintentionally, and it will damage the friendship," said Kiara Sanchez, the researcher who led that study.

"And white friends worry they'll say something prejudiced by accident. So there's a lot of anxiety on both sides."

But if we care about making the world more inclusive and fair, then talking about *Who Are We?* is crucial. "The problem of racism can be solved, in theory, with the right information, investment, strategy, and implementation," Harvard social psychologist Robert Livingston writes in his book *The Conversation.* "We have to start talking to one another—especially those outside our social circle. Nothing will improve until we begin to have honest and informed conversations about race and decide, as a community, to do something about it."

Conversations about who we are—and who we want to be—are essential if we hope society will change.

• • •

Conversations about race are some of the most difficult discussions, and so, for researchers, they have served as useful models for studying the dynamics that emerge during challenging dialogues. In 2020, for instance, in an attempt to figure out how to have more honest and open conversations about race and ethnicity, another group of scientists recruited more than a hundred pairs of close friends and brought them, face-to-face, to talk about their experiences with race and racism. The researchers' goal was to figure out if there is something that can be done *before* a discussion begins that makes it easier to talk about hard things.

Every pair of friends was similar in two ways: One person was Black and the other was white. And neither of them were informed, before the experiment, that they would be discussing race.

At the start of the experiment, some of the pairs were given generic instructions; they would serve as a control group. These pairs of friends were told to discuss "something that has happened to you recently or an experience you had that is related to your race or ethnicity." Black participants were invited to go first, and since each pair already knew each other, they were encouraged to tell "a story you have not shared with this friend before." The conversation, it was suggested, should last for around ten minutes.

The second group of participants—the experimental group—was prepared differently. They were also told to discuss "something that has happened to you recently or an experience you had that is related to your race or ethnicity." But before the discussion started, the individuals in this group received a quick training: "We want to take some time to share some things that we've learned [about] conversations about race with friends of different racial groups," these participants were told. "Sometimes it feels normal to talk about race, and sometimes it can feel a bit awkward or uncomfortable at first. And that's reasonable, because people have different experiences. However you feel is okay." Then the participants were asked to briefly write down "some benefits you think can happen from talking about race with friends of different racial groups." They were asked "What, if anything, might get in the way of you and a friend experiencing these benefits?" Finally, they were instructed to describe what they could "do to help overcome these obstacles, and experience these benefits."

This exercise—acknowledge that this discussion might be awkward; think about what obstacles might emerge, and then come up with a plan for overcoming them—took only a few minutes, and it occurred before the participants came face-to-face. The researchers didn't instruct anyone on how to speak to each other, and they didn't declare any topics off limits. They didn't remind people to be respectful or polite or explain how to avoid identity threats. Participants also weren't told to share their answers to these pre-discussion questions with each other. They could simply scribble some thoughts and then set them aside, if they wished.

But the researchers suspected that simply getting someone to acknowledge to themselves, up front, that a conversation about race or ethnicity can be uncomfortable might make that discomfort easier to withstand. And pushing people to think about the *structure* of their conversation—their hopes for the dialogue; what tensions might appear and how to handle them—might make those obstacles less likely or intimidating.

Put differently, the researchers hypothesized that nudging participants to think, just a little harder, about *how* a conversation will unfold, before it starts, might make identity threats a bit less threatening.

The conversations, when they finally occurred, were relatively similar for both groups. But when the pairs in the control group—those who had received no special training—began talking, some of them struggled. They seemed hesitant to dive in. They fled to safer topics, such as their classes or sports. For one pair, the conversation was so uncomfortable that, even though they were close friends, they said goodbye after just three minutes.

However, in the experimental group, conversations often went better. Some friends talked for a long time. They got deep, asked each other questions, debated their experiences. They discussed how race and racism *felt* and described painful or meaningful moments from their own lives, rather than bland generalizations. All the conversations generally went well, but among the experimental group, there were moments of real connection. In one conversation, a Black man told his white friend what it felt like when a clerk had followed him around a store. "I could feel the shop owner, like, looking at me, and watching me, and everything I touched," the Black man said. Both participants were college friends, but they had never talked about race with each other. "I can't forget, like, who I am in America, and stuff," the Black participant said. "I'm a Black man."

He had just described a situation that, in another setting, was ripe for identity threat. His white friend might have questioned if racism was actually at fault ("Maybe there were other reasons for the clerk's behavior?") or could have downplayed his partner's concerns ("Your friends aren't racist, though"). In a misguided attempt to console his Black friend, he might have minimized this experience by implying that he was being oversensitive or needlessly anxious. And the Black participant, in reply, might have suggested that his white partner was unwilling to acknowledge racism, was blinded by white privilege, and was inadvertently perpetuating a supremacist mindset. Both of them might have threatened the other's identity without intending to do so.

Instead, when the Black participant stopped speaking, his white friend, though clearly uncomfortable, began by acknowledging and validating what he had heard. "Anyone in our friend group seems shadier than you," he told him. "The idea that someone would . . ." He trailed off, looking upset. "I feel like, even though our friend group is really multiracial, we don't talk about it too much." The white participant didn't downplay or diminish his friend's emotions or question the details. He didn't offer solutions. He simply acknowledged what his friend had said.

"I appreciate that," the Black friend replied. He said there were tensions that came from being a Black man in a largely white environment, but "especially around you guys, it's always good. It feels like I can forget about those external racial pressures and just hang out."

During this and other conversations, there were few dramatic moments, or big revelations, or passionate outbursts. But to researchers, that was the point: These kinds of dialogues were noteworthy precisely because they seemed so *normal.* They were two friends discussing a tough subject, rather than avoiding it.

When the researchers tallied their data, they found that, after these conversations, participants often felt closer to each other and more comfortable talking about race. Black participants, especially those who had received the special training, said they felt they could be more authentic around their white friends. One of the researchers, Kiara Sanchez of Dartmouth, told me she thinks those results emerged "because, when you listen to the conversations, you hear a lot of support: 'That must have hurt,' 'I'm sorry that happened to you,' 'It's awful you were discriminated against.' Sometimes just acknowledging someone's experiences and feelings can make a big difference."

There are lessons here for tough conversations of all types, even beyond those related to our identities. The first insight is that, as we've seen before, preparing for a conversation before it begins—thinking just a little bit more when we open our mouths—can have enormous impacts. Anticipating obstacles, planning for what to do when they arise, considering what you hope to say, thinking about what might be important to others: Before any challenging conversation, think for a few moments about what you hope will happen, what might go wrong, and how you'll react when it does.

The second lesson is that just because we're worried about a conversation, that doesn't mean we ought to avoid it. When we need to deliver disappointing news to a friend, complain to a boss, or discuss something unpleasant with our partner, it's normal to feel a sense of hesitation. But we can reduce that tension by reminding ourselves why this conversation is important and diminish our anxieties by acknowledging, to ourselves and others, that these conversations may be awkward at first, but will get easier.

Third, thinking about *how* a conversation will occur is just as important as *what* is said, particularly during a *Who Are We?* conversation. Who will speak first? (Studies suggest the person with the least power should begin.) What kinds of emotions should we anticipate? (If we prepare for discomfort and tension, we make them easier to withstand.) What obstacles should we expect? When they emerge, what will we do?

Most important, what benefits do we expect will emerge from

this dialogue, and are they worth the risks? (Almost always, the answer is yes—nearly everyone in Sanchez's experiment said afterward they were glad they had participated.)

SOME QUESTIONS TO ASK YOURSELF BEFORE A CONVERSATION BEGINS

- **How do you hope things will unfold?**
- **How will this conversation start?**
- **What obstacles might emerge?**
- **When those obstacles appear, what is your plan to overcome them?**
- **Finally, what are the benefits of this dialogue?**

There's a final lesson here, as well: In any hard discussion, and particularly in a *Who Are We?* conversation, we are wise to avoid generalizations—and to speak, instead, about our own experiences and emotions. Identity threats typically emerge *because* we generalize: We lump people into groups ("Lawyers are all dishonest") or assign others traits they loathe ("Everyone who voted for that guy is a racist"). These generalizations take all of us—our unique perspectives and complicated identities—out of the conversation. They make us one-dimensional.

However, when we describe our own experiences, feelings, and reactions—when we feel safe enough to reveal who we are—we start to neutralize identity threats. This requires some work, because avoiding generalizations means not only describing ourselves with honesty, but also listening closely to our companions so we can hear their specific pain and frustrations. We must not give in to the temptation to minimize someone's struggles, or try to solve their problems, simply because witnessing their discomfort is so difficult. We must not imply that, because we have not personally experienced their suffering, it therefore is not real.

But when we embrace how others see the world and their identities within it, when we listen to their specific stories and acknowledge their feelings, we start to understand why two people, who otherwise agree about so much, might see some aspects of life—like policing, or parenting, or romantic relationships—so differently because of their dissimilar backgrounds. We begin to appreciate how our worlds have been shaped by our upbringings, our race and ethnicity, our gender, and other identities. We start to understand how much discussing *Who Are We?* can reveal. We begin to connect.

NETFLIX'S NO RULES RULES

When Vernā Myers arrived at Netflix as vice president for inclusion strategy, four months after Jonathan Friedland was fired, the company was still in turmoil. Everyone at Netflix said they abhorred discrimination. Everyone said they aspired to create an equitable workplace. But that didn't mean everyone was certain the company needed to *change.* "There were a lot of well-meaning, kind people who thought if you hate racism and believe in equality, that's enough," Myers said. "That's not how it works."

Before joining Netflix, Myers had worked as a lawyer and then had served as the executive director of a consortium of law firms pushing to increase racial diversity in the legal profession. She became deputy chief of staff to the Massachusetts attorney general, leading the office's diversity initiatives, and then had founded a consulting firm to help companies become more inclusive. "She's maybe the most charismatic person I've ever met," one of her former consulting employees told me. "She can make anyone feel comfortable." Myers had started spending time with Netflix as they grappled with the Friedland situation, so she had some sense of the culture. Most important, she knew how to help people think more deeply before they opened their mouths.

The issue at Netflix, however, was that the firm's culture was *designed* to push people to speak and act quickly, often before ideas were completely thought out. The company's culture deck proclaimed that the "goal is to be Big and Fast and Flexible," and "as we grow, minimize rules." Employees were encouraged to be unconstrained and unstructured, to challenge anything and everything. "You may have heard preventing error is cheaper than fixing it ... but not so in creative environments," the culture deck decreed. When Hastings wrote a book about his experiences, he urged readers to "operate a little closer toward the edge of chaos," and "keep things a little bit loose. Welcome constant change."

But when it came to the toughest, most sensitive topics—including prejudice and bias—that kind of unconstrained, chaotic culture could be disastrous. "No one at Netflix knew how to discuss this stuff without it going nuclear," an employee told me. And since Friedland's firing, there had been confusion over what kinds of conversations were okay. Is radical candor appropriate in discussing *Who Are We?* Are there topics that should be avoided? "No one understood where to draw the line," the executive said. "So everyone just completely stopped talking about it."

Myers's team sensed that this kind of silence was part of the problem. They needed to get the company talking about hard, sensitive issues so that people could understand what their colleagues were experiencing, could wrestle with inequities inside the firm and the world and grasp how they, without meaning to, might be contributing to problems.

But those conversations had to happen the correct way. They had to occur in a manner where everyone felt safe. Netflix's culture of ruthless honesty had to be nudged just so, in order to push people to ask themselves, and each other, the right questions.

In other words, Netflix needed some rules.

• • •

Of course, they couldn't call them rules. Rules were verboten at Netflix! So Myers and her team called them *guidelines.* As they began conducting employee workshops, hosting conversations with various divisions, and offering training sessions for leaders on diversity and inclusion, the guidelines were always made clear: When discussing issues of identity, no one is allowed to blame, shame, or attack anyone else. It is okay to ask questions, if they are asked in good faith.* Goals were detailed at the beginning of each session—"Do your best to connect with compassion and courage"; "Embrace the discomfort and sense of not knowing"—and conversations were structured by moderators through reminders such as "I want to bring our attention to some things that were just said" or "Some people are very emotional about this issue; maybe we can all take a breath."

It was acknowledged, up front, that these conversations would likely be awkward and that people would inevitably make mistakes. That was okay. Attendees were told to speak about their own experiences and describe their own stories. Don't generalize. When a colleague talks about something painful, listen. Don't solve or diminish. Tell them you're sorry it happened and acknowledge the pain that was expressed.

Everyone was encouraged to speak—it wasn't fair for some people to do the work of describing their lives, while others observed—

* Within Netflix, as within society, there are some limits on questions. "This happens a lot with trans and nonbinary people," Myers told me. "People ask them about their bodies, and that's inappropriate. We would never ask cisgender people these kinds of questions. And so we tell everyone, check your motivations. Are you asking just because you're personally curious, or because knowing the answer will help everyone succeed?"

SOME GUIDELINES FOR HARD CONVERSATIONS

Start a conversation by talking about guidelines.
What is okay, and what is out of bounds?

Acknowledge discomfort.
This may be a challenging conversation, and it may make people uncomfortable. That is okay.

We will make mistakes.
The aim is not perfection, but curiosity and understanding.

The goal is to share your experiences and perspectives, not convince someone to change their mind.

No blaming, shaming, or attacks.

Speak about your own views and experiences.
Don't spend time describing what other people think.

Confidentiality is important.
People must feel safe, and that means knowing our words won't be repeated.

Respect is essential.
Even if we disagree, we show we respect each other's right to be heard.

Sometimes we need to pause.
Some conversations can be re-traumatizing. Go slow, encourage people to pause or step away. Discomfort should be expected—but pain or trauma is a signal to stop.

and to reflect on how race and ethnicity and gender and other markers of identity had shaped their lives. This was important: Everyone has a racial and ethnic identity, employees were told, as well as a gender identity and a multitude of other selves. All of us can recognize the sting of exclusion. This commonality, instead of dividing us, can help us empathize.

Myers typically began her workshops by emphasizing her own mistakes. She would share how she had misgendered people; how, to her embarrassment, she had once told a trans friend that plural pronouns like *they* and *them* might not be the best way to go. She described one time when she was "on a plane and heard the voice of a woman pilot on the PA system, and it started getting turbulent, and I thought, 'I hope she can drive!'" Then she realized she had never wondered about the pilot's abilities when the pilot was male. "I didn't even know I had that bias inside my head," she told a group. "But there it was."

Next, she would ask participants to describe a time they had felt excluded. There was often a long silence, and then a smattering of quiet dialogue. Eventually Myers would raise the stakes and ask people to describe when they had excluded *others,* what they wish they had done differently. That was even more terrifying.*

In another workshop for executives, Wade Davis, one of Myers's lieutenants, began the session by describing his background: He was a gay Black man who had grown up poor in Louisiana and Colorado. Once an NFL cornerback, he had been released multiple times until he was out of the league completely. It stung to be rejected like that, he said. He had made plenty of mistakes in his life when it came to racism and sexism. He had made ignorant assumptions, had unwittingly said offensive things.

Then Davis asked the group to reflect on their own experiences with privilege and exclusion. Eventually, he mentioned that he had spent a lot of time talking to managers about Netflix's hiring practices. A number of people had told him they were committed to finding diverse candidates, but he had also noticed that some Netflix

* These workshops are just one facet of the work Myers and her team have pursued at Netflix. For details on other aspects, please see the endnotes.

job applicants, particularly those from underrepresented backgrounds, were ultimately rejected because someone said they didn't "meet the bar."

"So, what is the Netflix bar?" Davis asked. "And how do you know someone meets it?"

The executives in the room began describing what they looked for in hiring. A middle-aged designer said he sought out applicants who had studied at schools like RISD or Parsons, and who had experience at firms like Apple or Facebook. "Diversity is important to me," he told the room. "But what's most important is knowing someone can succeed here."

He stopped talking. "Oh, shit," he said. "I'm listening to myself, and I'm realizing, I just described me. I described my own background. I define the bar as myself." He looked around. "That's not good, is it?"

Davis later told me that, in these kinds of conversations, what's important is realizing how we might inadvertently contribute to problems like inequality. The aim is not to say the exact right thing, or to arrive at the perfect insight. Perfection can't be the goal, "because if you're trying to say the perfect thing, nothing authentic is going to happen," he said. "The goal is staying in the conversation, finding space for messy learning and supporting each other."

These workshops, at first, alarmed some Netflix employees. They didn't want to attend. When they did attend, they didn't want to speak. When they did speak, they didn't want to go first. People were scared of saying something offensive, of accidentally asking an insulting question, of revealing something about themselves that might indicate they were racist or sexist. But, slowly, word got out that the workshops weren't as risky as employees feared. People could be honest and ask questions. No one was attacked for making a mistake. The workshops got bigger, and talking about these topics became easier until, eventually, thousands of employees had attended a session, many of them more than once. They began asking one another the kinds of questions that can lead to real understanding: *What does it mean to be transgender? As a Black mother, how do you feel about the police? As a parent, do you worry about juggling work and fatherhood?** And because these discussions were shaped by guidelines, everyone understood there would be uncomfortable moments and that some people would misspeak—but grappling with that discomfort, and seeing how our words impact others, is part of the point.

In the toughest *Who Are We?* conversations—those where, say, we don't have the opportunity to play soccer together, or can't experiment with different approaches to discussing vaccines—what are we to do? How do we talk about racism, sexism, or other sensitive topics when we know that getting it wrong might impact friendships and careers?

Netflix's approach offers one solution: Establish guidelines and make sure they are clearly communicated. Invite everyone into the dialogue and give everyone a voice—and let everyone know they are expected to examine themselves. Focus on belonging, and creating a sense that everyone is welcome. "If the first lesson you hear is that you're biased and inherently prejudiced, that's not a comfortable place for most people to begin. It feels threatening," said Greg Walton, a professor of psychology at Stanford. But when conversations focus on creating belonging for everyone, as well as diversity and inclusion, "you're inviting people to participate and learn, to take responsibility for improving things."

It is important to note that these kinds of discussions will almost never be perfect. But perfection is not the goal. As Myers told me,

* It is important to note that, alongside encouraging such questions, guidelines must also allow people to decline to answer. This is critical because, historically, individuals from marginalized communities have been asked to do an outsized amount of work describing their lives. For more on this, please see the endnotes.

"most of the work is about gaining awareness of yourself, your culture, and the culture of others." The goal is to recognize our own biases, "who we might be excluding or including."

Or, as Kiara Sanchez put it, the aim is not to "neutralize the discomfort, but rather give people a framework for persevering through it. It seems like a minor distinction, but the underlying theory is that discomfort can be helpful." Discomfort pushes us to think before we speak, to try to understand how others see or hear things differently. Discomfort reminds us to keep going, that the goal is worth the challenge.

THE IMPACT

By 2021, nearly every Netflix employee had received some form of training on the concepts of belonging, diversity, and inclusion. There were employee resource groups for Black, South Asian, Hispanic, Indigenous, trans, and gay and lesbian employees, and for those who were veterans, parents, or impacted by disabilities or mental health. Whereas researchers had found that some prejudice-reduction programs were ineffective because they were too brief or did not draw everyone in, at Netflix, the prolonged interventions and clear guidelines had made it easier to talk about *Who Are We?*

Just three years after Myers was hired, Netflix released data showing that it now outpaced nearly every other big firm in Silicon Valley, as well as Hollywood, in hiring from underrepresented groups. Women made up 52 percent of Netflix's workforce, and 45 percent of the company's senior leadership. Half of Netflix's U.S. employees were from at least one historically excluded ethnic or racial group, and 19 percent of U.S. employees were Black or Hispanic.

Within the tech industry, those figures are astonishing. They are equally uncommon within the entertainment industry. When researchers from the University of Southern California compared Netflix to other entertainment companies, they found Netflix shows had more women writers than most studios, and an uncommonly large number of Black and other underrepresented filmmakers, actors, and producers. Netflix finally felt, to many employees, like a different company from the one where Jonathan Friedland had said a racial slur.

Then, in October 2021, Netflix released a new Dave Chappelle stand-up special named *The Closer.* Chappelle is one of the world's most popular comedians, known for biting commentaries on race, gender, and sexuality. In *The Closer,* he joked about being "tricked" into calling a trans woman beautiful. He said that "gender is a fact"—seen by many as delegitimizing the trans community—and lampooned survivors of sexual violence. He lamented society's treatment of the rapper DaBaby, who was embraced after he murdered another man, but became a pariah after making homophobic comments.

GLAAD, an organization that monitors media for bias against the LGBTQ community, said the special was "ridiculing trans people and other marginalized communities." One Netflix employee complained on Twitter that the special "attacks the trans community, and the very validity of transness." Protests by outside groups were planned and boycotts proposed.

The outcry prompted Ted Sarandos, co-CEO of Netflix, to publicly defend the program and argue in an email sent to all employees that "we have a strong belief that content on screen doesn't directly translate to real-world harm." He noted that *The Closer* "is our most watched, stickiest and most award winning stand-up special to date." That inspired even more criticism. Websites and newspapers jumped on the controversy, publishing more than two thousand articles in just two months. When demonstrators marched on Netflix's Los Angeles headquarters to protest the Chapelle special, counterprotesters showed up and scuffles broke out.

To the outside world, it once again seemed like Netflix was at war with itself. But inside the firm, employees saw things differently. Only a small number of those picketing were Netflix employees. "We didn't need to do that," said one employee who had lodged a formal complaint with executives about the Chappelle special. There were multiple internal town hall meetings where workers had the opportunity to voice their complaints and anger. Executives were confronted with questions; petitions were circulated suggesting reforms. Internal criticisms were widely shared—and the company had procedures in place for listening and responding. "We knew how to get heard," the employee told me. "There was a system to make sure everyone knew how we felt."

There were still disagreements, of course: The company's trans employee resource group urged executives to put a disclaimer on the special or edit the most offensive parts; executives declined and said they were devoted to artistic expression, even when it was offensive. A few workers, disappointed by executives' responses, left the company.

But even employees who complained about the special told me that, when tense discussions occurred, the tone was generally empathetic, structured to give everyone a voice. A few days after publicly defending the special, Sarandos approached *The Hollywood Reporter* with a mea culpa. "I screwed up," he said. He acknowledged failing to listen to employees' concerns. "I should have first and foremost acknowledged in those emails that a group of our employees were in pain, and they were really feeling hurt. . . . I'd say those emails lacked humanity." Since then, he continued, he'd been focused on "just listening to folks and hearing out how they're feeling."

One of the employees who helped organize internal petitions about the Chappelle special told me that "these kinds of conversations always have a lot of heated emotions," but that Netflix has learned how to have them. "We had a big town hall after all this started, and the rules were made clear at the beginning: Everyone was allowed to talk, but no shaming or blaming or attacks. You had to think before you spoke. You had to contribute, rather than just criticize." During that meeting, people critiqued the company's leadership to their faces, "and trans employees talked about what they had experienced at the company and what needed to change," the employee said. "And there were other people saying, 'I don't agree with you on everything, but thank you, I understand you're hurting and I'm committed to having this conversation.' It felt like a real dialogue."

Companies, like societies, will always have disagreements. Compromise is not always possible, or sometimes even the goal. Often the best we can hope for is understanding. It is through understanding, and dialogue, that a community, and a democracy, thrives. When we create space to discuss conflicting beliefs, we make connection more likely.

Netflix, of course, has not solved issues such as racism and prejudice. "Those are big, structural problems, and there's no silver bullet," Myers told me. Real change requires shifts in not only how Netflix hires, promotes, and supports employees, but society at large. "But if you don't teach people how to have these kinds of conversations, then you don't give them a chance to hear each other," Myers said. "That isn't the solution, but it's the first step."

The *Who Are We?* conversation may be hard, but it is also vital. "If we cannot end now our differences, at least we can help make the world safe for diversity," John F. Kennedy told students at American University in 1963, five months before he was assassinated. "In the final analysis, our most basic common link is that we all inhabit this small planet. We all breathe the same air. We all cherish our children's future. And we are all mortal."

Commonalities are what allow us to learn from each other, to bridge differences, to begin talking, understanding, and working together. Conversations about identity are what reveal these connections and allow us to share our full selves.

A GUIDE TO USING THESE IDEAS

PART IV

Making Hard Conversations Easier

Difficult conversations happen all the time. Sometimes they are centered on issues such as race, ethnicity, or gender. Just as frequently, they are challenging in other ways: An employee has performance problems and needs to hear some blunt feedback; a boss is underpaying you and needs to understand your complaints; a spouse has got to change if a relationship is going to survive; an uncle is drinking too much, and you are worried.

These kinds of conversations are hard because they can threaten someone's sense of self: Our discussion with an employee about their performance might seem, to them, like criticisms of their work ethic, intelligence, or personality. Telling a boss that you deserve a bigger paycheck could sound, to the boss herself, as if you are accusing her of being uncaring. Asking a spouse to change can sometimes come off as an attack on who they are. An uncle is likely to hear your concerns about his alcohol consumption as a criticism of how he lives.

But these conversations are not just essential, they are unavoidable. So it is important that we are mindful of the last rule for a learning conversation.

Fourth Rule:
Explore if identities are important to this discussion.

This rule tells us to consider our actions during three distinct periods: *before* a discussion, at the *beginning* of the discussion, and as the discussion *unfolds*.

BEFORE THE DISCUSSION

Before a word is spoken in a *Who Are We?* conversation, there are some questions you should consider. The goal of this exercise is to nudge yourself to think about *how* you hope a conversation will unfold, and *what* you hope will be said.

Ask yourself:

- **What do you hope to accomplish?** What do you most want to say? What do you hope to learn? What do you think *others* hope to say and learn? If we have elucidated goals before a discussion, we're more likely to achieve them.
- **How will this conversation start?** How will you ensure that everyone has a voice and feels they can participate? What is needed to draw everyone in?
- **What obstacles might emerge?** Will people get angry? Withdrawn? Will a hesitancy to say something controversial prevent us from saying what's necessary? How can we make it safer for everyone to air their thoughts?

- **When those obstacles appear, what's the plan?** Research shows that being preemptively aware of situations that make us anxious or fearful can lower the impact of those concerns. How will you calm yourself and others if the conversation gets tense, or encourage someone who has gone quiet to participate more?
- **Finally, what are the benefits of this dialogue?** Are they worth the risks? (The answer usually is yes.) When people get angry or upset, or it's easier to walk away, how will you remind yourself and others why this dialogue is so important?

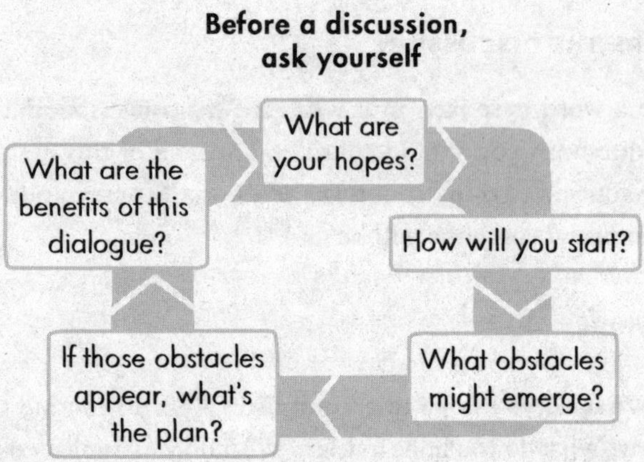

AT THE BEGINNING OF THE DISCUSSION

Tough conversations frequently begin on uncertain footing. Particularly when we're discussing *Who Are We?*, we're usually anxious we'll say the wrong thing, or tense about what we might hear.

We can lessen those anxieties by addressing a few things right away.

As a conversation begins:

- **First, establish guidelines.** It is useful to make clear the *norms*—for instance, no one is allowed to **blame, shame, or attack others.** The goal is to **share our feelings, not litigate who is at fault.** It is also helpful to define if **asking questions is okay,** and if there are some kinds of inquiries—about, say, very personal topics, or particularly sensitive issues—that require some forethought. We should affirm that **everyone is encouraged to speak,** that everyone belongs in this discussion, and perhaps identify someone to serve as a moderator to make sure everyone is given space. Finally, it is useful to ask people to **speak about their own experiences and describe their own stories.** Don't generalize. Don't solve or diminish others' problems, unless they ask for help. When a colleague describes something painful, **listen,** and tell them you're sorry it happened. Acknowledge what they felt.
- **Second, draw out everyone's goals.** You likely have some aims in mind. Share them. Then, ask others what they hope to get out of this discussion. Identify *emotional goals* ("I want to make sure we stay friends" or "I need to get something off my chest"); and *practical goals* ("I'd like to walk away from this with a plan"); as well as *group goals* ("It's important to me that we all show compassion for each other").
- **Finally, acknowledge, and keep acknowledging, that discomfort is natural—and useful.** We will misspeak. We will ask naïve questions. We will say things we didn't realize were offensive. When these discomforts emerge, rather than shutting down, we should use them as opportunities to learn.

At the beginning of a discussion

Establish the guidelines	- What are the norms? - No blaming, shaming, or attacks. - Are questions okay?
A moderator can encourage	...everyone to speak. ...people to tell their own stories and not diminish others' problems. ...everyone to listen.
Draw out everyone's	...emotional goals. ...practical goals. ...more ephemeral goals.
Acknowledge this will be uncomfortable	- We may misspeak. - We may ask naïve questions. - When those discomforts emerge, we won't shut down. Rather, we'll see them as opportunities to learn.

AS THE DISCUSSION UNFOLDS

Once we've prepared for a hard conversation, and have discussed guidelines and goals, we should remember to:

- **Draw out multiple identities.** Ask people about their backgrounds, communities, the organizations and causes they support, and where they come from. Share your identities in return. We all contain multiple selves; none of us are one-dimensional. It helps to be reminded of that.

- **Work to ensure everyone is on an equal footing.** *Who Are We?* discussions work best when everyone has an equal voice and the ability to speak. Focus on welcoming everyone's perspective. Don't trumpet your wealth or connections, your privilege or seniority, your expertise. Seek to frame topics so everyone is an expert, or everyone a novice. (This, in fact, is why discussing experiences is so powerful: We're all experts in what we've seen and felt.)
- **Acknowledge people's experiences and look for genuine similarities.** Ask people about their identities and build on what you have in common. ("You went to Valley High? So did I!") But remember: Similarities must be genuine. And connections become more meaningful when we push them a bit further, and use them to understand each other better. ("High school was tough for me. What was it like for you?") Even if we don't have similarities, simply acknowledging others' experiences showing you have heard them—can create a sense of togetherness.
- **Manage your environment.** Social identities gain and lose power based on their salience and the environment where a conversation occurs. Sometimes a simple shift—moving a discussion from a group setting to something more personal; talking away from the workplace; starting a meeting by discussing the weekend before getting to business—can shift what feels safe, and who feels welcomed. (And, by the same token, when an environment makes someone feel left out, it can undermine our sense of safety.)

During the discussion

1 Draw out multiple identities.

2 Put everyone on an equal footing.

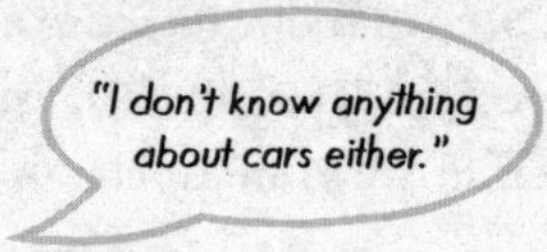

3 Look for similarities to create in-groups.

4 Manage your environment.

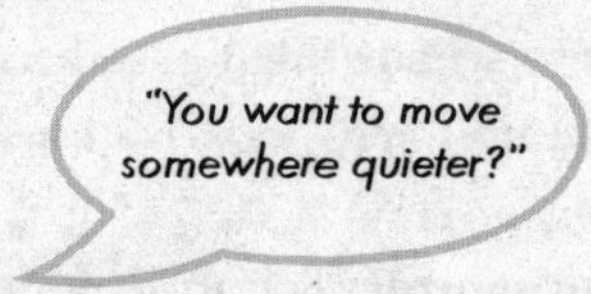

This can seem like a lot. Hard conversations, even with the most meticulous and thoughtful planning, can veer off in directions we haven't foreseen. But when we're aware of harmful influences such as identity threat and stereotype threat, when we have a plan and are prepared for obstacles, when we know that things will get uncomfortable and that's okay, it becomes a bit easier to discuss difficult things.

AFTERWORD

In the spring of 1937, a chain store magnate named Billy Grant approached Harvard University with a proposition. Grant had dropped out of high school decades earlier, but had gone on to make a fortune selling kitchen supplies and household wares at "25 Cent Stores" across the nation. Now, at the age of sixty-one, he had announced that he wanted to give back to society through a large donation—and, he told Harvard's administrators, also achieve a secondary, more practical goal: He oversaw a growing empire and was hiring rapidly. His executives needed research, data, and scientific insights to assist them in choosing the best store managers and the smartest employees. So Grant offered to give a small fortune to the university to fund the school's general research—as long as their scholars might consider his matter and offer some advice.

Harvard's administrators thought the request was a bit crass. But a donation is a donation, and they already knew how they would use the money, so they said yes. For years, faculty in the medical school had wanted to conduct a long-term, longitudinal study of, as they put it, "healthy young men." In particular, they wanted to recruit hundreds of Harvard undergraduates and follow them for decades, examining such issues as "the problem of nature vs. nurture; connections between personality and health; whether mental and physical illnesses can be predicted; how constitutional considerations might influence career choice." The plan, essentially, was to take Grant's money and—in addition to trying to figure out what made someone good at selling spatulas—collect data on people's fitness, families, schooling, work, emotional impulses, and physical characteristics. The participants would undergo extensive on-campus medical exams and psychological interviews, and then be asked to fill out detailed surveys, delivered via the mail and home visits by researchers, for the rest of their lives. Once all that data started rolling in, the researchers would look for patterns that explained why some participants became happy, gainfully employed, healthy adults, while others did not.

The project initially was known as the Grant Study, and over the following years it slowly expanded. Eventually, a group of teens from South Boston's tenements were enrolled, and then, as various participants married and had children, many of their spouses and offspring were included as well. Over time, more than two thousand men and women were poked, prodded, interviewed, and psychologically analyzed. Today the Harvard Study of Adult Development is one of the largest, longest, and most famous studies in the world.

Among the first of the participants to be interviewed were two young men who had enrolled at Harvard in the years leading up to World War II. The first was an undergraduate who, researchers eventually determined, was a neurotic hypochondriac. Godfrey Camille, one researcher wrote (not too kindly), "was a disaster." He had been raised away from other families and children because his parents were "pathologically suspicious." When a researcher interviewed Camille's mother, he deemed her "one of the most nervous people I have ever met," and a psychologist determined that Camille had one of "the bleakest childhoods I have ever seen." Camille arrived at Harvard in 1938 and almost instantly seemed overwhelmed. He visited the infirmary regularly, complaining of so many mysterious illnesses that one physician noted in his file that "this boy is turning into a regular psychoneurotic." He was skinny, physically weak, and struggled to make friends. When America entered the war, Camille, like most Harvard men, enlisted in the military. But whereas many of his classmates were commissioned as officers and returned home with ribbons and medals, Camille was still a private when he was honorably discharged, with no significant accomplishments to speak of. He then attended medical school, but shortly after graduation attempted suicide, which made him a pariah in Boston's medical community. He grew so distant from his family that, when his sister and mother died, he hardly mentioned their deaths in his follow-up surveys. At age thirty-five, he was hospitalized for fourteen months for pulmonary tuberculosis. "I was glad to be sick," he later told a researcher. "I can go to bed for a year."

The other young man from that period was different. John Marsden was an exceptional student and came from a wealthy and prominent family that ran a dry-goods franchise in Cleveland. Marsden also volunteered for World War II, served valiantly, and then, rather than accede to his father's wishes to join the family business, he followed his passion and enrolled in the University of Chicago's law school, where he graduated near the top of his class. He became a public-service lawyer, got married, and eventually started a successful private practice.

The Grant Study had been designed with the aim of objectivity. The researchers wanted to avoid guessing which of the participants were likely to soar or stumble, lest those pre-judgments taint the data. But when it came to Camille and Marsden, it was hard to avoid predictions. It was clear to everyone that Camille was likely to end up depressed and lonely—or, perhaps, dead by his own hand. "Everyone had predicted he would be a loser," one researcher wrote. Whereas Marsden, the scientists assumed, would become a leader in his community, another chapter in his family's proud legacy. Marsden, a researcher noted, is "one of the more professionally successful members of the Study."

Then, in 1954, sixteen years after it began, the study's funding ran out. Billy Grant had by now donated the equivalent of $7 million in today's dollars and was frustrated that the study hadn't revealed much that was helpful about selecting store managers. Even worse, Harvard had failed to sufficiently mention his generosity when it published papers from the study. Grant was done shelling out money, he told administrators. The researchers scrambled to find alternative sources of funding—at one point, they convinced a collection of tobacco companies to fund the project by suggesting their work might reveal "positive reasons" for smoking—but eventually that support dried up, as well. Final reports were written. Farewells were made. There were sporadic attempts at keeping in touch with some participants, but for the most part, the study was boxed up and stashed in the basement of the medical school.

That would have been the end of the story, except that, in the early 1970s, a group of young psychiatry professors started digging through those boxes and stumbled upon the project's surveys. Intrigued, they began tracking down the participants, sending them new questionnaires and scheduling follow-up interviews. They expected to find that most participants had kept traveling along the same trajectories as when the study had ended. When they spoke to Camille and Marsden, though, they discovered that assumption was completely wrong.

In the intervening decades, it seemed, Camille had become a different person. He was now in his fifties, married, a leader in his church, and had won over Boston's medical establishment by founding a large, independent clinic that specialized in allergy treatments. He was a nationally recognized expert on asthmatic patients, invited to symposiums, and interviewed on television. When researchers spoke to his daughters, who were now young adults, they called him an "exemplary father," someone with "the innate ability to just give. He could play like five-year-olds do."

Researchers, drawing on the study's previous protocols, conducted follow-up surveys every two years. Each time they spoke with Camille, he seemed happier than ever. "Before there were dysfunctional families, I came from one," Camille wrote in 1994, when he was seventy-five. But he had managed to escape that legacy, he continued, by changing "into the person I've slowly become: Comfortable, joyful, connected and effective." At eighty, Camille threw himself a potluck birthday party, and more than three hundred people showed up. A bit later, he let the scientists know that he was flying to the Alps for a climbing trek with friends. He died of a heart attack on that trip, at eighty-two years old. At his memorial, the church was packed. "There was a deep and holy authenticity about the man," the bishop eulogized. Camille's son told the crowd that "he lived a very simple life, but it was very rich." Camille, the Harvard researchers later determined, was among the top—perhaps *the* top—participant in the study by measurement of happiness, health, and satisfaction from life and work. "Who could have foreseen," one of them wrote, "that he would die a happy, giving, and beloved man?"

In contrast, Marsden, the lawyer, was in terrible shape when the researchers found him after the study's hiatus. In his fifties now, he was divorced and alienated from his children and his family in Cleveland. Though his law practice was successful, he had few friends and spent most of his time alone. He reported feeling angry, lonely, and disappointed by life. He eventually remarried, but just a few years later, reported that the relationship was "loveless." *Do you ever go to your wife when you're upset?* one survey asked. "No, definitely not,"

Marsden wrote. "I would get no sympathy. I would be told that it's a sign of weakness." When asked how he coped with difficulty, Marsden wrote: "I keep it to myself. I tough it out." One researcher broke protocol and offered to find Marsden a couples therapist. Marsden and his wife attended one session, but then abandoned the effort. "He seemed like a broken person," that researcher, Robert Waldinger, told me. Eventually, Marsden stopped responding to interview requests. The researchers discovered why when a survey was returned, unopened, by the U.S. Postal Service. The addressee had died, according to a note on the envelope. The current residents had no idea if there were next of kin.

How was it possible, the researchers wondered, that things could turn out so unexpectedly for these two men? It wasn't just Camille and Marsden. As the scientists compared other participants' contemporary lives to the plans and aspirations they had described as adolescents, they found that a number of them—men and women who seemed to have bright futures and were seemingly destined for greatness—had ended up, instead, lonely and depressed adults, dissatisfied by their lives. Whereas others, who had faced crippling obstacles, such as mental health and poverty, had arrived at old age happy, successful, and surrounded by family and friends.

The researchers, by now, had seven decades of data to draw upon, and they began crawling through it. They scrutinized people's genetics and childhoods, looked at their propensities for alcoholism and schizophrenia, measured how many hours each participant had worked and how many kids they had raised, all in hopes of determining which variables could reliably predict how things would turn out later in life. They discovered some correlations: Having loving parents made it easier to find happiness as an adult. Possessing genes related to physical hardiness and longevity was helpful—as was getting enough exercise and eating well. Education early in life, as well as a lifelong commitment to learning, also provided a leg up.

However, as important as these factors were, one thing seemed to matter much more than anything else. It didn't come as a surprise; it had been obvious to everyone, across the decades, as they had conducted their interviews. The most important variable in determining whether someone ended up happy and healthy, or miserable and sick, was "how satisfied they were in their relationships," one researcher wrote. "The people who were the most satisfied in their relationships at age 50 were the healthiest (mentally and physically) at age 80."

Another researcher put it more bluntly: "The most important influence, by far, on a flourishing life is love." Not romantic love, but, rather, the kinds of deep connections we form with our families, friends, and coworkers, as well as neighbors and people from our community. "Love early in life facilitates not only love later on, but also the other trappings of success, such as prestige and even high income. It also encourages the development of coping styles that facilitate intimacy, as opposed to ones that discourage it."

Participants who ended up happy all had "warm adult relationships" with numerous people. They had good marriages, were close to their children, and had invested in strong friendships. The people "who flourished found love," one researcher observed, "and that was why they flourished."

On the other hand, people who had not invested in relationships—who had prioritized their careers over families and friends or had struggled to connect for other reasons—were mostly miserable. Take John Marsden, for example. When he was forty-three years old—with almost half his life in front of him—this is what he wrote when asked by researchers to describe what he found himself thinking about often:

1. I'm growing old. Realize for the first time the reality of death.
2. Feel I may not achieve what I wanted.

3. Not sure I know how to bring up children. I thought I did.
4. Tensions at work are severe.

Marsden didn't mention other people, or relationships, except in a negative sense. When he felt depressed, rather than seek out companions, he went to his office and tried to use his legal practice to distract himself. When he argued with his wife or children, he stomped off and withdrew, rather than talking through issues until a resolution, or at least an understanding, emerged. "He was a very self-critical person," said Waldinger, who currently leads the Harvard project. "He pushed himself hard and judged himself pretty harshly, and that made him successful in his profession. But it also meant he was critical of other people, which is probably what alienated so many of them." As one summary of Marsden's surveys put it, "he developed a wariness of people and habitually negative ways of coping with the world. He had difficulty connecting with others, and when he encountered challenges, his instinct was to withdraw from the people closest to him. He married twice, and never felt that he was truly loved."

Compare that with Camille, the doctor. During the year he spent in the tuberculosis ward, Camille began developing relationships with fellow patients. He met some for Bible study, and with others to play cards, and formed relationships with nurses and orderlies. He later told researchers that his time in the hospital had felt like a rebirth. "Someone with a capital 'S' cared about me," he wrote on one survey. "Nothing has been so tough since that year." When he left the hospital, he joined a church and threw himself into committees, potlucks, Sunday school—anything where he could meet other people. Researchers later determined that, until the age of thirty, Camille didn't have one real, durable friendship; a decade later, he was among the most socially active people in the study, and as his network expanded, his career took off. "My professional life hasn't been disappointing—far from it—but the truly gratifying unfolding has been into the person I've slowly become," he wrote on a survey at the age of seventy-five. "Connectedness is something we must let happen to us. . . . What durable and pliable creatures we are, and what a storehouse of goodwill lurks in the social fabric." Talking to other people, connecting with them, sharing his joys and sorrows, he said, had transformed his life. "You know what I learned?" he told one interviewer. "I learned love."

Across the decades and surveys, similar findings emerged again and again: The happiest participants called others regularly, made lunch and dinner dates, sent notes to friends saying they were proud of them, or wanted to help them shoulder sad news. Most of all, happy participants engaged in many, many conversations over the years that brought them closer to others. "Through all the years of studying these lives, one crucial factor stands out for the consistency and power of its ties to physical health, mental health and longevity," reads a 2023 summary of the Harvard data. "Good relationships keep us healthier and happier." And, in many instances, those relationships were established, and kept alive, via long and intimate discussions.

This central finding has been replicated in hundreds of other studies over the past few decades. "We now have robust evidence indicating that being socially connected has a powerful influence on longevity, such that having more and better relationships is associated with protection and, conversely, that having fewer and poorer relationships is associated with risk," reads one paper published in 2018 in the *Annual Review of Psychology*. Another study, published in 2016, examined dozens of biomarkers of health, and found that "a higher degree of social integration was associated with lower risk" of illness and death at every stage of life. Social isolation, the researchers wrote, was more dangerous than diabetes and a host of other chronic diseases.

Put differently, connecting with others can make us healthier, happier, and more content. Conversations can change our brains, bodies, and how we experience the world.

• • •

Which brings me back to my confession from the prologue: In many ways I wrote this book for myself. After I had failed as a manager at work and was wondering why I had become someone who couldn't seem to read cues or hear what others were saying, I realized I might need to reevaluate how I communicated. So, one night—and I know this sounds a little strange—I sat down and scribbled out a list of all the times, over the last year, that I could remember screwing up a conversation. I wrote down the times I had only half-listened to my wife, when I had failed to empathize with coworkers as they told me something vulnerable, when I had ignored a good idea because I had already decided to follow my own notions, all those meals I had spent talking about myself instead of asking about others, the times (it shames me to say it) when I told my kids to please stop asking me stuff so I could get some work done. All of us, I think, carry some version of this list in our heads. But writing it out forced me to confront some hard questions: Why was it that, at times, I had so much trouble hearing what someone was trying to tell me? Why was I so quick to get defensive, or to glide past the emotions people were clearly trying to share? Why, sometimes, did I talk so much and listen so little? Why hadn't I understood when a friend needed comfort rather than advice? How could I put my kids aside when they so clearly wanted to be with me? Why did I struggle to explain what was inside my own head?

These struck me as meaningful questions, worthy of exploration, and I wanted answers. So I began calling neurologists and psychologists and sociologists and other experts, asking them how it was possible that I—someone who has been communicating my whole life!—could still get it so wrong. This book is the result of that journey. What all that reporting and reading studies and squinting at data offered, in the end, is something invaluable: It has helped me to connect better, to be more mindful when other people reveal something personal, to know that there is always a conversation going on—be it practical, emotional, or social—and that we won't be able to connect until we come to an understanding about what we all want and need. Most of all, it has convinced me of the importance of having learning conversations, where my aim is to pay attention to what *kind* of conversation is occurring; to identify our goals for a dialogue; to ask about others' emotions and share my own feelings; and to explore if our identities influence what we say and hear.

THE LEARNING CONVERSATION

Rule One:
Pay attention to what *kind* of conversation is occurring.
Rule Two:
Share your goals, and ask what others are seeking.
Rule Three:
Ask about others' feelings, and share your own.
Rule Four:
Explore if identities are important to this discussion.

I've tried to have learning conversations in every part of my life, and it has helped me listen more than I used to. (I'm getting better, though my wife, just last week, asked how a rambling dinnertime monologue might align with some of the advice in this book.) I try to ask more questions—both to determine what people want out of a conversation and to explore the deep, meaningful, and emotional parts of life where real connection occurs. I try to reciprocate others' happiness and sadness, as well as their admissions and vulnerabilities, when I'm lucky enough to encounter them, and own up more freely to my own mistakes, feelings, and who I am. As a result, I feel closer to the people around me, more connected to my family, friends, colleagues—and, most of all, more thankful for these relationships than ever before. (And I hope this only continues: If you send me an email at charles@charlesduhigg.com, I promise I'll respond.)

There is no single right way to connect with other people. There are skills that make conversations easier and less awkward. There are tips that increase the odds you'll understand your companions, and they'll be more likely to hear what you are trying to say. The effectiveness of various conversational tactics waxes and wanes based on our surroundings, the types of discussion we're having, the kind of relationships we hope to achieve. Sometimes we get there; sometimes we don't.

But what's important is *wanting* to connect, *wanting* to understand someone, *wanting* to have a deep conversation, even when it is hard and scary, or when it would be so much easier to walk away. There are skills and insights that can help us satisfy that desire for connection, and they are worth learning, practicing, and committing to. Because whether we call it love, or friendship, or simply having a great conversation, achieving connection—authentic, meaningful connection—is the most important thing in life.

ACKNOWLEDGMENTS

I must start by thanking the people who shared their thoughts, insights, and experiences with me. Over the three years I spent reporting this book, hundreds of scientists and thinkers have been generous with their time, for which I am enormously grateful. One unfortunate aspect of large reporting projects is that some of the most helpful—and fascinating—people never appear on the page, and so I wanted to offer special thanks to Dacher Keltner of Berkeley, Lisa Feldman Barrett of Northeastern University, and the many people affiliated with the Dartmouth Social Systems Lab, NASA, and the writing staff of *The Big Bang Theory*, among others, who agreed to speak with me.

Some of my favorite conversations—both in writing this book and life—have occurred with Andy Ward, my editor. He is a gifted, demanding, and farsighted wordsmith, and a dedicated friend. In the U.K., Nigel Wilcockson offered wonderful suggestions and support, and in Brooklyn, Scott Moyers was an invaluable early sounding board. Similarly, I was lucky enough to work with Gina Centrello, who made Random House a haven for writers, as well as Tom Perry, Maria Braeckel, Greg Kubie, Sanyu Dillon, Ayelet Durantt, Windy Dorresteyn, Azraf Khan, and Joe Perez. I owe a huge debt to the amazing Random House sales force.

Andrew Wylie, as all who know him are aware, has made the world immeasurably better for writers, and his colleague James Pullen, also of the Wylie Agency, does valiant battle overseas. I previously worked at *The New York Times*, where I had many wonderful colleagues, and now write for *The New Yorker*, where David Remnick and Daniel Zalewski prove, each day, that kindness, intelligence, and the highest standards in journalism are natural companions. And, a special thanks to David Kortava, who provided fact-checking for the book, Asha Smith and Olivia Boone, my assistants, and Richard Rampell, who always offers sage advice.

The book's graphics are by Darren Booth, a wonderful illustrator. Most of this book was written in Santa Cruz, California, which has welcomed my family.

Finally, my deepest thanks are to my sons, Oli and Harry, and, of course, my wife, Liz, whose constant love, support, guidance, intelligence, and friendship made this book possible.

—July 2023

A NOTE ON SOURCES AND METHODS

The reporting in this book is based on hundreds of interviews and thousands of papers and studies. Many of those sources are detailed in the text itself or the endnotes.

In most situations, individuals who were major sources of information or who published research that was integral to my reporting were provided with summaries of my reporting and given an opportunity to review facts and offer additional comments, address discrepancies, or register issues with how information was portrayed. Many of those comments influenced the book's final form and are reproduced in the endnotes. (No source was given access to the book's text prior to publication, and all comments were based on summaries that I, or a fact-checker, provided.)

In a very small number of cases, confidentiality was extended to sources who, for a variety of reasons, would not speak on a for-attribution basis. In such cases, and other situations, some identifying characteristics have been withheld or changed to protect anonymity, to conform with privacy laws and ethics, or for other reasons.

NOTES

PROLOGUE

xi **Even if you had nothing in common with Felix:** Felix Sigala spoke to me on the condition of anonymity. Details—including Sigala's name as well as specifics about his career—have been changed to obscure his identity. The FBI was presented with fact-checking inquiries regarding the events described. The Bureau, citing the agency's press policies, declined to comment beyond confirming general details.

xv **"The single biggest problem with communication":** The provenance of this quote, like many great quips, is somewhat murky, but it is widely attributed to George Bernard Shaw.

CHAPTER ONE: THE MATCHING PRINCIPLE

3 **a case officer for the Central Intelligence Agency:** Jim Lawler spent twenty-five years as an officer with the Central Intelligence Agency and is still bound by pledges of confidentiality on a number of topics. Though he spent many hours sharing his experiences with me, he did not, at any time, divulge confidential information. As a result, some of the details in his story have been changed, were

described to me only in general terms, or were confirmed by other sources. Yasmin is a pseudonym. Lawler did not specify which nation Yasmin came from, saying only that it was "an oil-rich country hostile to the United States." Lawler also declined to identify the nation where he was stationed, saying only that it was "an alpine nation in Europe." If you are interested in learning more about Lawler's experiences, please allow me to recommend his wonderful espionage novels: *Living Lies* and *In the Twinkling of an Eye.*

4 **"who truly understands him":** Randy Burkett, "An Alternative Framework for Agent Recruitment: From MICE to RASCLS," *Studies in Intelligence* 57, no. 1 (2013): 7–17.

8 **a flurry of research:** Marta Zaraska, "All Together Now," *Scientific American* 323 (October 2020): 4, 64–69; Lars Riecke et al., "Neural Entrainment to Speech Modulates Speech Intelligibility," *Current Biology* 28, no. 2 (2018): 161–69; Andrea Antal and Christoph S. Herrmann, "Transcranial Alternating Current and Random Noise Stimulation: Possible Mechanisms," *Neural Plasticity* 2016 (2016): 3616807; L. Whitsel et al., "Stability of Rapidly Adapting Afferent Entrainment vs. Responsivity," *Somatosensory & Motor Research* 17, no. 1 (2000): 13–31; Nina G. Jablonski, *Skin: A Natural History* (Berkeley: University of California Press, 2006).

9 **"Why people 'click' with some people":** Thalia Wheatley et al., "From Mind Perception to Mental Connection: Synchrony as a Mechanism for Social Understanding," *Social and Personality Psychology Compass* 6, no. 8 (2012): 589–606.

9 **"to connect with each other, against all odds":** Wheatley, here, is quoting the author Michael Dorris.

10 **scholars at the Max Planck Institute:** Ulman Lindenberger et al., "Brains Swinging in Concert: Cortical Phase Synchronization While Playing Guitar," *BMC Neuroscience* 10 (2009): 1–12; Johanna Sänger, Viktor Müller, and Ulman Lindenberger, "Intra- and Interbrain Synchronization and Network Properties When Playing Guitar in Duets," *Frontiers in Human Neuroscience* (2012): 312; Viktor Müller, Johanna Sänger, and Ulman Lindenberger, "Hyperbrain Network Properties of Guitarists Playing in Quartet," *Annals of the New York Academy of Sciences* 1423, no. 1 (2018): 198–210.

10 **the electrical impulses along their skin:** Daniel C. Richardson, Rick Dale, and Natasha Z. Kirkham, "The Art of Conversation Is Coordination," *Psychological Science* 18, no. 5 (2007): 407–13. In response to fact-checking inquiries, the author of this study, Daniel Richardson, said that while these kinds of physical effects have been documented by scientists, "those are not specifically effects that I have personally proved in my own lab. I have discussed these effects before in review papers, or introductions to my own related experiments (on eye movements or body movement coordination, for example)." Sievers noted that while we do see

these kinds of alignments in collaborative activities, researchers are uncertain about the direction of the causality.

10 **Sievers found other studies:** Ayaka Tsuchiya et al., "Body Movement Synchrony Predicts Degrees of Information Exchange in a Natural Conversation," *Frontiers in Psychology* 11 (2020): 817; Scott S. Wiltermuth and Chip Heath, "Synchrony and Cooperation," *Psychological Science* 20, no. 1 (2009): 1–5; Michael J. Richardson et al., "Rocking Together: Dynamics of Intentional and Unintentional Interpersonal Coordination," *Human Movement Science* 26, no. 6 (2007): 867–91; Naoyuki Osaka et al., "How Two Brains Make One Synchronized Mind in the Inferior Frontal Cortex: fNIRS-Based Hyperscanning During Cooperative Singing," *Frontiers in Psychology* 6 (2015): 1811; Alejandro Pérez, Manuel Carreiras, and Jon Andoni Duñabeitia, "Brain-to-Brain Entrainment: EEG Interbrain Synchronization While Speaking and Listening," *Scientific Reports* 7, no. 1 (2017): 1–12.

10 **a long and convoluted tale about her prom night:** Greg J. Stephens, Lauren J. Silbert, and Uri Hasson, "Speaker–Listener Neural Coupling Underlies Successful Communication," *Proceedings of the National Academy of Sciences* 107, no. 32 (2010): 14425–30; Lauren J. Silbert et al., "Coupled Neural Systems Underlie the Production and Comprehension of Naturalistic Narrative Speech," *Proceedings of the National Academy of Sciences* 111, no. 43 (2014): E4687–96.

10 **"extent of speaker-listener neural coupling":** Greg J. Stephens, Lauren J. Silbert, and Uri Hasson, "Speaker–Listener Neural Coupling Underlies Successful Communication," *Proceedings of the National Academy of Sciences* 107, no. 32 (2010): 14425–30.

11 **we must connect with them:** J. M. Ackerman and J. A. Bargh, "Two to Tango: Automatic Social Coordination and the Role of Felt Effort," in *Effortless Attention: A New Perspective in the Cognitive Science of Attention and Action,* ed. Brian Bruya (Cambridge, Mass.: MIT Press Scholarship Online, 2010); Sangtae Ahn et al., "Interbrain Phase Synchronization During Turn-Taking Verbal Interaction—A Hyperscanning Study Using Simultaneous EEG/MEG," *Human Brain Mapping* 39, no. 1 (2018): 171–88; Laura Astolfi et al., "Cortical Activity and Functional Hyperconnectivity by Simultaneous EEG Recordings from Interacting Couples of Professional Pilots," *2012 Annual International Conference of the IEEE Engineering in Medicine and Biology Society,* 4752–55; Jing Jiang et al., "Leader Emergence Through Interpersonal Neural Synchronization," *Proceedings of the National Academy of Sciences* 112, no. 14 (2015): 4274–79; Reneeta Mogan, Ronald Fischer, and Joseph A. Bulbulia, "To Be in Synchrony or Not? A Meta-Analysis of Synchrony's Effects on Behavior, Perception, Cognition and Affect," *Journal of Experimental Social Psychology* 72 (2017): 13–20; Uri Hasson et al., "Brain-to-Brain Coupling: A

Mechanism for Creating and Sharing a Social World," *Trends in Cognitive Sciences* 16, no. 2 (2012): 114–21; Uri Hasson, "I Can Make Your Brain Look Like Mine," *Harvard Business Review* 88, no. 12 (2010): 32–33; Maya Rossignac-Milon et al., "Merged Minds: Generalized Shared Reality in Dyadic Relationships," *Journal of Personality and Social Psychology* 120, no. 4 (2021): 882.

11 **synchronize as well:** In response to fact-checking inquiries, Sievers wrote that while understanding and neural alignment can be accompanied by physiological entrainment of pulse, facial expression, or emotional experience, it is not guaranteed. "It's possible to listen to someone, understand them, and not become physiologically entrained. . . . Part of what makes both conversation and music meaningful is seeing how people change as they interact, aligning and misaligning, steering each other and being steered."

11 **There is something about neural simultaneity:** Laura Menenti, Martin J. Pickering, and Simon C. Garrod, "Toward a Neural Basis of Interactive Alignment in Conversation," *Frontiers in Human Neuroscience* 6 (2012); Sivan Kinreich et al., "Brain-to-Brain Synchrony During Naturalistic Social Interactions," *Scientific Reports* 7, no. 1 (2017): 17060; Lyle Kingsbury and Weizhe Hong, "A Multi-Brain Framework for Social Interaction," *Trends in Neurosciences* 43, no. 9 (2020): 651–66; Thalia Wheatley et al., "Beyond the Isolated Brain: The Promise and Challenge of Interacting Minds," *Neuron* 103, no. 2 (2019): 186–88; Miriam Rennung and Anja S. Göritz, "Prosocial Consequences of Interpersonal Synchrony," *Zeitschrift für Psychologie* (2016); Ivana Konvalinka and Andreas Roepstorff, "The Two-Brain Approach: How Can Mutually Interacting Brains Teach Us Something About Social Interaction?" *Frontiers in Human Neuroscience* 6 (2012): 215; Caroline Szymanski et al., "Teams on the Same Wavelength Perform Better: Inter-brain Phase Synchronization Constitutes a Neural Substrate for Social Facilitation," *Neuroimage* 152 (2017): 425–36.

12 **achieved moments of supercommunication:** Sievers wrote that his research is primarily focused on how conversation creates alignment in the future, a distinction from alignment in the moment. Further, his dissertation research was on emotion perception in music and movement. B. Sievers et al., "Music and Movement Share a Dynamic Structure That Supports Universal Expressions of Emotion," *Proceedings of the National Academy of Sciences* 110, no. 1 (2012): 70–75; B. Sievers et al., "A Multi-sensory Code for Emotional Arousal," *Proceedings of the Royal Society B* 286 (2019): 20190513; B. Sievers et al., "Visual and Auditory Brain Areas Share a Representational Structure That Supports Emotion Perception," *Current Biology* 31, no. 23 (2021): 5192–203.

12 **stage an experiment:** In this study, Sievers "was interested in knowing who was better at creating consensus for being convincing," he wrote. "And I was inter-

ested in knowing why and then trying to lay down a scientific and neurobiological foundation for understanding why people might be more or less convincing or create more or less group cohesion. . . . I wasn't thinking about, like, supercommunication. [But] I think there are people that are much better at this than other people. And it makes sense to sort of scientifically try and understand why and if we can be better at communication."

12 **difficult to understand:** Beau Sievers et al., "How Consensus-Building Conversation Changes Our Minds and Aligns Our Brains," *PsyArXiv,* July 12, 2020.

14 **When he dominated the conversation:** Sievers wrote: "We found that groups with people judged to be high social status showed lower neural alignment, and that high-status people used different conversation strategies, including talking more, giving orders to others, and implicitly rejecting others' ideas. Subject 4 in Group D was rated as having high social status and this conversation did not produce increased alignment, so this feels like a good example. However, the statistical analysis doesn't let us 'zoom in' on a single person, so we can't know with certainty whether Subject 4 held his group back; other factors may have been at play."

14 **high centrality participants discussing:** The dialogue from study participants throughout this chapter has been edited and condensed, in some places, for brevity and clarity. In the original study, participants are referred to with coded signifiers and are not referred to, in the transcripts, as "high centrality participants."

15 **But the most important difference:** Sievers wrote that "the high centrality participants who facilitated consensus, they did not speak more or less than others, and they directed attention to other speakers, and they did so more than the high-status people. They requested clarification more frequently. . . . They were not rated to be more influential by their group, and they were more susceptible to neural influence. . . . This ties into a larger literature on the traits that people have called high self-monitoring . . . a tendency to adapt one's behavior to the groups that you're in. And we didn't measure that trait in our study, but we should have."

16 **"How do you think this movie will end?":** This transcript, like the previous one, was edited and condensed for brevity and clarity.

16 **"likely to adapt their own brain activity":** Sievers, "How Consensus-Building Conversation Changes Our Minds."

17 **Other people turned to them:** Sievers made clear that this study did not look at community leadership, and so while that is a "proposed explanation, [it is] not part of the science. . . . It could be that people become central in their social network and then other people have to talk to them, because they could have become central for some other reason, like they own a yacht or something."

18 **if our mind doesn't align:** Sievers noted that "the localization of brain function—which parts of the brain are responsible for what kinds of behavior or thinking—is one of the most debated topics in neuroscience. . . . However, generally speaking, it appears that brain areas and networks seem to perform multiple functions (Suárez et al., 2020). This seems to be true across the brain, from neural networks to individual neurons (Rigotti et al., 2013). So, the mindsets identified in this section are likely handled by several brain networks coordinating together over time. Put simply, the brain is very complex, and any claims that just one network or part of the brain is responsible for a certain kind of behavior or thinking—or a particular mindset—is inevitably oversimplified."

19 **we're attuned to *How Do We Feel?*:** Piercarlo Valdesolo and David DeSteno, "Synchrony and the Social Tuning of Compassion," *Emotion* 11, no. 2 (2011): 262.

20 **"about other people, oneself, and the relation":** Matthew D. Lieberman, *Social: Why Our Brains Are Wired to Connect* (Oxford: Oxford University Press, 2013). The default mode network incorporates the medial frontoparietal network, or MFPN. Sievers wrote that "some scientists have theorized that the medial frontoparietal network is specific to social stimuli (e.g., Schilbach et al., 2008), but there is also strong evidence that its function may be much more general. The MFPN may be involved in memory retrieval (Buckner & DiNicola, 2019) and creativity (Beaty et al., 2016; Beaty et al., 2021). It may be that the MFPN is involved in generating information internally, when that information is disconnected from immediate sensory input (Buckner & DiNicola, 2019), or integrating that information with sensory information (Yeshurun, Nguyen and Hasson, 2021). Moreover, there are other parts of the brain that likely play a role in social cognition outside of the MFPN, such as the fusiform gyrus for face recognition and the amygdala for recognition of emotion in facial expressions. And so, though a range of social tasks reliably recruit the MFPN, activation of the MFPN does not always imply social cognition."

21 **70 percent of our conversations are social in nature:** This is an oversimplification of how our brains work, but a useful one for illustrative purposes. Usually, many different parts of our brains are working at the same time, and the distinctions between these portions of our brains can be unclear.

21 **the decision-making mindset becoming dominant:** As Beau Sievers wrote, there is "evidence that strongly suggests that when people are using the same brain networks, this is no guarantee that they are in the same mindset, and vice versa." Sievers wrote that rather than rely on thinking of certain neural networks becoming activated, it is best to use the "notion of mindset that does not require specific and reliable recruitment of single brain networks. A mindset could just be a predisposition to use one's whole brain in a particular way when presented with certain kinds of information. On this account, a brain being in a mindset is

like an orchestra playing a symphony; many symphonies are possible, but only one at a time."

21 **Psychologists who study married couples:** Caleb Kealoha, "We Are (Not) in Sync: Inter-brain Synchrony During Interpersonal Conflict" (honors thesis, University of California, Los Angeles, 2020).

21 **one prominent researcher, John Gottman:** John M. Gottman, "Emotional Responsiveness in Marital Conversations," *Journal of Communication* 32, no. 3 (1982): 108–20. There are many different reasons couples experience conflict and tension, and many ways to overcome them. Some are described here and in chapter 5. It is also worth noting that approaches to diagnosing and dealing with marital challenges are myriad. Gottman, himself, has written extensively about the "Four Horsemen" of communication issues that can harm relationships: criticism, contempt, defensiveness, and stonewalling. In response to fact-checking inquiries, Gottman wrote that "there are several findings for the 'masters' of relationship: Maintaining trust and commitment, during conflict a positive-to-negative ratio equal to or exceeding 5 to 1, no four horsemen (criticism, defensiveness, contempt, stonewalling), turning toward bids for connection at least 86 percent of the time, love maps (knowing other person's inner psychological world), expressing fondness and admiration, using softened startup, effective repair during conflict, and effective psychological smoothing during conflict, an ability to deal with the existential part of gridlocked conflict."

22 **Happy couples ask each other more questions:** Adela C. Timmons, Gayla Margolin, and Darby E. Saxbe, "Physiological Linkage in Couples and Its Implications for Individual and Interpersonal Functioning: A Literature Review," *Journal of Family Psychology* 29, no. 5 (2015): 720.

24 **But she didn't seem to mind:** Lawler mentioned that his decision to play with her son while the woman was on the phone, in his opinion, was also what helped forge a connection. "That actually, I think, is what touched her," he told me. "I did that simply because it was the right thing to do, not because I was trying to sell her any steel. It was just being human and the right thing to do."

27 **"A case officer creates an ever-deeper relationship":** Randy Burkett, "An Alternative Framework for Agent Recruitment: From MICE to RASCLS," *Studies in Intelligence* 57, no. 1 (2013): 7–17.

A GUIDE TO USING THESE IDEAS, PART I: THE FOUR RULES FOR A MEANINGFUL CONVERSATION

31 **In one project:** This project was described to me by participants on the condition of confidentiality.

CHAPTER TWO: EVERY CONVERSATION IS A NEGOTIATION

37 **a cold November morning in 1985:** The jury deliberations in *Wisconsin vs. Leroy Reed* were filmed by television producers and portions of those recordings were eventually made into a program for *Frontline* titled "Inside the Jury Room." For information on this trial and deliberations, I am indebted to Douglas Maynard, who was kind enough to share transcripts of the full deliberations with me (the *Frontline* program contains only a partial selection of jurors' comments). I am also grateful to the producers of the *Frontline* episode. Transcripts are quoted nearly verbatim, though many exchanges, asides, and interstitial dialogues have not been included. I also relied upon "But Did He Know It Was a *Gun*?," International Pragmatics Association Meeting, Mexico City, July 5, 1996; "Truth, But Not the Whole Truth," *The Wall Street Journal*, April 14, 1986; Douglas W. Maynard and John F. Manzo, "On the Sociology of Justice: Theoretical Notes from an Actual Jury Deliberation," *Sociological Theory* (1993): 171–93.

39 **"not be swayed by sympathy":** Taken from Wis JI-Criminal 460, Wisconsin Criminal Jury Instructions.

43 **Dr. Behfar Ehdaie specialized in treating prostate cancer:** For more on the work of Drs. Ehdaie and Malhotra, please see "Negotiation Strategies for Doctors—and Hospitals," *Harvard Business Review*, October 21, 2013; "Bargaining Over How to Treat Cancer," *The Wall Street Journal*, September 2, 2017; Behfar Ehdaie et al., "A Systematic Approach to Discussing Active Surveillance with Patients with Low-Risk Prostate Cancer," *European Urology* 71, no. 6 (2017): 866–71; Deepak Malhotra, *Negotiating the Impossible: How to Break Deadlocks and Resolve Ugly Conflicts (Without Money or Muscle)* (Oakland, Calif.: Berrett-Koehler, 2016). In response to fact-checking, Ehdaie clarified that he felt that patients could hear him, but he was not discussing prostate cancer risk in an effective manner.

43 **doctors advise against surgery:** Laurence Klotz, "Active Surveillance for Prostate Cancer: For Whom?" *Journal of Clinical Oncology* 23, no. 32 (2005): 8165–69; Marc A. Dall'Era et al., "Active Surveillance for Prostate Cancer: A Systematic Review of the Literature," *European Urology* 62, no. 6 (2012): 976–83.

43 **Active surveillance carries its own risks:** Ehdaie explained that "active surveillance aims to monitor a cancer closely and intervene within the window of cure to treat the prostate cancer. . . . Dying with prostate cancer may apply only to older and more unhealthy men. . . . We also enroll younger men with prostate cancer into active surveillance because the evidence demonstrates that these men do as well as men with initial surgery or radiation therapy because we are monitoring their cancer closely and can intervene within the window of

cure, or the cancer will remain low risk for their lifetime and never require treatment."

43 **he felt active surveillance was the right decision:** Ehdaie stressed that the risk associated with active surveillance is not equivalent to a 3 percent mortality and that, in fact, "studies demonstrate that there are no differences in survival between immediate treatment and active surveillance for low-risk disease."

45 **Surveys indicate that:** According to the American Cancer Society, there are roughly 268,000 prostate cancer diagnoses per year, based on the most recent data. If roughly half of those are low-risk, and the rate of choosing active surveillance is roughly 60 percent (estimates provided by Dr. Ehdaie), then roughly 53,000 men per year are opting for surgeries that might not be necessary.

45 **opt for unnecessary surgeries:** Matthew R. Cooperberg, William Meeks, Raymond Fang, Franklin D. Gaylis, William J. Catalona, and Danil V. Makarov, "Time Trends and Variation in the Use of Active Surveillance for Management of Low-Risk Prostate Cancer in the US," *JAMA network open* 6, no. 3 (2023): e231439-e231439.

45 **negotiate a peace deal:** The Colombia Negotiations Initiative, Harvard Law School.

45 **Malhotra analyzed:** Deepak Malhotra and M.A.L.Y. Hout, "Negotiating on Thin Ice: The 2004–2005 NHL Dispute (A)," *Harvard Business School Cases* 1 (2006).

45 **describes formal negotiations:** Malhotra, in response to fact-checking inquiries, said, "I've worked on many different kinds of negotiations for a long time, not just what you refer to here as 'formal' negotiations" and that "Dr. Ehdaie's situation was not the first time I was dealing with something that most other people might not immediately think of as a 'negotiation.'"

46 **task in any negotiation:** "Ask Better Negotiation Questions: Use Negotiation Questions to Gather Information That Will Expand the Possibilities," Harvard Law School, August 8, 2022; Edward W. Miles, "Developing Strategies for Asking Questions in Negotiation," *Negotiation Journal* 29, no. 4 (2013): 383–412.

47 **a few weeks later:** In keeping with patient confidentiality, this case was only described to me in general terms, and some details were changed to protect patient privacy.

49 **training other surgeons:** In addition to the interventions described in this chapter, Ehdaie and Malhotra developed additional methods of encouraging these conversations. For more, please see "Negotiation Strategies for Doctors—and Hospitals"; "Bargaining Over How to Treat Cancer"; and Malhotra's *Negotiating the Impossible.*

49 **"tell you who they are":** Ehdaie wrote that he would describe his work this way: "We created a systematic approach using all of the communication tools adapted from negotiation theory with Dr. Malhotra. People find credibility in situations in which someone is recommending opposite their perceived bias. In this case, I wanted to make sure patients realized that I am also a surgeon (not just the AS physician) and believe strongly in surgery for the appropriate patients. However, in patients with low-risk prostate cancer, I believe that AS is the preferred option.... We reduced surgery by 30%. We do believe that a systematic approach using these methods helps better communicate risk to patients, strengthen patient autonomy in their decisions, and helps medical decision making across disciplines."

50 **Numerous studies have found:** In 2018—the last year for which reliable statistics are available—only 14 percent of people who opted for a jury trial for federal crimes were found innocent. Leroy Reed was being tried in state, rather than federal, court, but the trend is similar. John Gramlich, "Only 2% of Federal Criminal Defendants Go to Trial, and Most Who Do Are Found Guilty," Pew Research Center, June 11, 2019.

51 **"I want to listen":** In some places, including here, the transcript of deliberations has been edited or condensed for clarity.

52 **"improve the theory":** "History of the Harvard Negotiation Project," Harvard Law School.

53 **Fisher, a Harvard law professor:** Roger Fisher (1922–2012), Harvard Law School, August 27, 2012.

53 **Fisher and his colleagues wrote:** In response to a fact-checking email, Sheila Heen, a professor at Harvard Law School who worked with Fisher, wrote, "Fisher pointed out that each party actually needs to have their interests met in order to say yes to any agreement, and this means that each of us should care about finding ways to understand and meet others' interests as well as our own, if we are to find solutions to our shared challenges."

58 ***logic of costs*:** The *logic of costs and benefits* and the *logic of similarities* can also be referred to as the *logic of consequences* and the *logic of appropriateness.* For more on these kinds of thinking, please see: Long Wang, Chen-Bo Zhong, and J. Keith Murnighan, "The Social and Ethical Consequences of a Calculative Mindset," *Organizational Behavior and Human Decision Processes* 125, no. 1 (2014): 39–49; J. Mark Weber, Shirli Kopelman, and David M. Messick, "A Conceptual Review of Decision Making in Social Dilemmas: Applying a Logic of Appropriateness," *Personality and Social Psychology Review* 8, no. 3 (2004): 281–307; Johan P. Olsen and James G. March, *The Logic of Appropriateness* (Norway: ARENA, 2004); Daniel A. Newark and Markus C. Becker, "Bringing the Logic of Appropriateness into the

Lab: An Experimental Study of Behavior and Cognition," in *Carnegie Goes to California: Advancing and Celebrating the Work of James G. March* (United Kingdom: Emerald Publishing, 2021); Jason C. Coronel et al., "Evaluating Didactic and Exemplar Information: Noninvasive Brain Stimulation Reveals Message-Processing Mechanisms," *Communication Research* 49, no. 2 (2022): 268–95; Tim Althoff, Cristian Danescu-Niculescu-Mizil, and Dan Jurafsky, "How to Ask for a Favor: A Case Study on the Success of Altruistic Requests," *Proceedings of the International AAAI Conference on Web and Social Media* 8, no. 1 (2014): 12–21.

61 **They are now at nine votes:** The transcript is slightly ambiguous regarding this vote: One ballot was not read aloud. But, based on subsequent dialogue, it appears there were three votes for guilt, and nine votes for acquittal.

62 **"when the cop pulled me over":** This comment comes from an interview with juror James Pepper, not the transcript of the deliberations.

A GUIDE TO USING THESE IDEAS, PART II: ASKING QUESTIONS AND NOTICING CLUES

68 **researchers at Harvard:** Michael Yeomans and Alison Wood Brooks, "Topic Preference Detection: A Novel Approach to Understand Perspective Taking in Conversation," Harvard Business School Working Paper No. 20-077, February 2020.

70 **Researchers at Harvard and other universities have looked:** Ibid.; Anna Goldfarb, "Have an Upbeat Conversation," *New York Times,* May 19, 2020.

CHAPTER THREE: THE LISTENING CURE

80 **Epley was just the person:** For more on Nicholas Epley's fascinating research, please let me recommend his book *Mindwise: Why We Misunderstand What Others Think, Believe, Feel, and Want* (New York: Vintage, 2015).

81 **The key to starting:** For more on research into asking questions, let me recommend Alison Wood Brooks and Leslie K. John, "The Surprising Power of Questions," *Harvard Business Review* 96, no. 3 (2018): 60–67; Karen Huang et al., "It Doesn't Hurt to Ask: Question-Asking Increases Liking," *Journal of Personality and Social Psychology* 113, no. 3 (2017): 430; Einav Hart, Eric M. VanEpps, and Maurice E. Schweitzer, "The (Better Than Expected) Consequences of Asking Sensitive Questions," *Organizational Behavior and Human Decision Processes* 162 (2021): 136–54.

84 **"I had to sit with that":** Epley wrote to me that some of the most powerful conversations after the second drunk-driving incident also occurred with his par-

ents. "It hit me like a sledgehammer during this time that I had the capacity to really ruin my life. I stopped drinking immediately . . . including all through college . . . and have not been drunk a single time since."

86 **Psychology journals noted:** Rachel A. Ryskin et al., "Perspective-Taking in Comprehension, Production, and Memory: An Individual Differences Approach," *Journal of Experimental Psychology: General* 144, no. 5 (2015): 898.

86 **"perspective taking":** Roderick M. Kramer and Todd L. Pittinsky, eds., *Restoring Trust in Organizations and Leaders: Enduring Challenges and Emerging Answers* (New York: Oxford University Press, 2012).

86 **"constitutes a vital skill":** Sandra Pineda De Forsberg and Roland Reichenbach, *Conflict, Negotiation and Perspective Taking* (United Kingdom: Cambridge Scholars Publishing, 2021).

87 **psychology textbooks had it wrong:** Epley wrote that "I wouldn't say that 'perspective-getting' ever struck any of us as particularly insightful. It seemed ridiculously obvious."

88 **focused on perspective *getting*:** Tal Eyal, Mary Steffel, and Nicholas Epley, "Perspective Mistaking: Accurately Understanding the Mind of Another Requires Getting Perspective, Not Taking Perspective," *Journal of Personality and Social Psychology* 114, no. 4 (2018): 547; Haotian Zhou, Elizabeth A. Majka, and Nicholas Epley, "Inferring Perspective Versus Getting Perspective: Underestimating the Value of Being in Another Person's Shoes," *Psychological Science* 28, no. 4 (2017): 482–93. Epley said that "By perspective-taking, you're trying to imagine what's on the mind of another person, trying to put yourself in their shoes and see things from their point of view. Perspective-getting is when you actually ask them what's on their mind, and what their point of view is, and you just listen to what they have to say. When I use the term 'perspective-taking' scientifically, typically what I mean is what psychologists are asking people to do in an experiment—to take somebody's perspective, imagine trying to see things from their point of view. It's all in-your-head mental gymnastics. 'Perspective-getting' is asking them what they think about X, Y, or Z, and then listening to what they say. You're getting their perspective from them. Those are two very different things."

89 **"a practical methodology":** Arthur Aron et al., "The Experimental Generation of Interpersonal Closeness: A Procedure and Some Preliminary Findings," *Personality and Social Psychology Bulletin* 23, no. 4 (1997): 363–77. As Arthur Aron noted in response to a fact-checking inquiry, students helped collect data in this experiment.

89 **"We have taken great care":** The full quote is "We have taken great care in matching partners. Based on our experience in previous research we expect that you and your partner will like one another—that is, you have been matched with someone we expect you will like and who will like you."

89 **A series of thirty-six questions:** Some questions from the Fast Friends Procedure have been edited for brevity. The full list of thirty-six questions is:

1. Given the choice of anyone in the world, whom would you want as a dinner guest? 2. Would you like to be famous? In what way? 3. Before making a telephone call, do you ever rehearse what you are going to say? Why? 4. What would constitute a "perfect" day for you? 5. When did you last sing to yourself? To someone else? 6. If you were able to live to the age of ninety and retain either the mind or body of a thirty-year-old for the last sixty years of your life, which would you want? 7. Do you have a secret hunch about how you will die? 8. Name three things you and your partner appear to have in common. 9. For what in your life do you feel most grateful? 10. If you could change anything about the way you were raised, what would it be? 11. Take four minutes and tell your partner your life story in as much detail as possible. 12. If you could wake up tomorrow having gained any one quality or ability, what would it be? 13. If a crystal ball could tell you the truth about yourself, your life, the future, or anything else, what would you want to know? 14. Is there something that you've dreamed of doing for a long time? Why haven't you done it? 15. What is the greatest accomplishment of your life? 16. What do you value most in a friendship? 17. What is your most treasured memory? 18. What is your most terrible memory? 19. If you knew that in one year you would die suddenly, would you change anything about the way you are now living? Why? 20. What does friendship mean to you? 21. What roles do love and affection play in your life? 22. Alternate sharing something you consider a positive characteristic of your partner. Share a total of five items. 23. How close and warm is your family? Do you feel your childhood was happier than most other people's? 24. How do you feel about your relationship with your mother? 25. Make three true "we" statements each. For instance, "We are both in this room feeling . . ." 26. Complete this sentence: "I wish I had someone with whom I could share . . ." 27. If you were going to become a close friend with your partner, please share what would be important for them to know. 28. Tell your partner what you like about them, be very honest this time, saying things that you might not say to someone you've just met. 29. Share with your partner an embarrassing moment in your life. 30. When did you last cry in front of another person? By yourself? 31. Tell your partner something that you like about them [already]. 32. What, if anything, is too serious to be joked about? 33. If you were to die this evening with no opportunity to communicate with anyone, what would you most regret not having told someone? Why haven't you told them yet? 34. Your house, containing everything you own, catches fire. After saving your loved ones and pets, you have time to safely make a final dash to save any one item. What would it be? Why? 35. Of all the people in your family, whose death would you find most disturbing? Why? 36. Share a personal problem and ask your partner's advice on how they

might handle it. Also, ask your partner to reflect back to you how you seem to be feeling about the problem you have chosen.

91 **if a question was likely:** These questions come from the first study in "The Experimental Generation of Interpersonal Closeness: A Procedure and Some Preliminary Findings," which was focused on establishing small-talk conditions.

91 **reveal vulnerabilities:** It is worth noting that there are some downsides to revealing vulnerabilities. As Margaret Clark, a psychology professor at Yale, said: "In general, it's absolutely correct that you are not going to get people being empathic or giving you the support that you need, unless you're vulnerable and revealing your needs and feelings and so forth. People need that in order to provide support. I can be vulnerable with a friend who really cares about me. However, there are circumstances where it's very unwise. The most obvious one is if the other person doesn't care about you and could use that information to take advantage of you rather than support you. You've got to read if the other person cares for you correctly. In the early stage of a relationship, vulnerability is good, but revealing too much too soon can go wrong. There's a pacing to it. In developing relationships, you do want to be vulnerable *and* you want to maintain some self-protection."

91 **"emotional contagion":** Kavadi Teja Sree, "Emotional Contagion in Teenagers and Women," *International Journal of Scientific Research and Engineering Trends* 7, no. 2 (2021): 917–24.

92 **"10-week-old infants":** Elaine Hatfield, John T. Cacioppo, and Richard L. Rapson, "Primitive Emotional Contagion" in *Emotion and Social Behavior,* ed. M. S. Clark (Newbury Park, Calif.: Sage, 1992), 151–77.

93 **In a separate experiment:** The one-at-a-time study mentioned in this section was not conducted by the Arons. In a fact-checking discussion, Arthur Aron clarified that subsequent experiments have revealed two things: First, one of the major factors influencing interpersonal closeness is whether someone believes the other person likes them. Second, responsiveness and reciprocity—rather than just self-disclosure—is the predominant factor in establishing a sense of closeness. "Feeling like your partner is responsive to you is a huge factor," Aron told me.

94 **thirty-six questions are effective:** Arthur Aron wrote: "What we know today is that the key thing is that this provides an opportunity for each party to provide meaningful responsiveness."

94 **"Reciprocity is nuanced":** Professor Clark of Yale elaborated: "When my husband had a medical problem, a cousin of mine provided lots of support and didn't talk about his own problems at all. A couple of years later, his wife got sick and he called me and was revealing what was going on and how upset he was.

And *then* I provided the reciprocal support—two years later. The rule is not reciprocity in the moment, it's being responsive to each other's needs, and that responsiveness going both ways."

94 **"they are more likely":** Jacqueline S. Smith, Victoria L. Brescoll, and Erin L. Thomas, "Constrained by Emotion: Women, Leadership, and Expressing Emotion in the Workplace," in *Handbook on Well-Being of Working Women* (Netherlands: Springer, 2016), 209–24.

96 **people tended to ask:** Huang et al., "It Doesn't Hurt to Ask," 430. In response to fact-checking questions, Michael Yeomans, one of the researchers on this study, said that the "paper was about follow-up questions—that build on topics that go deeper." For more on topic starters, please see Hart, VanEpps, and Schweitzer, "(Better Than Expected) Consequences of Asking Sensitive Questions," 136–54.

98 **"that's sometimes enough to get":** It's important to note that though deep questions can undermine some stereotypes, to rid workplaces of double standards requires sustained effort and examining structural causes of bias. Heilman stressed that simply teaching people to ask a certain kind of question, alone, is not enough. For more on how to undermine these prejudices and stereotypes, please see chapters 6 and 7.

98 **"Follow-ups are a signal":** Michael Yeomans is now affiliated with Imperial College London.

99 **a few specific questions:** These questions have been edited for brevity. The full list of questions can be found in Michael Kardas, Amit Kumar, and Nicholas Epley, "Overly Shallow?: Miscalibrated Expectations Create a Barrier to Deeper Conversation," *Journal of Personality and Social Psychology* 122, no. 3 (2022): 367. For this version of the experiment, the questions included: 1. For what in your life do you feel most grateful? Tell the other participant about it. 2. If a crystal ball could tell you the truth about yourself, your life, your future, or anything else, what would you want to know? 3. Can you describe a time you cried in front of another person?

99 **Epley suspected:** Epley elaborated: "I think what our data suggests is that the runway up to the more meaningful questions can be a lot steeper than you'd guess. . . . Treat somebody as a close friend—that's kind of the heuristic that I take from our work."

99 **chance to test his theory:** Epley emphasized that "we design experiments to *test* hypotheses, not 'to show' or 'to prove' anything. Designing experiments 'to show' a result or 'to prove' a belief is what propaganda looks like. So, I would say, I wanted to test our theory, with data, that deeper conversations would be more positive than people expected." He also wrote that, although emotional contagion is one of the mechanisms making deep conversations powerful, there are other

mechanisms that may be even more impactful, "such as reciprocating trust in each other, which builds over time, while also really learning meaningful things about the other person through the content of the conversation. That's what really builds connection."

100 **Epley later reported:** Kardas, Kumar, and Epley, "Overly Shallow?," 367.

101 **Dozens of other studies:** Huang et al., "It Doesn't Hurt to Ask," 430; Nora Cate Schaeffer and Stanley Presser, "The Science of Asking Questions," *Annual Review of Sociology* 29, no. 1 (2003): 65–88; Norbert Schwarz et al., "The Psychology of Asking Questions," *International Handbook of Survey Methodology* (2012): 18–34; Edward L. Baker and Roderick Gilkey, "Asking Better Questions—A Core Leadership Skill," *Journal of Public Health Management and Practice* 26, no. 6 (2020): 632–33; Patti Williams, Gavan J. Fitzsimons, and Lauren G. Block, "When Consumers Do Not Recognize 'Benign' Intention Questions as Persuasion Attempts," *Journal of Consumer Research* 31, no. 3 (2004): 540–50; Richard E. Petty, John T. Cacioppo, and Martin Heesacker, "Effects of Rhetorical Questions on Persuasion: A Cognitive Response Analysis," *Journal of Personality and Social Psychology* 40, no. 3 (1981): 432.

101 **"questioners assumed":** "The Case for Asking Sensitive Questions," *Harvard Business Review,* November 24, 2020.

CHAPTER FOUR: HOW DO YOU HEAR EMOTIONS NO ONE SAYS ALOUD?

104 **the man would take forever:** In an email responding to fact-checking questions, Prady provided further detail: "Specifically it was that despite his mathematical genius (he was capable of doing things like converting from decimal to hexadecimal in his head), he was unable to process the phrase 'quality of service.' The formula for a tip is 15%–20% depending on 'quality of service.' Despite his mathematical prowess, he was unable to evaluate the *human* factor present in 'quality of service.' In fact, we once suggested he always tip 17½% and he pointed out that the odds that the service was *exactly middling* were infinitesimally small, and that 17½% would ensure he was nearly always over or undertipping."

105 **Computer programmers, they decided:** In response to a fact-checking inquiry, Prady explained, "The decision to not make them computer programmers was twofold. First, in the time that had passed since my time in the software industry, it had evolved from garage start-ups to big Microsoft-sized businesses, and we didn't want the characters engaged in business. Second, the specific work of programming, which involves staring at screens and typing, is difficult to depict

on television and might be boring for the viewer." Prady felt strongly that it should be emphasized that the vocation of programming, itself, is not boring, "Nothing could be further from the truth—programming is exhilarating."

105 **be the kind of people:** For background on *The Big Bang Theory,* I am indebted to Jessica Radloff, *The Big Bang Theory: The Definitive, Inside Story of the Epic Hit Series* (New York: Grand Central Publishing, 2022); "There's a Science to CBS' *Big Bang Theory,*" *USA Today,* April 11, 2007; "Why the *Big Bang Theory* Stars Took Surprising Pay Cuts," *Hollywood Reporter,* March 29, 2017; "TV Fact-Checker: Dropping Science on *The Big Bang Theory,*" *Wired,* September 22, 2011; Dave Goetsch, "Collaboration—Lessons from *The Big Bang Theory,*" *True WELLth,* podcast, June 4, 2019; "*The Big Bang Theory:* 'We Didn't Appreciate How Protective the Audience Would Feel About Our Guys,'" *Variety,* May 5, 2009; "Yes, It's a *Big Bang,*" *Deseret Morning News,* September 22, 2007.

106 **"you have an entire lifetime":** *The Big Bang Theory,* season 3, episode 1, "The Electric Can Opener Fluctuation," aired September 21, 2009.

106 **"People's emotions are rarely":** Daniel Goleman, "Emotional Intelligence: Why It Can Matter More than IQ," *Learning* 24, no. 6 (1996): 49–50.

107 **shot the pilot:** "*The Big Bang Theory* Creators Bill Prady and Chuck Lorre Discuss the Series—And the Pilot You Didn't See," *Entertainment Weekly,* September 23, 2022.

107 **Were the physicists innocent:** Prady said that "I think the audience was protective of [Sheldon and Leonard] and felt that the characters around them, especially Katie, represented danger for them. We were surprised at how protective test audiences were of Leonard and Sheldon."

108 **Their body language:** Judith A. Hall, Terrence G. Horgan, and Nora A. Murphy, "Nonverbal Communication," *Annual Review of Psychology* 70 (2019): 271–94; Albert Mehrabian, *Nonverbal Communication* (United Kingdom: Routledge, 2017); Robert G. Harper, Arthur N. Wiens, and Joseph D. Matarazzo, *Nonverbal Communication: The State of the Art* (New York: John Wiley and Sons, 1978); Starkey Duncan, Jr., "Nonverbal Communication," *Psychological Bulletin* 72, no. 2 (1969): 118; Michael Eaves and Dale G. Leathers, *Successful Nonverbal Communication: Principles and Applications* (United Kingdom: Routledge, 2017); Martin S. Remland, *Nonverbal Communication in Everyday Life* (Los Angeles: Sage, 2016); Jessica L. Tracy, Daniel Randles, and Conor M. Steckler, "The Nonverbal Communication of Emotions," *Current Opinion in Behavioral Sciences* 3 (2015): 25–30.

108 **lulls us into ignoring:** In response to fact-checking inquiries, Professor Judith Hall of Northeastern University said that this process of "overlooking" nonverbal signals is complex, "as many nonverbal signals and leakages do penetrate, nonconsciously, into our brains. We might choose to 'ignore' something while the

cues have actually been registered at a nonconscious level. Then, of course, sometimes we do actually miss cues."

108 **psychiatrist named Terence McGuire:** I interviewed Terence McGuire in 2017. He passed away in 2022, and as a result was not able to participate in fact-checking for this chapter. For fact-checking purposes, the contents of this chapter, as it applies to NASA and McGuire, were shared with NASA, which confirmed some details but declined to comment on specifics regarding candidate interviews, and with McGuire's daughter, Bethany Sexton, who confirmed the details in this chapter, including the methods McGuire used in analyzing candidates. In addition, I spoke to numerous people who worked with McGuire, as well as people who have worked with NASA in screening astronaut applicants. I am also indebted to: "This Is How NASA Used to Hire Its Astronauts 20 Years Ago—And It Still Works Today," Quartz, August 27, 2015; "The History of the Process Communication Model in Astronaut Selection," SSCA, December, 2000; T. F. McGuire, *Astronauts: Reflections on Current Selection Methodology, Astronaut Personality, and the Space Station* (Houston: NASA, 1987); Terence McGuire, "PCM Under Cover," Kahler Communications Oceania.

109 **had been relatively brief:** Soviet cosmonauts had done much longer missions.

109 **Reagan ordered NASA:** "History and Timeline of the ISS," ISS National Laboratory.

109 **"advent of the space station":** McGuire, *Astronauts.*

109 **"social intelligence that involves":** Peter Salovey and John D. Mayer, "Emotional Intelligence," *Imagination, Cognition and Personality* 9, no. 3 (1990): 185–211.

110 **had found that this despondency:** "It's Not Rocket Science: The Importance of Psychology in Space Travel," *The Independent,* February 17, 2021.

110 **mission control's tone of voice:** Schirra had said, prior to this mission, that he intended to retire. In response to fact-checking inquiries, Andrew Chaikin, a historian of space travel, said, "The basic fact is that Schirra had a strong belief that during a flight the mission commander—that is, himself—was in charge, not mission control."

112 **Robert Provine had started:** Robert R. Provine, *Laughter: A Scientific Investigation* (New York: Penguin, 2001); Chiara Mazzocconi, Ye Tian, and Jonathan Ginzburg, "What's Your Laughter Doing There? A Taxonomy of the Pragmatic Functions of Laughter," *IEEE Transactions on Affective Computing* 13, no. 3 (2020): 1302–21; Robert R. Provine, "Laughing, Tickling, and the Evolution of Speech and Self," *Current Directions in Psychological Science* 13, no. 6 (2004): 215–18; Christopher Oveis et al., "Laughter Conveys Status," *Journal of Experimental Social Psychol-*

ogy 65 (2016): 109–15; Michael J. Owren and Jo-Anne Bachorowski, "Reconsidering the Evolution of Nonlinguistic Communication: The Case of Laughter," *Journal of Nonverbal Behavior* 27 (2003): 183–200; Jo-Anne Bachorowski and Michael J. Owren, "Not All Laughs Are Alike: Voiced but Not Unvoiced Laughter Readily Elicits Positive Affect," *Psychological Science* 12, no. 3 (2001): 252–57; Robert R. Provine and Kenneth R. Fischer, "Laughing, Smiling, and Talking: Relation to Sleeping and Social Context in Humans," *Ethology* 83, no. 4 (1989): 295–305.

112 **"naturally occurring human laughter":** Robert R. Provine, "Laughter," *American Scientist* 84, no. 1 (1996): 38–45.

113 **"immediate and involuntary":** Provine, *Laughter: A Scientific Investigation.*

115 **tell when people felt aligned:** Gregory A. Bryant, "Evolution, Structure, and Functions of Human Laughter," in *The Handbook of Communication Science and Biology* (United Kingdom: Routledge, 2020), 63–77. In response to fact-checking inquiries, Bryant said that "listeners could distinguish between friends laughing together and strangers laughing together. . . . I think it's a reasonable speculation that people are detecting alignment in some sense, but technically the task was just to detect friends versus strangers. Our interpretation was more general, which is that friends are more aroused when engaged in conversation, reflected in their genuine laughter, as opposed to the lower arousal volitional laughter more common between strangers. Listeners are highly sensitive to it. I do like the idea that people are looking for evidence of attempts to connect."

115 **"mood," or what psychologists:** The use of words *mood* and *energy* in this context, though conforming to dictionary definitions, does not align perfectly with how those words are sometimes used by research psychologists. Lisa Feldman Barrett, a professor of psychology at Northeastern University, explained that " 'mood' is described by two properties, valence and arousal. Mood is not a synonym for valence. We use 'affect' to mean properties of consciousness, whether or not a person is emotional. We use 'affect' as synonymous with 'mood.' Some scientists use 'mood' to refer to moments of feeling that are not emotions, which they define as not linked to events in the world. I think that is incorrect, because a brain is always processing internal sensations, which gives rise to . . . your feelings, in conjunction with sense data from the world." For more on these topics, please see James A. Russell, "A Circumplex Model of Affect," *Journal of Personality and Social Psychology* 39, no. 6 (1980): 1161; James A. Russell and Lisa Feldman Barrett, "Core Affect, Prototypical Emotional Episodes, and Other Things Called Emotion: Dissecting the Elephant," *Journal of Personality and Social Psychology* 76, no. 5 (1999): 805; Elizabeth A. Kensinger, "Remembering Emotional Experiences: The Contribution of Valence and Arousal," *Reviews in the Neurosciences* 15, no. 4 (2004): 241–52; Elizabeth A. Kensinger and Suzanne Corkin, "Two Routes to

Emotional Memory: Distinct Neural Processes for Valence and Arousal," *Proceedings of the National Academy of Sciences* 101, no. 9 (2004): 3310–15.

115 ***feeling positive or negative*****:** While some psychologists use the words *positive* or *negative* in this context, Barrett argues that a more appropriate framing "is 'pleasant-unpleasant.' . . . 'Positive' or 'negative' . . . can be descriptive (like *I feel good*) or it can be evaluative (like *it's good that I feel this way*). . . . So it's really 'pleasant,' 'unpleasant.'"

116 **your brain has evolved:** Dacher Keltner et al., "Emotional Expression: Advances in Basic Emotion Theory," *Journal of Nonverbal Behavior* 43 (2019): 133–60; Alan S. Cowen et al., "Mapping 24 Emotions Conveyed by Brief Human Vocalization," *American Psychologist* 74, no. 6 (2019): 698; Emiliana R. Simon-Thomas et al., "The Voice Conveys Specific Emotions: Evidence from Vocal Burst Displays," *Emotion* 9, no. 6 (2009): 838; Ursula Hess and Agneta Fischer, "Emotional Mimicry as Social Regulation," *Personality and Social Psychology Review* 17, no. 2 (2013): 142–57; Jean-Julien Aucouturier et al., "Covert Digital Manipulation of Vocal Emotion Alter Speakers' Emotional States in a Congruent Direction," *Proceedings of the National Academy of Sciences* 113, no. 4 (2016): 948–53.

117 **match someone's mood:** Barrett said that mirroring can be counterproductive if what your interlocutor needs is *instrumental support*: "I was trained as a therapist, like, a million years ago. But what a good communicator does is they figure out whether the person wants empathy, or they want instrumental support. If the person wants empathy, then you mirror them. If they want instrumental support, then you try to counteract what's happening to them. . . . If I try to calm my daughter down when she just wants me to be empathic, it will be bad. On the other hand, if I'm empathic with her when she needs me to be instrumental, it might make things worse. . . . So a good communicator tries to figure out, do they want empathy or do they want an instrumental support? . . . In the lingo, we call it pacing and leading. When I was the therapist, I would pace the person first. I would actually match their breath, and then I'd slow my breath down and then they would slow theirs down. So first I would entrain them, and then I would manipulate my own signal and they would manipulate theirs too, because they're already synced with me."

120 **McGuire suspected:** It is worth noting that McGuire's approach was informed by his interest in the "Process Communication Model," which attempts to identify someone's personality type by examining how they communicate. McGuire's daughter, Bethany Sexton, in response to fact-checking inquiries, wrote that the approach described in this chapter "was something that Terry used not only with the astronauts but throughout his practice for decades. Additionally he formed a very keen relationship with a colleague named Taibi Kahler,

PhD. At the time Taibi was studying transactional analysis and had put together a psychological and behavioral model called process communication. When Terry learned of Dr. Kahler's work, they connected and became fast friends. Terry used Taibi's model in the analysis of the astronauts. . . . Terry felt the model was so powerful it enabled him to assess the astronauts in a matter of minutes based on their word choice, mannerisms and ways of expression." It is also worth noting that some of the approaches McGuire used in interviewing candidates did not align with the facts of his life. For instance, he never had a sister.

123 **NASA selected the class:** "90-006: 1990 Astronaut Candidates Selected," NASA News; "Astronaut's Right Stuff Is Different Now," Associated Press, October 13, 1991.

124 **"I was so close":** Radloff, *Big Bang Theory.*

125 **"Significant improvement":** Some dialogue was excluded for brevity and appropriateness.

129 **"the audience went wild":** Radloff, *Big Bang Theory.*

129 **"characters you like":** "Emmy Watch: Critics' Picks," Associated Press, June 22, 2009.

CHAPTER FIVE: CONNECTING AMID CONFLICT

132 **the lockdown was over:** Jeffcoat told me the lockdown was caused by an altercation near the campus, but not on it.

132 **daughters to a movie:** Earlier that year, a gunman in Aurora, Colorado, had opened fire in a theater, killing twelve people.

133 **a public figure in the fight for gun control:** Jeffcoat prefers the term "gun safety" to "gun control."

133 **final season of *Lost*:** The final season of *Lost*, in case you were wondering, was great.

134 **Roughly half the nation:** Charles Duhigg, "The Real Roots of American Rage," *The Atlantic*, January/February, 2019; "Political Polarization," Pew Research Center, 2014.

134 **Roughly four in ten:** "Political Polarization and Media Habits," Pew Research Center, October 21, 2014.

134 **Over 80 percent:** Jeff Hayes, "Workplace Conflict and How Businesses Can Harness It to Thrive," *CPP Global Human Capital Report,* 2008.

134 **"Peace is not the absence":** This quote has also been attributed to Gandhi. Its original provenance, like many oft-quoted statements, is somewhat murky.

135 **event Jeffcoat had agreed:** The organizers of this project included Spaceship Media, Advance Local, Alabama Media Group, Essential Partners, journalists from various newspapers, and others.

135 **conduct an experiment:** In response to fact-checking inquiries, John Sarrouf of Essential Partners wrote, "I would say that the question at hand is whether we could sufficiently steep participants enough in a two-day dialogue experience and skill building to have them continue the conversation online for a month and keep the same kind of open and complex exchange that we were able to build in person."

135 **the vast majority of Americans:** "The Vast Majority of Americans Support Universal Background Checks. Why Doesn't Congress?," Harvard Kennedy School, 2016.

135 **Large majorities support bans:** "Polling Is Clear: Americans Want Gun Control," *Vox,* June 1, 2022.

135 **"Everyone is so focused":** Sarrouf clarified that he believes "there is a lack of trust of one another and . . . the language we have to discuss this issue pulls people further apart." His hope was to "illustrate the power of structured, intentional communication to repair trust, build relationships on mutual understanding, and generate the resilience to forces of polarization needed for collective action."

136 **Sheila Heen, a professor:** Heen is a coauthor of one of my favorite books on communication: *Difficult Conversations: How to Discuss What Matters Most* (New York: Penguin, 2010).

138 **"acknowledge the emotions":** Heen elaborated that "the deeper problem is a relationship problem, spurred by how we each feel treated by the other. This involves feelings, to be sure, but the feelings are a symptom rather than the problem. . . . The deeper problem is how we feel treated by the other person. And that's producing frustration, feeling alone or misunderstood and dismissed. . . . I think that for people who tend to say 'you just shouldn't be emotional' they're missing that actually it's how you're treating the other person that is the issue and possibly is a solution."

139 **furious and sad and worried:** Heen added that it's not just whether or not people in conflict admit their emotions, but also how they do so. "It could also be that they're *both* saying that they're furious and they're both just blaming each other. They're not getting to 'okay, I'm listening, let me try to understand why you're so mad.'"

141 **no less important goal:** Sarrouf described his goals this way: "Creating a space where what is invited from people is their deep listening, curiosity, desire to understand and be understood and experience a different way of engaging this

topic; and teaching participants communication skills." Sarrouf also emphasized that all the organizers' goals were explained to participants before the event began.

141 **"sense of psychological safety":** Dotan R. Castro et al., "Mere Listening Effect on Creativity and the Mediating Role of Psychological Safety," *Psychology of Aesthetics, Creativity, and the Arts* 12, no. 4 (2018): 489.

142 **expose their emotions:** Sarrouf explained that while feelings are part of this dialogue, "my point is to get them to talk about reasons. I want to hear about their stories. I want to hear about the values that underlie their beliefs. And I want them to talk about the complexity of their beliefs. Emotions are just a part of what comes out when people talk about those. . . . I don't want anybody to expose an emotion that they're not comfortable exposing. What I want them to do is to tell us a story about themselves rather than having other people tell a story about them, which is what we do to each other when we're in conflict. I have a story about you, and you have a story about me, and those stories are usually inaccurate. And this is an opportunity for you to re-author your own story."

142 ***looping for understanding*:** I first learned about *looping for understanding* from the journalist Amanda Ripley in her wonderful book *High Conflict: Why We Get Trapped and How We Get Out* (New York: Simon and Schuster, 2021). During the communication training in Washington, D.C., organizers did not refer to this technique as *looping for understanding*, or teach it as such, but rather taught a more general approach. Sarrouf explained that he calls his approach "full-spectrum listening" and that it is often used in "an exercise where four people get together. . . . You tell a story and three people are listening to you. One of them is listening for what happens, you know, the facts of what happened to you. The second person is listening for your values, and the things that you most care about in that story. . . . And the third person is listening [for] what emotions are coming through for you. . . . And then each of the three people listening reports back what they heard—and not just tell them whether they heard it right or not (although yes, there's definitely a little bit of that). More of what they're doing is actually learning from the three people who listened about themselves—things that they didn't even know were true for them, but because people were listening so deeply to them on different channels for different things, they came away with new insights about their own experience. . . . If you can learn to listen to all of the different messages that people are sharing when they speak you can actually learn not just the facts about their lives, but what's important to them, about what's important in their lives, what relationships they had, what their emotional journey was like, their commitments, their dilemmas."

143 **The goal is not to repeat:** G. Itzchakov, H. T. Reis, and N. Weinstein, "How to Foster Perceived Partner Responsiveness: High-Quality Listening Is Key," *Social*

and Personality Psychology Compass 16, no. 1 (2021); Brant R. Burleson, "What Counts as Effective Emotional Support," *Studies in Applied Interpersonal Communication* (2008): 207–27.

143 **"beginning of a conversation":** The researchers in this paper were studying conversational receptiveness, of which techniques like looping for understanding can be considered a component, but not the totality of this approach. The full quote from this paper reads: "Using field data from a setting where conflict management is endemic to productivity, we show that conversational receptiveness at the beginning of a conversation forestalls conflict escalation at the end. Specifically, Wikipedia editors who write more receptive posts are less prone to receiving personal attacks from disagreeing editors." Michael Yeomans et al., "Conversational Receptiveness: Improving Engagement with Opposing Views," *Organizational Behavior and Human Decision Processes* 160 (2020): 131–48.

145 **Heen teaches approaches:** Heen wrote, "I think that there are really three purposes for looping (or skillful active listening). 1. To help the talker better understand themselves(!). In a complicated conflict, I explain my perspective to you, but when you summarize it back to me, I often think, 'Well, yeah, but there's more to it for me. . . . It's also that . . .' So as the talker, my listener is helping me sort out a bunch of layers of why this matters to me and what my own interests and concerns and feelings are about it; 2. To help the listener better and more fully understand. (I sometimes ask each side, 'What do you think the other side doesn't "get" about your perspective?' and once explained, the listener actually says, 'Oh, gosh, yeah, I didn't get that part of it'); and 3. To let the talker *know* that the listener understands more fully—which also SHOWS the talker that the listener cares enough about the issue, and about the relationship, to work hard to get what's most important to them. So looping is doing all of this work, which is why it can so dramatically change the dynamic when it is done—and reciprocated—with sincerity."

145 **began in a curious way:** Sarrouf wrote, "What is described here is the first of three questions that were asked and responded to in the dialogue experience: 1. Could you tell us about a life experience you've had that has shaped your perspective or beliefs about firearms? 2. What's at the heart of the matter when you think about the role of firearms in our nation? 3. In what ways do you experience mixed feelings or feel pulled in different directions on the issue? Where do you find some of your values bumping up against other values as you think about this issue? We have people go around the circle answering these questions and then we open up the conversation to have them ask people questions of genuine curiosity. The purpose of the questions of genuine curiosity is to deepen understanding, follow curiosity, invite nuance and complexity, not just clarity."

149 **about 8 percent:** "How and Why Do American Couples Argue?," YouGov America, June 1, 2022.

149 **when it finally occurred:** In response to fact-checking questions, Benjamin Karney wrote that "it is accurate that the associations between marital conflict, as observed in the lab, and concurrent marital satisfaction, change in marital satisfaction, and divorce, is significant but not that strong. That means that, on average, couples who experience more conflict are at higher risk for poorer marital outcomes, but that still leaves plenty of couples who fight a lot and are perfectly fine for long periods of time. Why? Because the quality of couples' conflict is not the only thing that matters to their feelings about the relationship. It is just one element in an array of variables (including personality, family background, external stress, financial status) that also contribute to understanding how marriages succeed and fail."

149 **fought about similar issues:** Though it is generally true that couples argue about similar issues across demographics, there is research indicating that impoverished couples argue more about the stressors that accompany poverty, and that couples with specific problems—including medical or addiction issues—argue with greater frequency about those issues. Moreover, Karney emphasized that "a lot (virtually all) of this early work was conducted on relatively affluent, white couples. We are learning lots about conflict in recent years by expanding our focus beyond these samples, studying couples from lower-income neighborhoods. One finding: The way couples handle conflict is powerfully affected by factors that partners cannot control. Couples often cannot choose the sources of their disagreements, or the severity of them. It takes a lot of privilege to be able to choose the timing of your conflicts, and to have the time to process conflicts at all. We have also learned that teaching couples to have better conflicts is very hard to do, and that getting better . . . does not always improve relationships, especially when those relationships are challenged in other ways that the interventions do not touch. The wisdom of Integrative Behavioral Couples Therapy is not that it teaches self-control but that it encourages accepting your partner as a whole person with a history and limits."

150 **Benjamin Karney, who:** Karney wrote, "My understanding of this literature is that there were significant differences between satisfied and distressed couples in how they approached [discussions about disagreements]. For one thing, distressed couples exchanged more negative behaviors with each other than satisfied couples did. For another thing, some research using a 'talk table' approach that separated the intent of each partner's behavior from its impact found that satisfied and distressed couples did not differ in the intent behind their behaviors, but differed a lot in the impact of those behaviors. That is, in satisfied couples, intentions matched impact, but in distressed couples, intentions did not predict impact."

151 **more in control:** It is important to note that control is just one factor that influences couples' conflict. Karney wrote, "There is a whole lot going on in couples' conflicts, and struggles over control are one slice. . . . It's not just one thing that is going on when couples disagree. . . . Conflict arises when each partner wants something different, so whenever there is conflict, each partner is trying to get the other person to change or compromise. You can call that control, or you can call that trying to get what you want."

151 **session taped by researchers:** Transcripts were shared with me on the condition that the identities of participants, as well as other specifics that might reveal identities such as the location of the conversations, remain confidential.

154 **"when everyone feels in control":** Stanley wrote, "If I get a couple to structure a bit, slow down, and get pretty behavioral about how they are talking with turn-taking and listening (and cutting out the swipes), people calm down fast and the good stuff comes out. A couple can get to enacting all the great good stuff."

155 **plenty of ugliness:** Quotes from the Facebook discussion throughout this chapter include both posts made on the private Facebook page devoted to this group, as well as direct messages that were shared with me by participants.

155 **called each other idiots:** Sarrouf wrote, "One of the flaws of the design was that we brought six times more people into the group who were never really trained or oriented to our work. . . . I think it became harder when people who did not have the experience came in. The people we did train used some of their skills to help others, but it was not the same."

155 **"models of curiosity":** "Dialogue Journalism: The Method," Spaceship Media; "Dialogue Journalism Toolkit," Spaceship Media.

155 **speak with civility:** Sarrouf wrote that moderators also worked to "reemphasize the purpose of the engagement. So purpose is very important to us. We would remind people that purpose is to help understand one another, and to learn from each other, rather than to try to convince each other. That's a huge element of the work, so you'd step in to reemphasize purpose. You'd step in to reemphasize some of the communication agreements that were laid out which are also there to support people and their purpose. And maybe some of the skills that we learn like, you know, listening to understand, speaking to be understood, asking what is a genuinely curious question. Let's remember to ask genuinely curious questions, rather than gotcha questions or rhetorical questions."

156 **struggles for control:** As this chapter notes, there were multiple dynamics, beyond struggles over control, that disrupted the online conversations. As Sarrouf wrote in response to fact-checking inquiries, these other factors included marginalization of some participants; instances when participants did not adhere

to communication agreements the group had struck; and other patterns that prevented an open and diverse conversation. He wrote: "The purpose is to create an equality of speaking, invite people to speak to the point, help people who are listening hang in there."

158 **"hard to metabolize":** Heen added that this process can take a long time, because "our own views shift over time, and as we integrate how the other person sees it into our own perspective, our own perspective changes."

159 **"I am beginning to lose interest":** This is an edited version of the entire quote, which reads, in its entirety: "I am beginning to lose interest in this group. There is nothing to talk about. Nobody is interested in changing their mind. You either believe in the most fundamental human right there is—the right to defend one's self, family, community, and country—or you believe in the denial of that most fundamental right and the concentration of arms and monopolization of force in the hands of the political elite and their minions. I know that my mind is set on the issue, and that yours probably is too. That's OK. I appreciate the civility here, but I guess in the end I will see you at the ballot box."

159 **"I've used these skills":** These quotes come from multiple polls conducted by Essential Partners.

159 **"used to be intolerant":** Sarrouf wrote, "I think the thing to understand here is that it is less about some people rising above and others not, and more about building patterns and tendencies that make it more likely to choose to listen openly and ask honest questions than not. . . . I think we know and have known for a long time that we have tools and structures to help people talk about very difficult topics. . . . We learned that as people move to an online space with some good grounding training and awareness, communication agreements, good moderation, supportive journalists who contribute some balanced reporting, [and] a few people like Melanie and Jon who are really bought in, [then] you can make a better conversation."

A GUIDE TO USING THESE IDEAS, PART III: EMOTIONAL CONVERSATIONS, IN LIFE AND ONLINE

168 **Numerous studies have shown:** Tim Althoff, Cristian Danescu-Niculescu-Mizil, and Dan Jurafsky, "How to Ask for a Favor: A Case Study on the Success of Altruistic Requests," *Proceedings of the International AAAI Conference on Web and Social Media* 8, no. 1 (2014): 12–21; Cristian Danescu-Niculescu-Mizil et al., "How Opinions Are Received by Online Communities: A Case Study on Amazon.com Helpfulness Votes," *Proceedings of the 18th International Conference on World Wide Web,* April 2009, 141–50; Justine Zhang et al., "Conversations Gone Awry: Detect-

ing Early Signs of Conversational Failure," *Proceedings of the 56th Annual Meeting of the Association for Computational Linguistics* 1 (July 2018): 1350–61.

168 **When we criticize:** Zhang et al., "Conversations Gone Awry"; Justin Cheng, Cristian Danescu-Niculescu-Mizil, and Jure Leskovec, "Antisocial Behavior in Online Discussion Communities," *Proceedings of the International AAAI Conference on Web and Social Media* 9, no. 1 (2015): 61–70; Justin Cheng, Cristian Danescu-Niculescu-Mizil, and Jure Leskovec, "How Community Feedback Shapes User Behavior," *Proceedings of the International AAAI Conference on Web and Social Media* 8, no. 1 (2014): 41–50.

CHAPTER SIX: OUR SOCIAL IDENTITIES SHAPE OUR WORLDS

173 **these drugs without question:** Dewesh Kumar et al., "Understanding the Phases of Vaccine Hesitancy During the COVID-19 Pandemic," *Israel Journal of Health Policy Research* 11, no. 1 (2022): 1–5; Robert M. Jacobson, Jennifer L. St. Sauver, and Lila J. Finney Rutten, "Vaccine Hesitancy," *Mayo Clinic Proceedings* 90, no. 11 (2015): 1562–68. Charles Shey Wiysonge et al., "Vaccine Hesitancy in the Era of COVID-19: Could Lessons from the Past Help in Divining the Future?" *Human Vaccines and Immunotherapeutics* 18, no. 1 (2022): 1–3; Pru Hobson-West, "Understanding Vaccination Resistance: Moving Beyond Risk," *Health, Risk and Society* 5, no. 3 (2003): 273–83; Jacquelyn H. Flaskerud, "Vaccine Hesitancy and Intransigence," *Issues in Mental Health Nursing* 42, no. 12 (2021): 1147–50; Daniel L. Rosenfeld and A. Janet Tomiyama, "Jab My Arm, Not My Morality: Perceived Moral Reproach as a Barrier to COVID-19 Vaccine Uptake," *Social Science and Medicine* 294 (2022): 114699.

173 **"social identities":** References to *social identity* as a monolithic concept sometimes overlook the impact various identities can have. For instance, someone's race might have a much greater impact on their life than their gender, and so it is important to recognize that, while *social identity* is a useful term for capturing this concept, it, alone, is often not sufficient. Similarly, the concept of intersectionality, or "the interconnected nature of social categorizations such as race, class, and gender as they apply to a given individual or group, regarded as creating overlapping and interdependent systems of discrimination or disadvantage," is an important component of understanding social identities, as further endnotes explain. For help in understanding these concepts, I am indebted to Kali D. Cyrus, MD MPH, an ABPN-certified psychiatrist and assistant professor at Johns Hopkins Medicine, who reviewed these chapters and offered suggestions to make them more robust and inclusive.

174 **"our membership in social groups":** Joshua L. Miller and Ann Marie Garran, *Racism in the United States: Implications for the Helping Professions* (New York: Springer Publishing, 2017).

174 **All of us have a personal identity:** Michael Kalin and Nicholas Sambanis, "How to Think About Social Identity," *Annual Review of Political Science* 21 (2018): 239–57; Russell Spears, "Social Influence and Group Identity," *Annual Review of Psychology* 72 (2021): 367–90.

174 **influence our thoughts:** Jim A. C. Everett, Nadira S. Faber, and Molly Crockett, "Preferences and Beliefs in Ingroup Favoritism," *Frontiers in Behavioral Neuroscience* 9 (2015): 15; Matthew D. Lieberman, "Birds of a Feather Synchronize Together," *Trends in Cognitive Sciences* 22, no. 5 (2018): 371–72; Mina Cikara and Jay J. Van Bavel, "The Neuroscience of Intergroup Relations: An Integrative Review," *Perspectives on Psychological Science* 9, no. 3 (2014): 245–74; Thomas Mussweiler and Galen V. Bodenhausen, "I Know You Are, but What Am I? Self-Evaluative Consequences of Judging In-Group and Out-Group Members," *Journal of Personality and Social Psychology* 82, no. 1 (2002): 19.

174 **One famous experiment:** Muzafer Sherif, University of Oklahoma, and Institute of Group Relations, *Intergroup Conflict and Cooperation: The Robbers Cave Experiment,* vol. 10 (Norman, Okla.: University Book Exchange, 1961).

174 **Other experiments have demonstrated:** Jellie Sierksma, Mandy Spaltman, and Tessa A. M. Lansu, "Children Tell More Prosocial Lies in Favor of In-Group Than Out-Group Peers," *Developmental Psychology* 55, no. 7 (2019): 1428; Sima Jannati et al., "In-Group Bias in Financial Markets" (2023), available at https://ssrn.com/abstract=2884218; David M. Bersoff, "Why Good People Sometimes Do Bad Things: Motivated Reasoning and Unethical Behavior," *Personality and Social Psychology Bulletin* 25, no. 1 (1999): 28–39; Alexis C. Carpenter and Anne C. Krendl, "Are Eyewitness Accounts Biased? Evaluating False Memories for Crimes Involving In-Group or Out-Group Conflict," *Social Neuroscience* 13, no. 1 (2018): 74–93; Torun Lindholm and Sven-Åke Christianson, "Intergroup Biases and Eyewitness Testimony," *The Journal of Social Psychology* 138, no. 6 (1998): 710–23.

174 **that intersect in complicated ways:** It is important to note that intersectionality—how someone is impacted by numerous identities that transcend binary pairings, and how those intersecting identities can expose people to increased discrimination and disadvantage—is an important component in understanding the power of social identities. For more on this, please see the work of Kimberlé Williams Crenshaw, Patricia Hill Collins, Sirma Bilge, Arica L. Coleman, Lisa Bowleg, Nira Yuval-Davis, Devon Carbado, and other scholars. I would particularly suggest the following works, which I found helpful: Sumi Cho, Kimberlé Williams Crenshaw, and Leslie McCall, "Toward a Field of Intersectionality

Studies: Theory, Applications, and Praxis," *Signs: Journal of Women in Culture and Society* 38, no. 4 (2013): 785–810; Ange-Marie Hancock, *Intersectionality: An Intellectual History* (New York: Oxford University Press, 2016); Edna A. Viruell-Fuentes, Patricia Y. Miranda, and Sawsan Abdulrahim, "More Than Culture: Structural Racism, Intersectionality Theory, and Immigrant Health," *Social Science and Medicine* 75, no. 12 (2012): 2099–106; Devon W. Carbado et al., "Intersectionality: Mapping the Movements of a Theory," *Du Bois Review: Social Science Research on Race* 10, no. 2 (2013): 303–12.

174 **"exaggerate the differences":** Saul Mcleod, "Social Identity Theory: Definition, History, Examples, and Facts," Simply Psychology, April 14, 2023.

175 **whenever we talk:** Matthew D. Lieberman, "Social Cognitive Neuroscience: A Review of Core Processes," *Annual Review of Psychology* 58 (2007): 259–89; Carolyn Parkinson and Thalia Wheatley, "The Repurposed Social Brain," *Trends in Cognitive Sciences* 19, no. 3 (2015): 133–41; William Hirst and Gerald Echterhoff, "Remembering in Conversations: The Social Sharing and Reshaping of Memories," *Annual Review of Psychology* 63 (2012): 55–79; Katherine D. Kinzler, "Language as a Social Cue," *Annual Review of Psychology* 72 (2021): 241–64; Gregory M. Walton et al., "Mere Belonging: the Power of Social Connections," *Journal of Personality and Social Psychology* 102, no. 3 (2012): 513.

176 **more influential than others:** It is useful to note how the power granted to some identities by society—what is sometimes referred to as privilege—can impact lives greatly. For more on this topic, let me recommend Allan G. Johnson, *Privilege, Power, and Difference* (Boston: McGraw-Hill, 2006); Devon W. Carbado, "Privilege," in *Everyday Women's and Gender Studies* by Ann Braithwaite and Catherine Orr (New York: Routledge, 2016), 141–46; Linda L. Black and David Stone, "Expanding the Definition of Privilege: the Concept of Social Privilege," *Journal of Multicultural Counseling and Development* 33, no. 4 (2005): 243–55; and Kim Case, *Deconstructing Privilege* (New York: Routledge, 2013).

177 **"nearly one-fifth":** Matt Motta et al., "Identifying the Prevalence, Correlates, and Policy Consequences of Anti-Vaccine Social Identity," *Politics, Groups, and Identities* (2021): 1–15.

178 **In June of that year:** "CDC Museum COVID-19 Timeline," Centers for Disease Control and Prevention, https://www.cdc.gov/museum/timeline/covid19.html.

178 **roughly 85 percent:** James E. K. Hildreth and Donald J. Alcendor, "Targeting COVID-19 Vaccine Hesitancy in Minority Populations in the US: Implications for Herd Immunity," *Vaccines* 9, no. 5 (2021): 489; Lea Skak Filtenborg Frederiksen et al., "The Long Road Toward COVID-19 Herd Immunity: Vaccine Platform

Technologies and Mass Immunization Strategies," *Frontiers in Immunology* 11 (2020): 1817.

179 **"math was important":** Claude M. Steele, *Whistling Vivaldi: How Stereotypes Affect Us and What We Can Do* (New York: W. W. Norton, 2011).

179 **As he later described:** Ibid.

179 **might be the instructors' fault:** In response to a fact-checking email, Steele wrote that he eventually determined this discrepancy wasn't due to implicit bias because "1) we got underperformance in our lab studies when there was no possibility of implicit bias since participants took the exams alone in a lab room and 2) when you remove stereotype threat, as we did in the critical conditions of these experiments, underperformance vanished completely, making it clear that in these experiments, at least, nothing but [stereotype threat] could have caused the underperformance since removing it totally eliminated all underperformance."

180 **hobbled by social identities:** Steele wrote: "They are not so much worrying about their actual abilities as they are worried about how they will be judged and seen and about what that will mean for their futures."

181 **For his experiment:** Steven J. Spencer, Claude M. Steele, and Diane M. Quinn, "Stereotype Threat and Women's Math Performance," *Journal of Experimental Social Psychology* 35, no. 1 (1999): 4–28.

181 **"because they were multitasking":** Steele wrote: "We know now that they don't underperform because they are overwhelmed, they underperform because they are trying too hard, they are multitasking, trying very hard to do well while they are also constantly monitoring how they are doing and worrying about how it all will affect their performance and the outcomes tied to that performance."

182 **Black and white students:** Claude M. Steele and Joshua Aronson, "Stereotype Threat and the Intellectual Test Performance of African Americans," *Journal of Personality and Social Psychology* 69, no. 5 (1995): 797.

182 **"white students did a lot better":** In response to a fact-checking inquiry, Aronson, the coauthor on this study, said, "Black students did much better when they didn't feel that they were being evaluated by the test, whereas it didn't matter for white students and this is presumably because there's not a stereotype operating." Aronson cautioned about comparing the scores of Black and white test takers, and rather emphasized that "Black students were susceptible to being confronted with a stereotyping situation: they did worse when they were reminded of the stereotype in some way or when they thought the test was diagnosing their abilities."

182 **hundreds of other studies:** Charlotte R. Pennington et al., "Twenty Years of Stereotype Threat Research: A Review of Psychological Mediators," *PLOS One* 11,

no. 1 (2016): e0146487. Today, Steele is the Lucie Sterns Professor Emeritus in the Social Sciences at Stanford University. He previously served as provost at both Columbia University and UC Berkeley.

182 **a stereotype exists:** Steele wrote: "It's not that women or Blacks think they have been assigned to their group by other people. Like men or whites they just know that that is their group. They don't have to assume anything about bigoted people assigning them to it. They simply know that there are stereotypes about their group afoot in the broader society. That's all it takes for them to feel threatened by the possibility of being judged or treated in terms of those stereotypes when they are in a situation or experiencing something consistent with the stereotype."

183 **counteracting stereotype threats:** An enormous amount of research has been done on how to fight stereotype threat, with many solutions proposed and tested. For more details, I would recommend chapter 9 of Claude Steele's book *Whistling Vivaldi*.

183 **changed the protocol:** Dana M. Gresky, "Effects of Salient Multiple Identities on Women's Performance Under Mathematics Stereotype Threat," *Sex Roles* 53 (2005).

188 **Qaraqosh, Iraq:** Salma Mousa, "Building Social Cohesion Between Christians and Muslims Through Soccer in Post-ISIS Iraq," *Science* 369, no. 6505 (2020): 866–70.

188 **Hundreds of Christians:** Richard Hall, "Iraqi Christians Are Slowly Returning to Their Homes, Wary of Their Neighbors," Public Radio International (2017).

188 **assaulted Christian women:** "For Persecuted Christian Women, Violence Is Compounded by 'Shaming,'" World Watch Monitor, March 8, 2019.

188 **"They know what they did":** Hall, "Iraqi Christians Are Slowly Returning."

189 **additional players would be Muslims:** In reply to a fact-checking email, Mousa clarified that, while it is accurate that three additional players would be Muslim, at the meeting people were told only that "in the interests of making sure that members of all communities participate in the leagues, we will be randomly adding players to your team, who may or may not be Christian." Attendees, however, realized this likely meant the additional players would be Muslim.

189 **Salma Mousa:** Mousa was aided by a close collaboration with community leaders in Qaraqosh and a research manager, Rabie Zakaria. Mousa was a PhD student when this work was done. She is now an assistant professor of political science at Yale.

189 ***contact hypothesis*:** Thomas F. Pettigrew and Linda R. Tropp, "Allport's Intergroup Contact Hypothesis: Its History and Influence," in *On the Nature of Preju-*

dice: Fifty Years After Allport by John F. Dovidio, Peter Samuel Glick, and Laurie A. Rudman (Malden, Mass.: Blackwell, 2005): 262–77; Marilynn B. Brewer and N. Miller, "Beyond the Contact Hypothesis: Theoretical," *Groups in Contact: The Psychology of Desegregation* (Orlando, Fla.: Academic Press, 1984): 281; Yehuda Amir, "Contact Hypothesis in Ethnic Relations," *Psychological Bulletin* 71, no. 5 (1969): 319; Elizabeth Levy Paluck, Seth A. Green, and Donald P. Green, "The Contact Hypothesis Re-Evaluated," *Behavioural Public Policy* 3, no. 2 (2019): 129–58.

190 **When Mousa surveyed:** Mousa, "Building Social Cohesion," 866–70.

191 **Muslim players told pollsters:** Salma Mousa, "Contact, Conflict, and Social Cohesion" (diss., Stanford University, 2020).

192 **old rivalries and grudges:** Mousa added another context that helped ensure equal footing: All the players on the teams, both Muslim and Christian, had been impacted by the ISIS militiamen. "The Muslims in the study were mostly from the Shabak Shia community, who were persecuted as heretics by ISIS. . . . So this wasn't a 'perpetrator vs. victim' dynamic per se, but rather a case of deep distrust and prejudice toward Muslims who were seen as diluting the Christian character of Qaraqosh by slowly moving into the city, and being stereotypically less educated, poorer, and more conservative. The shared displacement experience did little to bond the two groups together. Instead, the occupation hardened in-group identities, distrust, and segregation."

194 **more than two million:** "COVID-19 Weekly Epidemiological Update," World Health Organization, February 23, 2021.

194 **persuading people:** In response to fact-checking inquiries, Rosenbloom said that "the goal of Boost Oregon is not to convince people to get the shots. It's to help educate them to make a well-informed decision. Yes, we're teaching people about why they're good and why they're safe, but . . . what we need to do is we need to help them to get their questions answered, without having an agenda, or else we're dooming ourselves before we start."

194 ***motivational interviewing*****:** Jennifer Hettema, Julie Steele, and William R. Miller, "Motivational Interviewing," *Annual Review of Clinical Psychology* 1 (2005): 91–111; William R. Miller and Gary S. Rose, "Toward a Theory of Motivational Interviewing," *American Psychologist* 64, no. 6 (2009): 527; William R. Miller, "Motivational Interviewing: Research, Practice, and Puzzles," *Addictive Behaviors* 21, no. 6 (1996): 835–42; W. R. Miller and S. Rollnick, *Motivational Interviewing: Helping People Change* (New York: Guilford Press, 2013).

194 **subtly guides the client:** Ken Resnicow and Fiona McMaster, "Motivational Interviewing: Moving from Why to How with Autonomy Support," *International Journal of Behavioral Nutrition and Physical Activity* 9, no. 1 (2012): 1–9.

CHAPTER SEVEN: HOW DO WE MAKE THE HARDEST CONVERSATIONS SAFER?

198 **The Problem Netflix Lives With:** There are a number of missteps one can make in writing about race and ethnicity, particularly when the author is, like myself, a heterosexual white man who has enjoyed numerous advantages and privileges. One risk is failing to see insights that would be obvious to other writers. To that end, in writing this chapter I spoke to scholars of racism, prejudice, and interracial communication who were generous with their time, many of them thinkers with lived experiences of exclusion. I was grateful for their insights and asked some of them to review this chapter and give me their thoughts and suggestions. In some instances, their contributions are included in the text, or detailed in these notes. It is also important to note that while different kinds of prejudice often have some commonalities, they should not be lumped together. Racism is distinct from sexism, and from homophobia. Every prejudice—and every instance of injustice—is, in its own way, unique. Finally, in choosing how to refer to sensitive topics in this and other chapters, including how to refer to specific ethnicities, I have tried to adhere to the standards of the Associated Press Stylebook.

199 **he said the n-word:** "At Netflix, Radical Transparency and Blunt Firings Unsettle the Ranks," *The Wall Street Journal,* October 25, 2018.

199 **another thought:** It is important to note that statements that give offense might be blatant—such as using a racial slur—but they can also be much more subtle, which some scholars refer to as *microaggressions.* For more on this topic, please see Derald Wing Sue and Lisa Spanierman, *Microaggressions in Everyday Life* (Hoboken, N.J.: John Wiley and Sons, 2020); Derald Wing Sue et al., "Racial Microaggressions in Everyday Life: Implications for Clinical Practice," *American Psychologist* 62, no. 4 (2007): 271; Derald Wing Sue, "Microaggressions: More Than Just Race," *Psychology Today* 17 (2010); Anthony D. Ong and Anthony L. Burrow, "Microaggressions and Daily Experience: Depicting Life as It Is Lived," *Perspectives on Psychological Science* 12, no. 1 (2017).

199 **Reed Hastings:** Reed Hastings cofounded Netflix with Marc Randolph.

200 **the culture deck:** For my understanding of Netflix, I am indebted to many sources, including Reed Hastings's book, written with Erin Meyer: *No Rules Rules: Netflix and the Culture of Reinvention* (New York: Penguin, 2020); Corinne Grinapol, *Reed Hastings and Netflix* (New York: Rosen, 2013); Patty McCord, "How Netflix Reinvented HR," *Harvard Business Review* 92, no. 1 (2014): 71–76; James Morgan, "Netflix: Reed Hastings," *Media Company Leader Presentations* 12 (2018); Bill Taylor, "How Coca-Cola, Netflix, and Amazon Learn from Failure," *Harvard Business Review* 10 (2017); Kai-Ingo Voigt et al., "Entertainment on De-

mand: The Case of Netflix," in *Business Model Pioneers: How Innovators Successfully Implement New Business Models* (Switzerland: Springer International Publishing, 2017): 127–41; Patty McCord, *Powerful: Building a Culture of Freedom and Responsibility* (San Francisco: Silicon Guild, 2018).

200 **Netflix would either match it:** In response to fact-checking questions, a representative for Netflix said this practice does not happen as often today, and that as the company has grown and become more sophisticated, the firm does a better job of setting salaries at industry standards without employees needing to solicit outside offers.

200 **A note was sent:** In response to fact-checking questions, a representative for the company said this happens less frequently today.

202 **Businessperson of the Year:** This award was bestowed in 2010.

202 **don't seem particularly effective:** Evelyn R. Carter, Ivuoma N. Onyeador, and Neil A. Lewis, Jr., "Developing and Delivering Effective Anti-bias Training: Challenges and Recommendations," *Behavioral Science and Policy* 6, no. 1 (2020): 57–70; Joanne Lipman, "How Diversity Training Infuriates Men and Fails Women," *Time* 191, no. 4 (2018): 17–19; Peter Bregman, "Diversity Training Doesn't Work," *Harvard Business Review* 12 (2012); Frank Dobbin and Alexandra Kalev, "Why Doesn't Diversity Training Work? The Challenge for Industry and Academia," *Anthropology Now* 10, no. 2 (2018): 48–55; Hussain Alhejji et al., "Diversity Training Programme Outcomes: A Systematic Review," *Human Resource Development Quarterly* 27, no. 1 (2016): 95–149; Gwendolyn M. Combs and Fred Luthans, "Diversity Training: Analysis of the Impact of Self-Efficacy," *Human Resource Development Quarterly* 18, no. 1 (2007): 91–120; J. Belluz, "Companies Like Starbucks Love Anti-bias Training but It Doesn't Work—and May Backfire," *Vox* (2018); Dobin and Kalev, "Why Doesn't Diversity Training Work?," 48–55; Edward H. Chang et al., "The Mixed Effects of Online Diversity Training," *Proceedings of the National Academy of Sciences* 116, no. 16 (2019): 7778–83.

203 **team of researchers:** Elizabeth Levy Paluck et al., "Prejudice Reduction: Progress and Challenges," *Annual Review of Psychology* 72 (2021): 533–60.

203 **A 2021 *Harvard Business Review*:** Francesca Gino and Katherine Coffman, "Unconscious Bias Training That Works," *Harvard Business Review* 99, no. 5 (2021): 114–23.

203 **Another examination of three:** Frank Dobbin and Alexandra Kalev, "Why Diversity Programs Fail," *Harvard Business Review* 94, no. 7 (2016): 14.

203 **"the likelihood that Black men and women":** This quote comes from "Unconscious Bias Training That Works," and is a summary of another study: Alexandra Kalev, Frank Dobbin, and Erin Kelly, "Best Practices or Best Guesses? Assessing

the Efficacy of Corporate Affirmative Action and Diversity Policies," *American Sociological Review* 71, no. 4 (2006): 589–617.

203 **2021 *Annual Review of Psychology*:** Elizabeth Levy Paluck et al., "Prejudice Reduction: Progress and Challenges," *Annual Review of Psychology* 72 (2021): 533–60. It is worth noting that among the methods that seem consistently effective at reducing incidents of prejudice and biased attitudes is "face-to-face intergroup contact" and encouraging "interpersonal conversations over time," as researchers wrote in the 2021 *Annual Review of Psychology.*

204 **seemed as if every one:** In response to fact-checking inquiries, Netflix said that not every single employee had heard about the incident and had formed an opinion.

205 **hadn't worked hard enough:** A great deal of research suggests that these kinds of standards, whether formal or informally applied through employee norms and comments, can disproportionately disadvantage workers from minoritized backgrounds. For more on this, please see James R. Elliott and Ryan A. Smith, "Race, Gender, and Workplace Power," *American Sociological Review* 69, no. 3 (2004): 365–86; Ashleigh Shelby Rosette, Geoffrey J. Leonardelli, and Katherine W. Phillips, "The White Standard: Racial Bias in Leader Categorization," *Journal of Applied Psychology* 93, no. 4 (2008): 758; Victor Ray, "A Theory of Racialized Organizations," *American Sociological Review* 84, no. 1 (2019): 26–53; Alice Hendrickson Eagly and Linda Lorene Carli, *Through the Labyrinth: The Truth About How Women Become Leaders* (Boston: Harvard Business Press, 2007).

207 **Columbia and UC Berkeley:** Michael L. Slepian and Drew S. Jacoby-Senghor, "Identity Threats in Everyday Life: Distinguishing Belonging from Inclusion," *Social Psychological and Personality Science* 12, no. 3 (2021): 392–406. In response to fact-checking inquiries, Slepian clarified that the question about tough conversations "was just one situation out of about 29 more that we talked about."

208 **found there were lots of things:** Slepian noted that these results draw on multiple studies and papers.

209 **escape or fight back:** Sarah Townsend et al., "From 'in the Air' to 'Under the Skin': Cortisol Responses to Social Identity Threat," *Personality and Social Psychology Bulletin* 37, no. 2 (2011): 151–64; Todd Lucas et al., "Perceived Discrimination, Racial Identity, and Multisystem Stress Response to Social Evaluative Threat Among African American Men and Women," *Psychosomatic Medicine* 79, no. 3 (2017): 293; Daan Scheepers, Naomi Ellemers, and Nieska Sintemaartensdijk, "Suffering from the Possibility of Status Loss: Physiological Responses to Social Identity Threat in High Status Groups," *European Journal of Social Psychology* 39, no. 6 (2009): 1075–92; Alyssa K. McGonagle and Janet L. Barnes-Farrell, "Chronic

Illness in the Workplace: Stigma, Identity Threat and Strain," *Stress and Health* 30, no. 4 (2014): 310–21; Sally S. Dickerson, "Emotional and Physiological Responses to Social-Evaluative Threat," *Social and Personality Psychology Compass* 2, no. 3 (2008): 1362–78.

209 **"on multiple identities":** Slepian noted that the advertisements recruiting participants for this study specifically sought people who had been made to feel they didn't belong because of a social group, which likely resulted in a sample with an outsized experience of identity threat. It therefore follows that, for the population at large, the frequency of identity threat is likely smaller.

210 **identity threat:** Nyla R. Branscombe et al., "The Context and Content of Social Identity Threat," *Social Identity: Context, Commitment, Content* (1999): 35–58; Claude M. Steele, Steven J. Spencer, and Joshua Aronson, "Contending with Group Image: The Psychology of Stereotype and Social Identity Threat," in *Advances in Experimental Social Psychology* (Cambridge, Mass.: Academic Press, 2002), 34:379–440; Katherine T. U. Emerson and Mary C. Murphy, "Identity Threat at Work: How Social Identity Threat and Situational Cues Contribute to Racial and Ethnic Disparities in the Workplace," *Cultural Diversity and Ethnic Minority Psychology* 20, no. 4 (2014): 508; Joshua Aronson and Matthew S. McGlone, "Stereotype and Social Identity Threat," in Handbook of *Prejudice, Stereotyping, and Discrimination* (New York: Psychology Press, 2009); Naomi Ellemers, Russell Spears, and Bertjan Doosje, "Self and Social Identity," *Annual Review of Psychology* 53, no. 1 (2002): 161–86.

210 **70 percent of participants:** In response to a fact-checking inquiry, Sanchez expanded upon her comments to note that, in her study, 80 to 90 percent of participants also said they expected important benefits from these conversations. Kiara Lynn Sanchez, "A Threatening Opportunity: Conversations About Race-Related Experiences Between Black and White Friends" (PhD diss., Stanford University, 2022).

211 **Robert Livingston:** Robert Livingston, *The Conversation: How Seeking and Speaking the Truth About Racism Can Radically Transform Individuals and Organizations* (New York: Currency, 2021).

211 **face-to-face:** Because of the pandemic, most of these conversations occurred via video conferencing.

211 **Black participants were invited:** It is useful to note that, in less formal settings, asking a Black friend to speak first about their experiences with racism might create barriers to connection. As Dr. Kali Cyrus wrote, in reviewing this chapter, sometimes a Black person is asked to share their trauma, and the "[person of color's] experiences are put on display to be commented on, apologized for, or used in some way as an experience that is different or othered compared to

white people.... [It is important to acknowledge] that it is not the responsibility of the Black or less privileged person to put themselves in tough conversations for the sake of unity! Because, typically, they must do this at baseline to succeed in a job or setting that is predominantly white. HOWEVER, there are some POC (like me), who are willing and emotionally able to participate."

212 **prepared differently:** This is an edited version of the instructions. The full version reads: "A little later, you'll have the chance to talk with [friend]. But first, we want to take some time to share some things that we have learned. We asked other people about their conversations about race with friends of different racial groups. We are sharing this with both you and [friend name]."

213 **easier to withstand:** Sanchez said that the goal was to "give people a framework for persevering.... The underlying theory is that discomfort can be helpful. So it's not our goal to get rid of it, but rather help people see that it doesn't have to be a barrier to meaningful conversations or relationships."

213 **just three minutes:** Sanchez noted that, for the experimental versus control group, "there was no statistical difference between conditions in how long the conversation was. We also have no evidence yet that the content of the conversation was deeper or more vulnerable. In general, what we've been finding is that the conversation actually went pretty well in both conditions. Both friends reported having a positive experience, feeling engaged, and authentic in the conversation. And we haven't yet detected significant differences in the content of the conversation."

213 **"I can't forget":** In response to fact-checking inquiries, Sanchez wrote that what this Black participant is "discussing is his internal conflict about being a Black man in a white place and on one hand forgetting that sometimes, but very often being reminded of it and balancing those two experiences. [Such complexity] highlights the nature of these conversations and interracial relationships in general."

214 **tallied their data:** Kiara Lynn Sanchez, "A Threatening Opportunity: Conversations About Race-Related Experiences Between Black and White Friends" (PhD diss., Stanford University, 2022).

215 **could be more authentic:** Sanchez wrote that the strongest outcomes occurred immediately after the conversations, when "both friends experienced a boost in feelings of closeness (from before the conversation to immediately afterward). In addition, a few months later, Black friends felt more comfortable talking with their white friends about race, and more authentic in that relationship." She continued in response to further fact-checking inquiries: "The immediate outcomes were across both conditions, regardless of whether they got there with training, but the training had a unique benefit on Black friends' 'authenticity' and

'closeness' over time—this is the long-term benefit. Immediately everyone increased in 'authenticity' and 'closeness' across conditions. In the long term, Black friends in the training condition increased in 'closeness' and 'authenticity.' So just having the conversation was helpful, but in order to see long term benefits, the training was really helpful for Black friends."

215 **prepare for discomfort:** It is important to note the difference between preparing for discomfort and fixating on it. As Dr. Kali Cyrus noted, fixation can contribute to confirmation bias.

216 **out of the conversation:** In response to fact-checking inquiries, Sanchez wrote that "identity threat emerges often without anybody 'doing' anything. Just talking to somebody from a different group can trigger worries that that person might see you through the lens of a stereotype (before they say a thing!). . . . There is something to be said about the power of sharing personal experiences and perspectives, but I wouldn't say that avoiding generalizations is a surefire way to decrease another person's identity threat."

217 **"that's enough":** In response to fact-checking inquiries, Myers expanded on this statement: "One has to be actively anti-racist which means that as individuals and as a company we had to first recognize and understand our own unconscious biases and their unintended impact on our colleagues and the business."

217 **Massachusetts attorney general:** Netflix clarified that at the AG's office, Myers's remit was "to increase diversity and retention within the AG's office, sexual harassment and anti-discrimination training and enhance outreach and engagement to underserved communities in the Commonwealth, as well as advising the AG and his leadership staff."

218 **culture deck proclaimed:** Hastings and Meyer, *No Rules Rules.*

219 **conducting employee workshops:** Myers noted that her team "came in to create a long-term strategic change process which meant we worked with our HR partners and leaders within business units to shape these strategies. Doing workshops and conversations was just part of the strategy."

219 **acknowledged, up front:** Myers said that "most of the work is about awareness of yourself, your culture, and the culture of others and understanding how your identity, experience and culture shape your world view, your relationships and behavior and your judgments. Also learning to recognize your biases and how to check them, to notice who we might be excluding or including (consciously and unconsciously) and why, so that we can each do our job of creating an inclusive and respectful environment."

220 **sting of exclusion:** It is worth noting that although we can all recognize the sting of exclusion, that does not mean we have all experienced exclusion equally.

Some exclusion hurts more than others, and some people, because of their social identities, experience exclusion more often, and in different ways, than others.

220 **help us empathize:** Myers wrote that "it was important for people to see that it is not just the people of color or women who have identities, everyone does, and that diversity is something that exists within all of us, since we all have multiple identities and experiences that makes each of us quite unique as individuals. However, in many corporate spaces, there is a dominance of certain identities due to historical exclusion and racism and sexism, and they become the norm by which everything is shaped and judged.... It's not enough to bring in people who are different than the norm, we have to create an environment where they are respected and reflected in our teams, ways of working, language, policies, etc.... At all times the work is multi-faceted to create change on four levels: The personal level (how people think, believe, feel), the interpersonal level (people's behaviors and relationships), the organizational level (policies and practices) and the cultural level (what is seen as right, beautiful, true)."

221 **describe a time:** Myers wrote that these conversations were designed to draw out comments "not only about race; it was usually about difference, any kind of difference and how they reacted to that difference. Race came up a lot but it could have been gender, disability, income, sexual orientation, accent, language, etc."

222 **weren't as risky:** Myers wrote that "for some people these conversations are difficult and will never feel safe. In some cases, we changed content to address concerns." Not everyone, she noted, felt safe and comfortable.

223 **kinds of questions:** These kinds of questions can be uncomfortable, so the company had norms for when the discomfort became too much. "When someone doesn't feel comfortable discussing something about themselves or about an issue related to one or more of their identities, we encourage them to let their colleague know that they don't want to have that conversation," said Toni Harris Quinerly, Netflix's director of inclusion strategy. "As an Inclusion Team, we work hard to normalize this kind of boundary setting, so that people feel more comfortable communicating when they do and don't want to discuss something, and so that people on the receiving end are more likely to honor and respect those boundaries. This includes letting people know that there are multiple ways to learn about experiences you don't fully understand (e.g. finding related articles/books and/or seeking insights from other people or allies who may have knowledge or perspectives on that issue)."

223 **"If the first lesson":** Greg Walton, in response to fact-checking inquiries, specified that the goal of an exercise like this is not creating comfort for people who already have power, but rather creating atmospheres where people can re-

flect on themselves and society, and hear others' perspectives. The focus is on finding "trainings [that] can facilitate more positive and less biased behavior." Walton, in an interview, told me that "we have to create space in the culture for people who are imperfect. We can't just have a 'gotchya' culture. The goal is to take people who are imperfect and make them into allies, rather than enemies."

224 **every Netflix employee:** Vernā Myers, "Inclusion Takes Root at Netflix: Our First Report," Netflix.com, January 13, 2021.

224 **Netflix released data:** Vernā Myers, "Our Progress on Inclusion: 2021 Update," Netflix.com, February 10, 2022.

224 **Half of Netflix's:** These figures reflect 2022 demographics.

224 **compared Netflix:** Stacy L. Smith et al., "Inclusion in Netflix Original U.S. Scripted Series and Films," *Indicator* 46 (2021): 50–56.

226 **a small number:** It is unclear exactly how many employees participated in these demonstrations. Reporters on-site estimated the number at less than two dozen. Some employees also stopped working at noon to protest the Chappelle special.

227 **Real change requires shifts:** In reply to a fact-checking email, Netflix said, "Netflix is trying to entertain the world and believes that DEI can help accomplish that goal; so it isn't just about social good and each of us learning to work respectfully with each other and take advantage of our differences, but how this will enable all of us and the business to thrive." Myers added: "Increasing representation and applying an inclusion lens to everything we do helps us to innovate and be creative. It also helps us to tell authentic and new stories that haven't been told before, [and] see and give a platform to talent that has been excluded in the past. . . . This is good for the business, and it's really good for our members and members to be."

227 **"it's the first step":** Myers stepped down from her position at Netflix in September, 2023, after five years with the company. She remains an advisor to Netflix, and was succeeded by Wade Davis.

AFTERWORD

235 **consider his matter:** For my understanding of this study, I am indebted to: Robert Waldinger and Marc M. D. Schulz, *The Good Life* (New York: Simon and Schuster, 2023); George E. Vaillant, *Triumphs of Experience* (Cambridge, Mass.: Harvard University Press, 2012); George E. Vaillant, *Adaptation to Life* (Cambridge, Mass.: Harvard University Press, 1995); John F. Mitchell, "Aging Well: Surprising Guideposts to a Happier Life from the Landmark Harvard Study of Adult

Development," *American Journal of Psychiatry* 161, no. 1 (2004): 178–79; Christopher Peterson, Martin E. Seligman, and George E. Vaillant, "Pessimistic Explanatory Style Is a Risk Factor for Physical Illness: A Thirty-Five-Year Longitudinal Study," *Journal of Personality and Social Psychology* 55, no. 1 (1988): 23; Clark Wright Heath, *What People Are; a Study of Normal Young Men* (Cambridge, Mass.: Harvard University Press, 1945); Robert C. Intrieri, "Through the Lens of Time: Eight Decades of the Harvard Grant Study," *PsycCRITIQUES* 58 (2013); Robert Waldinger, "Harvard Study of Adult Development" (2017).

236 **Godfrey Camille:** The researchers in this project, when they have published case studies, have always referred to participants with pseudonyms and have altered biographical details to preserve confidentiality. The information included here relies upon those published reports, and thus includes names and details altered by the researchers. However, whenever possible, I have supplemented my understanding by interviewing those and other researchers, and consulting publications, both published and unpublished, to ensure accuracy.

241 **himself thinking about:** The wording of the question was: "Please use the last page(s) to answer all the questions we should have asked, if we'd asked about the things that matter most to you."

243 **one paper published:** Julianne Holt-Lunstad, "Why Social Relationships Are Important for Physical Health: A Systems Approach to Understanding and Modifying Risk and Protection," *Annual Review of Psychology* 69 (2018): 437–58.

243 **the researchers wrote:** Yang Claire Yang et al., "Social Relationships and Physiological Determinants of Longevity Across the Human Life Span," *Proceedings of the National Academy of Sciences* 113, no. 3 (2016): 578–83.

INDEX